Florida's Fabled Inns

with best wishes –

Louise K. Frisbie

Other Books by Louise K. Frisbie

Peace River Pioneers
Yesterday's Polk County
Here's How—Notes on News Writing *(out of print)*
R. H. Williams, Florida Pioneer *(out of print)*

Florida's Fabled Inns

by Louise K. Frisbie

Imperial Publishing Company
P. O. Box 120
Bartow, Florida 33830

Acknowledgments

Four and a half years were spent in researching and writing **Florida's Fabled Inns**, and many persons contributed to its creation.

Special appreciation is expressed to these persons, knowledgeable in regional Florida history, who consented to read parts of the manuscript for accuracy:

Mrs. Maxine Banash, Palm Beach
E. W. Carswell, Chipley
Dr. James W. Covington, Tampa University
Miss Clara Farley, Marianna
Thomas Graham, Flagler College, St. Augustine
Charles E. Harner, Nokomis
C. H. Harris, Jacksonville Public Library
Frank T. Hurley, Jr., St. Petersburg Beach
Malcolm Johnson, Tallahassee
Mrs. James N. LaRoche, Valparaiso
Gene Leedy, Architect, Winter Haven
Mrs. John Linehan, Lantana
Gary Lloyd, Tallahassee
Richard Mancini, Milton
Hart McKillop, Winter Haven
Helen (Mrs. William W.) Muir, Miami
Harris H. Mullen, Tampa
Mrs. John C. Packard, Marianna
Arva M. (Mrs. Robert) Parks, Coral Gables
Marjorie D. Patterson, Fort Lauderdale
Jane Patton, Panama City
Dr. Thelma Peters, Coral Gables
Norman Simons, Pensacola
Dean Zipf, Key West

Those who offered assistance in various other ways:

Mrs. Karl P. Abbott, Indialantic
Stayton Addison, The Breakers, Palm Beach
Elizabeth Alexander, Gainesville
Mrs. E. C. Bates, Altamonte Springs
Mrs. Josephine Bearden, St. Augustine
Mrs. Leonard Blankner, Bartow
Mrs. R. S. Bly, Lakeland
Mrs. Robert Bradford, Altamonte Springs
Quintilla Bruton, Plant City
Mrs. Kathryn Brock, Orlando
Miss Audrey Broward, Jacksonville
E. B. Browning, Sr., Madison
E. F. Callaway, Avon Park
Paul Eugen Camp, Tampa
T. Mabry Carlton, Sr., Wauchula
Robert Cauthen, Leesburg
Ramona M. Chergoski, Winter Haven
Fred H. Cooper, Stetson University, DeLand
Kathryn Cooke, Plant City
Mrs. Nan Dennison, Henry Morrison Flagler Museum, Palm Beach
Mrs. Nancy Dobson, Tallahassee
Mrs. John R. DuBois, Jupiter
Hampton Dunn, Tampa
Mrs. Bernice H. Gibson, Mulberry
Barbara Goddard, Orange City
Marian B. Godown, Fort Myers
Mrs. Calvin Grossenbacher, Apopka
Leland Hawes, Tampa
Glenn Hooker, Haines City
Joan B. Hoffman, Apalachicola
Mrs. Fred Houser, Lake Wales
Bob Hudson, Titusville
Walter Jubinsky, Daytona Beach
Mrs. Essie Eddy Joiner, Marianna
Mrs. Holland A. Kelley, Bartow
Mr. and Mrs. Robert Kloeppel, Jr., Jacksonville
James E. Knauff, the Belleview Biltmore, Belleview
Judge James R. Knott, Palm Beach
Mrs. Henry W. Land, Tangerine
Mrs. Louise LeGette, Tampa Tribune
Sam Lupfer, Sr., Kissimmee
Mary O. McRory, Tallahassee
Mrs. Thomas Mickler, Chuluota
Mrs. Allen Morris, Tallahassee
Ken Musson, Tampa
Randy F. Nimnicht, Miami
Mrs. Inez Nychyk, Fort Myers
Mrs. Lucy O'Brien, Tampa
Vernon Peeples, Punta Gorda
Miss Beulah Pipkin, Lakeland
Palmer Purser, Lake City
Stephanie Raine, the Don Ce-Sar, Pass-a-Grille
F. Blair Reeves, Gainesville
Sue Schaal, the Boca Raton Hotel and Club, Boca Raton
Charles Simmons, Flagler Museum, Palm Beach
Ed Skinner, Vero Beach
Barbara S. Smart, The Breakers, Palm Beach
Ernest M. Smith, Bartow
Orren Smith, Bonifay
Rebecca Smith, Miami
Mrs. W. B. Sutton, Pensacola
Wayne Thomas, Tampa
Frances L. Wright, Sorrento
Mrs. O. H. Wright, Bartow
Jean Yothers, Orlando

Libraries and Historical Organizations:

Apopka Historical Society
Bartow Public Library
Cocoa Public Library
Florida Historical Society
Fort Lauderdale Historical Society, Inc.
Gainesville Public Library
Henry Morrison Flagler Museum, Palm Beach
Historical Association of Southern Florida
The Historical Society of Okaloosa & Walton Counties, Inc.
Historical Society of Palm Beach County
Historic Tallahassee Preservation Board
Jacksonville Historical Society
Jacksonville Public Library, Florida Collection
Lake County Historical Society
Lakeland Public Library
Mount Dora Historical Society
Northwest Regional Library System, Panama City
Orange County Historical Museum
Orange County Historical Society
Pensacola Historical Society Museum
P. K. Yonge Library of Florida History, Gainesville
Peace River Valley Historical Society
Polk County Historical Association
Polk County Historical and Genealogical Library, Bartow
St. Augustine Historical Society
Santa Rosa Historical Society
Southwest Florida Historical Society
State Library of Florida, Tallahassee
State Photographic Archives, Tallahassee
Swisher Library, Jacksonville University
Tampa-Hillsborough County Public Library System
Tampa Historical Society
University of South Florida Library, Tampa
Volusia County Library Center, Daytona Beach

Fully annotated copies of the typescript of **Florida's Fabled Inns** have been accepted for reference by the P. K. Yonge Library of Florida History, Gainesville, the State Library of Florida, Tallahassee, and the University of South Florida Library, Tampa.

Second Printing, 1980

ISBN 0-9602960-O-X
Library of Congress Catalog Card Number 78-56754

MANUFACTURED IN THE UNITED STATES OF AMERICA
BY THE STORTER PRINTING COMPANY, INC.
GAINESVILLE, FLORIDA

To S. L. Frisbie, IV,
his dear wife, Mary,
and their son, Loyal,
whose roots in central Florida
reach back for more
than a century.

A Special Acknowledgment
of Appreciation
to
LOYAL FRISBIE
The Man in My Life

Contents

MAP OF THE CITY OF JACKS

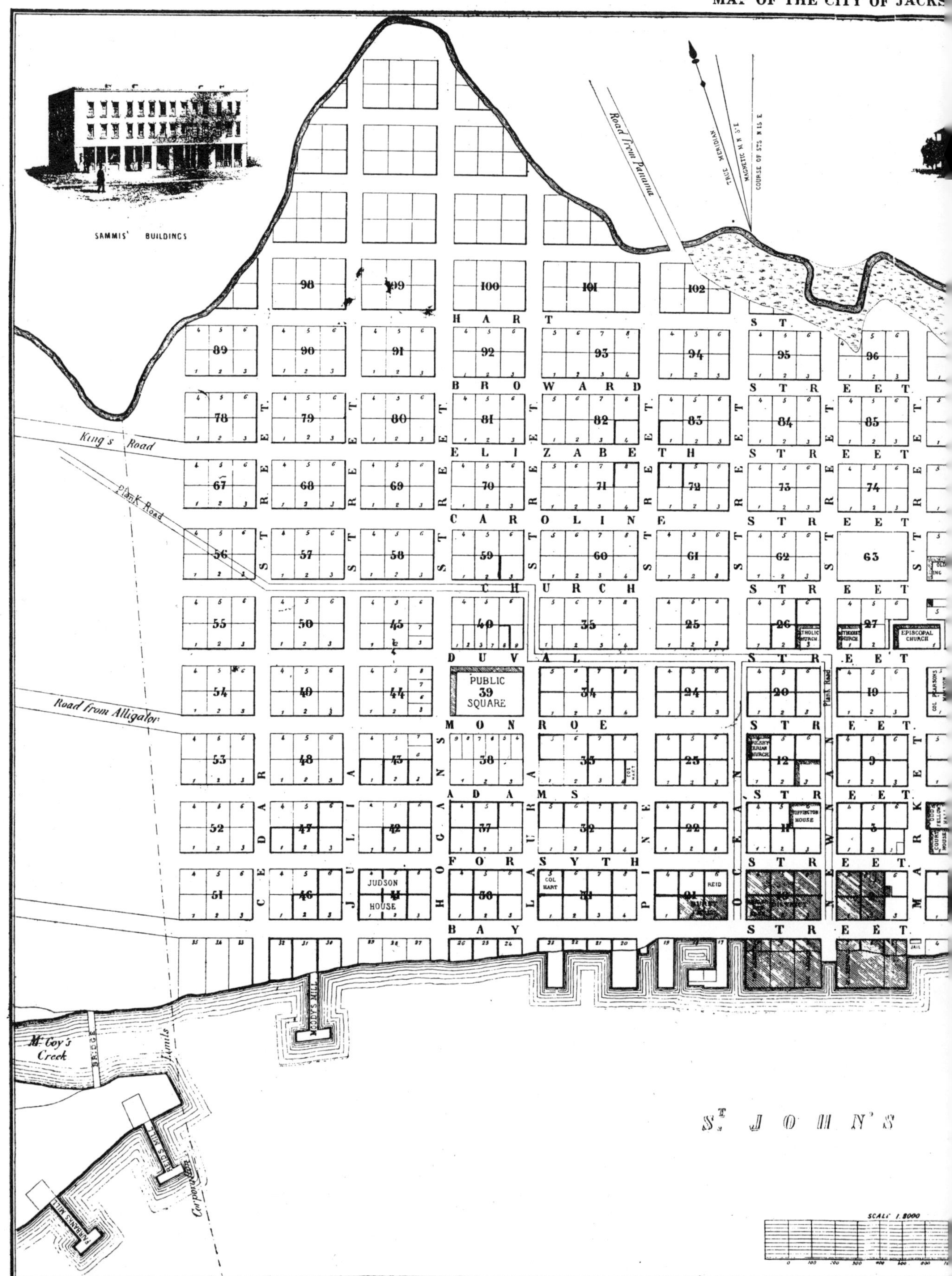

Original at Public Library: Gift of G. D. Ackerly.

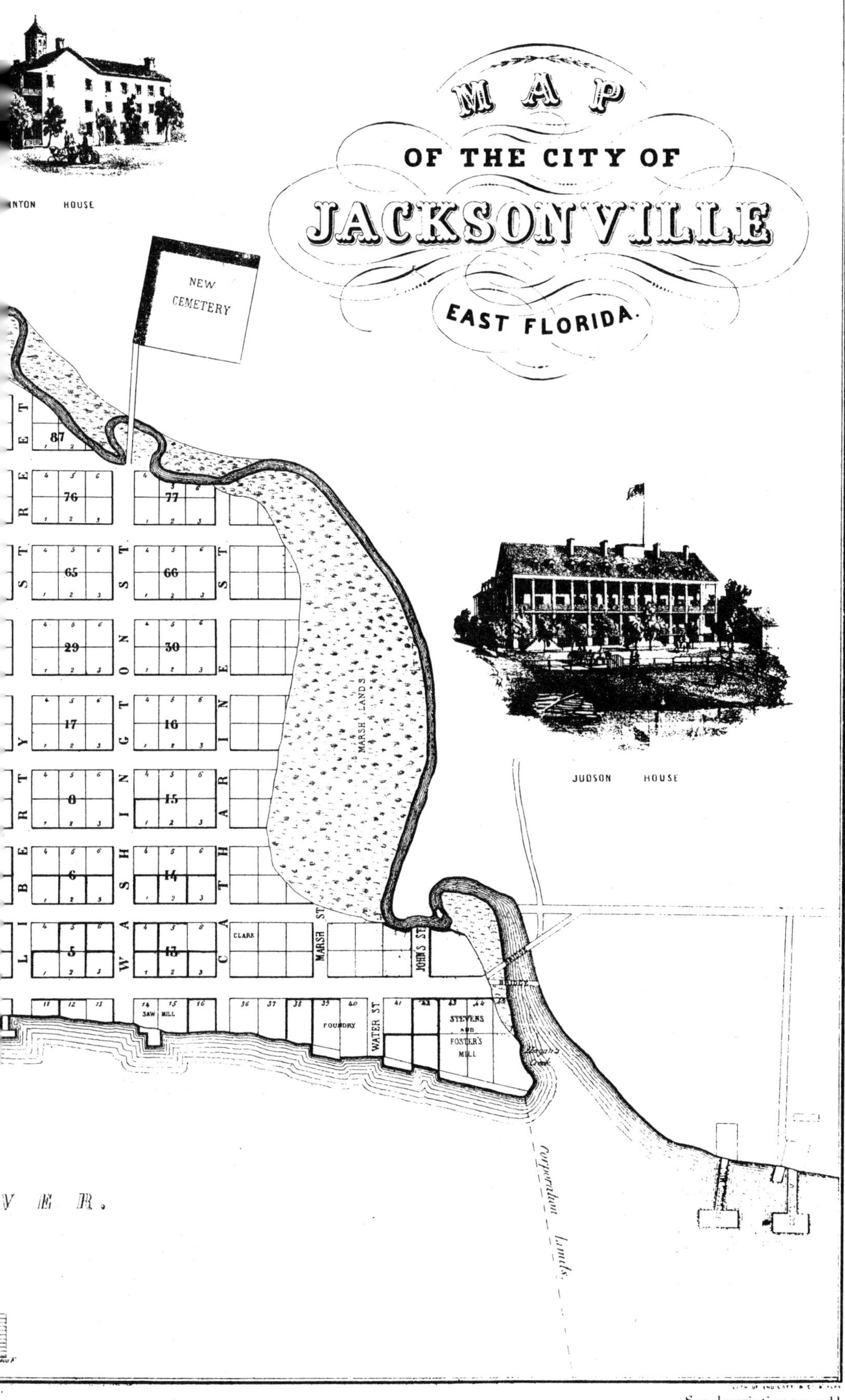

Two of the city's earliest hotels are sketched in the margin of this 1859 map of Jacksonville. The Buffington House (originally Wood's Hotel, in the late 1840s) stood in Block 11, just above the shaded area at the bottom of the map. The Judson House, which was opened in November, 1854, was in Block 41, at lower left. The shaded area shows the section covered by a devastating fire in 1854. I. D. Hart, known as the founder of Jacksonville, at various times owned nearly all the land later known as the Old City and most of the Springfield section. The locations of four churches are shown on this map—Catholic, Methodist and Episcopal in Blocks 26-28, and Presbyterian in Block 12.

See description page 11

The oldest inn in Florida still in existence in its original form is the Ximenez-Fatio House at St. Augustine, shown here in a photograph taken in the 1850s. It was built by Andres Ximenez in 1798 as a private residence and grocery store. After Ximenez' death in 1806, the building passed through several hands before it was purchased in 1855 by Miss Louisa Fatio. By that time an ell and a balcony had been added, and the building had been operated for some years—the exact time has not been determined—as an inn. Under Miss Fatio's ownership it was widely publicized and "was considered by the fastidious tourist to be as charming and comfortable as any in the town," according to a report of the Ximenez-Fatio House Study Committee of The National Society of the Colonial Dames of America in the State of Florida. It continued in use as an inn for twenty years. When Miss Fatio died in 1875, the property passed to her nephew, David L. Dunham, and the house was rented to many persons until it was purchased in 1939 by the Colonial Dames. Since then it has been open to the public as a historic exhibit for several months of the year. Archeological digs are conducted periodically in the grounds of the house. The period of the photo has been authenticated by the Library of Congress.

Foreword

Florida has had accommodations, of a sort, for travelers for two centuries—perhaps even longer. The first primitive taverns were located in the village of St. Augustine, which was 400 years old in 1965.

Food and drink—especially the latter—were dispensed on the first floor, while upstairs there were dormitory-like quarters for male travelers.

Respectable women were obliged to find shelter in private homes.

Ample evidence exists that the long-distance traveler in Florida has been received and welcomed in the homes of its residents since the first families settled in the state, whether at the wealthy rice-and-indigo plantations of Governor James Grant, Lieutenant Governor John Moultrie, Richard Oswald and Francis Fatio, or the home of the humblest stage-station keeper.

Florida had thirty innkeepers in 1850, as shown by the census of that year.

With a few notable exceptions, the era of the big American plan resort hotel in Florida is over. Not only the turn-of-the-century luxury hotels—often frame buildings impossible to modernize—but the hundreds, large and small, which came on the scene during the early decades of the 20th Century, and which might still be structurally sound, are being razed or turned into retirement homes. They are not dying of old age.

To paraphrase a story by Harris H. Mullen in *Florida Close-Up* deploring destruction of the Tampa Terrace Hotel in 1965-66, these hotels are being killed by the modern glut of urban automobile traffic. Hemmed in on all sides, they suffocate for lack of parking space, with no place to find it or build parking storage. The automobile is king. Every assistant clerk and bus boy drives his car to town and leaves it as near as possible to his work.

Students of Florida history disagree as to the veracity of certain anecdotes about colorful early developers such as Henry B. Plant. Several of these have been included in *Florida's Fabled Inns*—to be taken with as many grains of salt as the reader may choose.

Among Florida's first considerations after achieving statehood was that of bringing settlers into the state.

It had no money to provide the internal improvements which would attract settlers—which, in fact, were essential if prospective newcomers were to have access to the interior. What Florida did have in abundance was land, millions upon millions of acres which were, and would become, the state's property. In lieu of cash, no bargaining medium could compare with land.

The Internal Improvement Fund was established in 1855 to administer these vast acreages, and a board of trustees named to determine how they should be disposed of for the state's maximum benefit. The encouragement of railroad building had a very high priority. The trustees decided that the state would provide assistance to railroad builders by guaranteeing interest on construction bonds and, more importantly by far, would reward them with thousands of acres of property in return for each mile of railroad laid within a certain time.

It was a magic lure.

Florida's early hotels were operated entirely on the American plan, with all meals included in the daily or weekly rates, as a matter of course, for there were no other places where meals were served to the public. The dining rooms of the early hotels, in fact, regularly received local as well as transient guests, and often became popular for certain dishes.

The independent restaurant came on the scene toward the turn of the century. A business directory of Jacksonville in 1905 (population c. 45,000) lists only five restaurants and an oyster house. The Miami City Directory for 1904 (population 4,000) lists only one, the Epicurean, which emphasized its catering service and delicatessen, as well as "first-class cooking."

By the end of the first World War, many of the hotels in large cities changed from American to European plan. Among these were most of the major Jacksonville and Tampa hotels, about ten in Miami, and a scattered few in medium-size towns.

The account of Julia Tuttle's role in the history of Miami given in this book coincides with that of highly respected contemporary historians. Biographical sketches of Mrs. Tuttle and her son published in Rerick's *Memoirs of Florida* in 1902, four years after her death, however, indicate that her proposition to Henry Flagler that he extend his railroad to the village of Miami in November, 1892, was "favorably received, but owing to the financial panic of 1893 there was a delay in carrying out the somewhat venturesome undertaking." When the 1895 freeze demonstrated the Miami area's relative freedom from cold weather, Flagler "reopened negotiations with Mrs. Tuttle and in a few weeks all the preliminaries were settled."

Her son, thirty-two years of age in 1902, living in the Fort Dallas home he had helped to develop, was identified as Henry Ethelbert Tuttle, rather than Harry.

This source notes also that one of Julia Tuttle's most valuable achievements was "the building up of the Fort Dallas dairy, which supplies the milk for the famous chain of Flagler hotels, as well as the adjacent city and passing steamers."

Only a sampling of the state's hotel history can be given here. To estimate its scope, one might consider that in 1912, a year of no special significance, Daytona had thirty-five hotels and major boarding houses; St. Petersburg, thirty-seven.

For the most part, the scope of *Florida's Fabled Inns* begins with the time the United States acquired Florida from Spain in 1821 and ends with the early to middle 1950s.

1
Jacksonville and the St. Johns

THEY CALLED IT WACCA PILATKA, that narrow point of the St. Johns River in its tortuous rush to the ocean. The Atlantic was only sixteen miles to the east as the crow flies, but the route taken by the river—east, then north, then east again, with half a dozen creeks swelling its channel—was twice that distance.

When the English took over the Floridas, East and West, the name Wacca Pilatka was translated to Cow Ford. Near the Cow Ford was "a rather bold spring of clear, good water" and a little Timucuan village. The site was a bluff sloping down to the river; many years later it would comprise the foot of Liberty and Washington Streets, in Jacksonville, according to T. Frederick Davis in his 1925 *History of Jacksonville, Florida, and Vicinity.*

The first efforts to accommodate travelers at the Cow Ford were made by two Georgians, William G. Dawson and Stephen E. Buckles, early travelers to the St. Johns country, who believed the spot might one day become a settlement. They remained (probably in 1819) to open a store. The log house they built was located near the King's Road on what would be Adams Street, near Market.

A sailing vessel from New York brought Dawson & Buckles' stock of merchandise and the two men opened the first store in the area. Among the items they sold to the widely-separated farmers were blankets, saddles, bridles, farming implements, buckets, and other such basic supplies.

The two merchants had been preceded in 1818 by John Brady, who occupied the one-room log cabin built by Juan Maestre in the Spring of 1817, and abandoned later that year. It was situated at the place which was to become the southwest corner of Forsyth and Liberty Streets. Still earlier (1816), Lewis Zachariah Hogans and his wife, the former Mrs. Maria Taylor, built a home near what would be the northwest corner of Hogan and Forsyth Streets. It was made of logs but was larger and more carefully constructed than other log cabins of that time. The old Hogans well was a landmark remembered for nearly a century. The land grant had been made to Maria Taylor before her marriage to Hogans.

After Brady, Juan Maestre, L. Z. and Maria Hogans, and the partners Dawson & Buckles, came Isaiah David Hart, in January, 1821. His brother, Daniel C. Hart, came about the same time.

Prior to this time, travelers wishing to pass the night at the Cow Ford "had a miserable experience ahead," wrote Davis. "John Brady was kind-hearted and offered such as he had, but his cabin afforded little that was inviting, and his guests usually slept under the trees with a saddle for a pillow."

Dawson & Buckles also did what they could, offering the use of the attic above the store, occasionally spreading stock blankets on the storehouse floor for the comfort of some special visitor.

The merchant partners were the first to recognize the need for proper accommodations for the increasing numbers of travelers, since the Cow Ford was a natural overnight stop on the King's Road. They built a frame house east of their store, at the place which would later be the southwest corner of Adams and Market Streets, to be used as a boarding house, later called the Inn.

When it was completed in 1821, Mrs. Sarah Waterman was brought in from St. Johns Bluff to take charge of it. She brought her four daughters and two sons, and their arrival doubled the population of the settlement, Davis noted. This was the first frame house in that section of the country constructed of lumber "sawed in a saw-pit."

I. D. Hart in 1830 built what was then considered "a very large two-story boarding house" at the northwest corner of Bay and Market Streets—a place which was to remain in use as a boarding house or hotel site for more than seventy years.

Hart's Inn furnished accommodations for people who desired to spend the Winter there, wrote Davis. Sons and other relatives of wealthy northerners came during the Winter months to be helped by the climate; they went back to their homes greatly benefited, taking with them an enthusiasm that was easily communicated to others.

"So the healthfulness of the locality was established—the greatest asset in the upbuilding of a place and the greatest advertisement it could have. People continued to come. Some stayed and entered into business; some settled in the surrounding localities. In 1830, it is estimated that the population of Jacksonville was about one hundred."

Thus it began, and thus it was destined to continue. People came, or brought loved ones, to bask in Florida's sunshine and breathe its pure, healthful air. Respiratory illness—often tuberculosis, referred to by such euphemisms as "weakness of the lungs"—was the principal offender; and, as it was eventually learned, the farther south in the state one could stay, the more health benefits accrued.

Later, Florida was to become a playground, a Winter retreat for the wealthy and famous—the socially correct place to be in cold weather. But in the beginning, from the time Florida became a United States territory in 1821, it was those "weak lungs" that brought people to the Sunshine State.

When Jacksonville was incorporated in 1832, it was the ninth settlement so designated in Florida. The earlier ones were St. Augustine, Pensacola, Fernandina, Key West, Quincy, Magnolia, Apalachicola and Ochesee. All of these except isolated Key West were in north, middle and west Florida.

Jacksonville, by the late 1840s, could boast "a regular hotel," built by Oliver Wood and called Wood's Hotel. Several years later he sold it to Samuel Buffington, who changed its name to the Buffington House. The new owner built additions and made improvements until it contained nearly one hundred rooms. The Buffington was a fashionable hotel and many prominent local people lived there, at the southwest corner of Adams and Newnan Streets.

Jacksonville had two other hotels as early as 1852—the Crespo House (southeast corner of Adams and Ocean Streets), and the Coy House on the site of the old blockhouse (c. 1836, northeast corner of Monroe and Ocean Streets).

Another ante-bellum hotel in Jacksonville was the Judson House, completed and opened in November, 1854. During the previous year, A. Judson Day had come to Jacksonville from Maine, and bought the west half of the block between Hogan and Julia Streets from Forsyth Street to the St. Johns River. The seller was J. P. Sanderson and the price, $3,000. The Judson House was a three-and-a-half story frame structure which fronted 136 feet on Bay Street, extending the same distance on Julia.

It contained 110 guest rooms, spacious parlors, and a dining room which was eighty feet in length. Broad piazzas were built along the front of the first and second stories. The hotel, complete and ready for business, cost $125,000. It was burned during the Civil War, on March 11, 1862, "by a mob of men whose identity never became known."

The Buffington House burned in 1859, and was not rebuilt. The Crespo likewise burned, and was rebuilt.

Davis noted that a large percentage of the citizens of Jacksonville were men of education and ability, some of them being specialists in their professional lines. "Given to entertaining among themselves and the 'strangers within their gates,' they formed a distinct set where culture and refinement were the dominant characteristics, thus creating a social condition that was morally healthful and uplifting."

Entertainments included dinners, card parties and dances—the traditional square dance and waltz, the reel, and the graceful Spanish dances. A gifted musician with "fiddle and bow" provided the music for these ante-bellum dances—and a fond reputation which was to survive for a century and a quarter. He was "an old Spanish Negro," named Marcellini. All danced, grandfather and granddaughter alike. Propriety decreed that only a married couple could sponsor such an event. Other diversions were picnics, oyster roasts, and camping by the river on moonlight nights, known as marooning. Barbecues and patriotic celebrations were frequent and popular.

It was a time in Florida (what little of it was settled), and in other southern states, that was soon to be gone with the wind. Residents who experienced it described this era later as "the happy days before the war."

By 1860 Jacksonville was a city (so designated the preceding year) of more than 2,000 persons, having doubled in population during the preceding ten years, despite adversities.

The steamboat played a vital role in opening up sections of northeast Florida prior to the coming of the Iron Horse in the 1880s. Aside from the wagon, oxcart, horseback, and a few lines covered by rickety stages drawn over all-but-impassable "roads," they were the only means of transporting people, farm implements and the like.

Hotels and settlements dotted the river routes and seaports.

As early as 1830, the *George Washington* became the first steamer to ply the St. Johns. Four years later, a more or less regular run was established between Savannah and Picolata on the St. Johns, *via* Jacksonville. Troops and supplies were carried up and down the river during the Second Seminole War, 1835-42. In the 1840s the *Sarah Spaulding,* a high-pressure boat used often for short excursions, chugged her way between Jacksonville and Lake Monroe. "She made a fearful noise while in operation," wrote Davis.

Between 1852 and the Civil War, the *Darlington* provided the principal means of travel between Jacksonville and Enterprise.

These early steamers used lightwood knots for fuel, and a great volume of dense black smoke was emitted from their stacks. Some person at each landing would serve as lookout, and when the smoke of the steamer was seen, he would start the cry, "Steamboat, steamboat, coming 'round the point," Davis noted, and the local people gathered at the wharf to hear the latest news. The arrival of a steamboat meant a link with the outside world.

Bay Street, Jacksonville, in 1897.

Union officers were still stationed in Jacksonville in 1865, although the Civil War, as it affected that city, virtually ended with the evacuation of Confederate troops on July 26, 1864, from nearby Camp Milton.

These officers remaining in Jacksonville after the war made their unofficial headquarters in the St. Johns House, built in 1865 by Mrs. E. Hudnall. It was a frame house of two-and-a-half stories, located on the north side of Forsyth Street, between Pine (Main) and Laura Streets, and had forty rooms for guests. The St. Johns was favored by political figures as well, and doubtless within its walls many of the political schemes of that day

The St. James Hotel in Jacksonville, opened to the public on January 1, 1869, enlarged in 1872 and 1881, was the largest (with rooms for 500 guests) and probably the most elegant of the seasonal pre-railroad era hostelries in the state. It provided not only fine food and lodgings, but also telegraph, baggage and ticket facilities, a laundry, barber shop, wine room, reading rooms, bowling alleys and a billiard room. A passenger elevator was installed in 1876. This photo was made between the time of the last enlargement of the hotel in 1881 and introduction of the first electric lights in 1883. The St. James burned in the 1901 fire.

were hatched. It served until 1901, and was burned in the big fire of that year.

Next came the storied St. James, which was to become "the most famous hotel in the South and for a long time the mecca of the wealthy tourist in Florida." Its owners—New England capitalists—had purchased the two lots on the west side of Laura Street between Duval and Church Streets, at $900 each, and planned a hotel which cost $30,000—a very large sum at that time. It faced the public square (which in 1899 became Hemming Park) from the north.

The building was constructed in three stages, the first completed in time for the hotel to be opened on January 1, 1869.

At first it contained 120 rooms in a frame building three full stories high, and a fourth under a French roof. A novel attraction was provision for hot and cold baths. It also provided a billiard room and bowling alleys. The building—105 feet wide—faced Duval Street, and its gardens were at the rear, facing Church Street.

A brick addition, three stories high, was constructed toward Hogan Street in 1872; nine years later the French roof was removed, another four-story wooden section was added, and the central brick portion was increased to four stories. Thus it stood until the 1901 fire, continuously under the supervision of J. R. Campbell, entertaining guests of national prominence, as well as European dignitaries.

Although it was a Winter hotel, Jacksonville looked on the St. James as her own, wrote Davis.

Grand National Hotel, 1873, successor to the old Judson House.

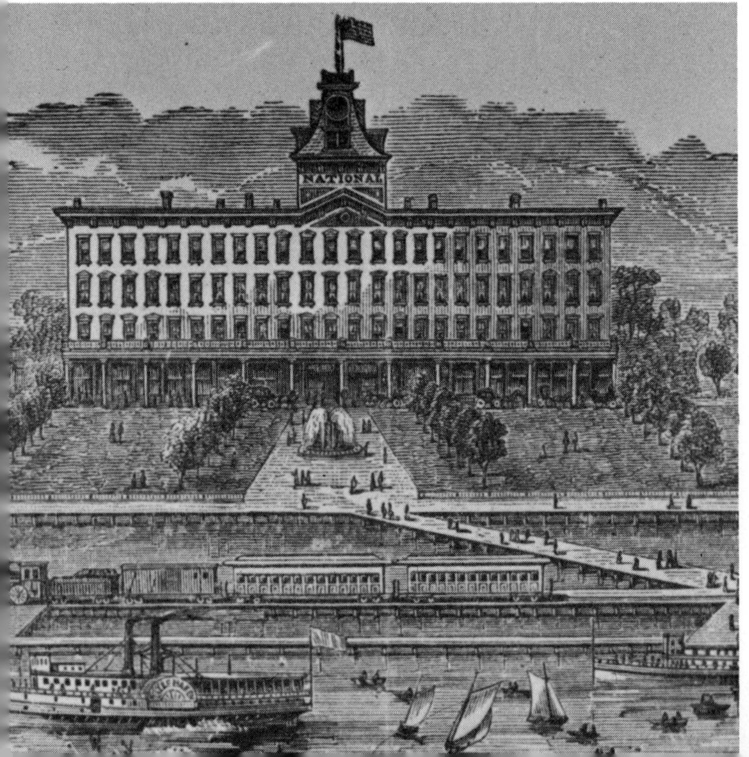

Above—Jacksonville's Water Works and artesian well (inset). Below—The Park Building (left) and Broward Building. Both were at the intersection of Pine (Main) and Forsyth Streets. All are shown about 1886.

"Here local society danced with famous personages from everywhere at the Saturday night hops; danced the schottische, the polka, the true waltz and the reels—those beautiful, graceful dances that, like the St. James itself, appear now to be a part of the past."

The site of the St. James remained vacant for eleven years after the 1901 fire. In 1912 Jacob E. Cohen, a founder of Cohen Brothers store (earlier located at 29 to 35 West Bay Street) erected a building there to house the department store and a number of business and professional offices. This structure, occupying the entire "St. James lot" directly north of Hemming Park, was named to memorialize the famous old hotel. The building still stands, housing May-Cohen department store.

The Grand National was the next substantial hotel in Jacksonville. In 1873 it was built on the site of the old Judson House, on Bay Street at Julia, facing the river across an ornamental park. The Grand National was a mammoth pile of brick surmounted by a grand central clock tower, which offered a view "far and wide." It had 150 guest rooms.

This hotel was not successful financially, and was not properly maintained; by 1879 it was closed, badly down-at-heels. During the next two years it became "almost a wreck." In 1881 the property was bought by Nathaniel Webster, who restored it (for $90,000) and renamed it the

Bay Street, Jacksonville, looking east from Hogan, about 1875. At right, the Astor Building; at left, barely visible in the distance, the Grand National Hotel.

The original St. James, opened in 1869.

"Professor Gwynn of the St. James"—whose function was not specified.

The McConihe block on Bay Street in the 1880s.

Hotel Aragon in the early 1900s, built in 1885 as an enlargement of the Grand National.

Everett. In 1885 Webster enlarged the hotel by building a six-story structure facing on Forsyth Street. This cost $100,000, mostly borrowed.

In a foreclosure sale in 1898 the Bay Street section (the Everett) was bought by Harry Mason. The Forsyth side (which became the Aragon) was sold in 1900 to Dr. Neal Mitchell, for a published price of $30,000.

Both of these hotels survived the 1901 fire. The name of the Everett was changed over the years to the Milner, then the Earle. It was razed in 1959. The Aragon was closed in 1971, after which it, too, was demolished.

The three-story Nichols House came next, in 1875, at the northwest corner of Hogan and Forsyth Streets. Built by W. M. Nichols, it was a three-story brick structure, costing $63,000. Several years later it was sold to J. S. Turner and leased by him to General B. Lewis. Lewis renamed it the Duval Hotel. It burned in 1892, was rebuilt the following year, survived the 1901 fire and remained to serve the public for many years.

In 1925 Davis wrote: "It (the Duval) occupies the most historic spot in Jacksonville, for it stands partly on the site of the log-cabin home of L. Z. Hogans, the first house built within the city limits of Old Jacksonville."

Another major Jacksonville hotel built the same year as the Nichols House—1875—was the Windsor. A three-story frame structure, it occupied the northwest corner of the intersection of Hogan and Monroe Streets. Passing through several ownerships and several enlargements (to Duval Street), it was sold in 1897 to the firm of Dodge & Cullins, which also operated the rebuilt Duval Hotel. Guest rooms of the original Windsor were on the two upper floors, while the first floor was occupied by dining rooms, offices, parlors and "a number of large sleeping apartments." (This probably implied suites, but at that time, private hotel rooms frequently were referred to as apartments.) Enlargements between 1875 and 1897 more than doubled its capacity. By the time it burned in 1901 it had accommodations for 450 guests.

The Windsor was the only one of Jacksonville's large hotels destroyed in that massive conflagration to be rebuilt. Construction of the new Windsor (by Dodge & Cullins) was begun three months after the fire, and it was opened on February 15, 1902. It covered the whole block directly west of Hemming Park, and was the last hotel built in Jacksonville on the old plan of covering a large area rather than of conserving ground space by building upward. The Windsor was of Spanish Renaissance architecture, constructed of brick, steel and stone, and could accommodate 500 guests.

Still another major hotel, built only a year after the Nichols (Duval) and Windsor, was the Carleton, located at the northwest corner of Bay and Market Streets. Much of the material, including the face brick, was shipped down from New England. Its builders were E. C. Stimpson and George A. Devnell. It contained 105 guest rooms, on four floors.

"For a long time the Carleton was one of Florida's famous hotels, and its history is inseparably linked with that of the Jacksonville of former days," wrote Davis.

The Carleton was another casualty of the 1901 fire. Although it was officially renamed the United States Hotel in the 1890s, the old name continued in use to the end.

"In the palmy tourist days of 1876-86, when Jacksonville was known as the 'Winter City in Summer Land,' the names 'St. James,' 'Carleton' and 'Windsor' were widely known throughout the North and East, for they were popular hotels and enjoyed a lucrative business in the Winter-time," wrote Davis.

The era beginning in 1879 was portentous in the history of Jacksonville and, indeed, of all Florida. Means of transportation—dependable, if not always comfortable—became available. Two factors brought about this circumstance: travel to Florida, which was destined to grow beyond any imaginings at that time, and the production of oranges for the market from lands around the St. Johns, an industry which before many years would find its home in the milder climes of central and south Florida.

The number of visitors coming to the state grew steadily, year by year, beginning in 1870, and Jacksonville's hotels and boarding houses were often filled to overflowing. Its Winter population during this time was four times the number of its permanent residents.

"Getting there" in those years was definitely not "half the fun." On the contrary, it was a tedious, exhausting experience. When the final change of railroad cars was made at Live Oak, and the last lap finished over the Florida Central into Jacksonville, Davis recorded, the tired tourist gave a sigh of relief.

There were few points of interest in Jacksonville at that time; the traveler came partly for the climate and partly because Florida was in vogue.

River boat trips out of Jacksonville, which were

Top right, Hibernia Hotel and pier, Fleming's Island. Clockwise from right center, four 19th Century Jacksonville hotels—the Acme, with French roof; the elegant Windsor, which burned in 1901; Ocean House, with guests and servants posing for the photographer; Moncrief House, Charles Evans, proprietor.

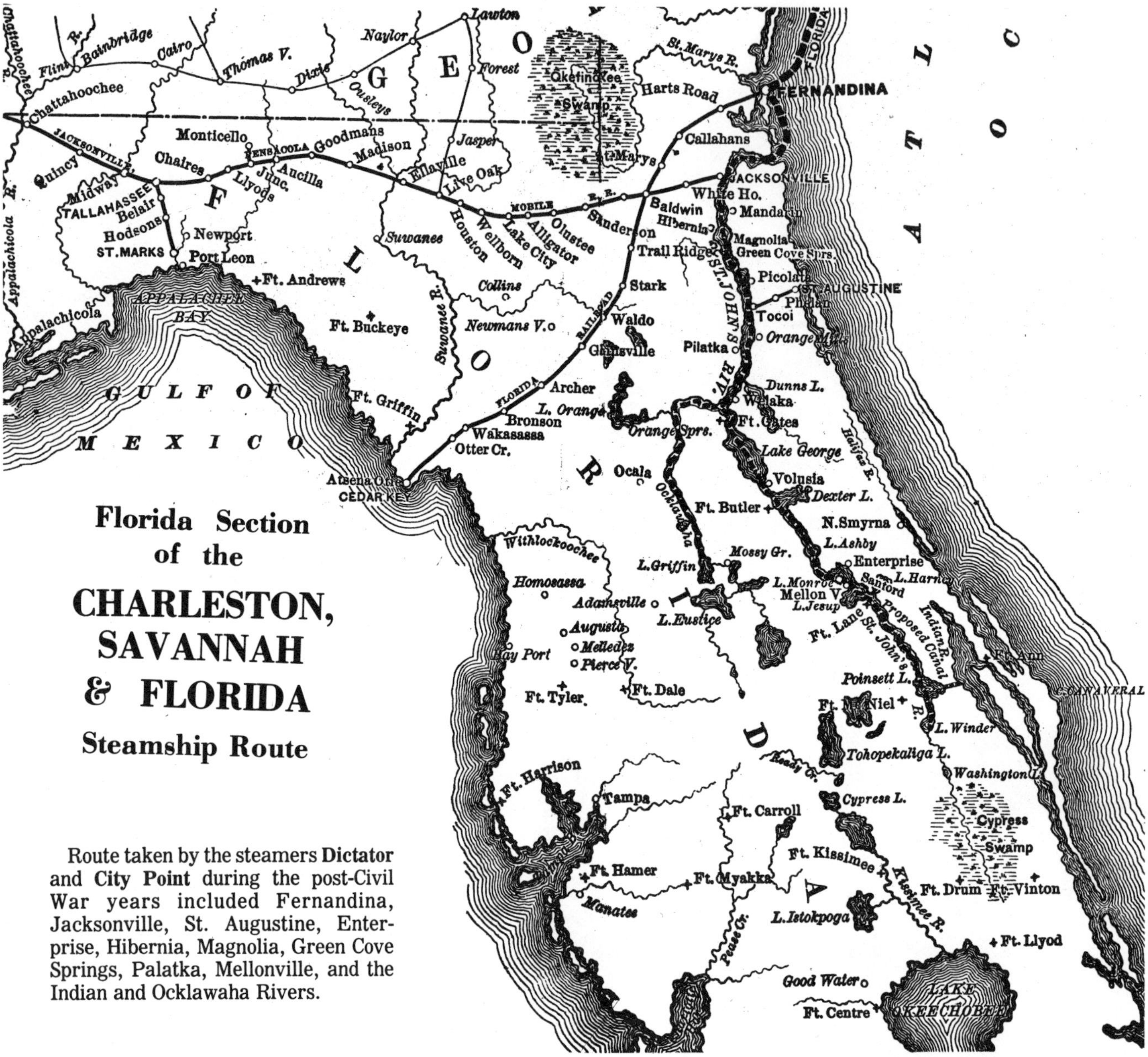

Florida Section of the CHARLESTON, SAVANNAH & FLORIDA Steamship Route

Route taken by the steamers **Dictator** and **City Point** during the post-Civil War years included Fernandina, Jacksonville, St. Augustine, Enterprise, Hibernia, Magnolia, Green Cove Springs, Palatka, Mellonville, and the Indian and Ocklawaha Rivers.

Magnolia Hotel at Magnolia Springs, c. 1885.

Night cruise on the St. Johns.

Nichols House, built in 1875. It burned in 1892, was rebuilt as the Duval Hotel, and escaped the 1901 fire. Note the second story porch and the flaring superstructure of the pillars.

Automobiles and horse-drawn carriages wait for passengers at Jacksonville's first Union Station, built in 1894-95.

St. Luke's Hospital, 1888.

Law Building (top), corner of Forsyth and Market Streets. Trinity Methodist Church (bottom), southwest corner of Monroe and Laura Streets (later Snyder Memorial Methodist). Both are shown in the 1880s.

Carleton House, built in 1876. Awnings shaded the windows against the sun; cooling devices were far in the future.

Hotel advertisements in the (Jacksonville) Florida Times-Union, January 1, 1891, page 2. Resorts on both coasts and in central Florida beckoned the traveler.

PORT TAMPA.

The "Inn" Hotel and Restaurant is open for the Season

—FOR PERMANENT AND TRANSIENT GUESTS.—

Key West, Havana, Manatee River, New Orleans, and Mobile Steamers

—NEAR THE HOTEL.—

C. E. HOADLEY,

Superintendent

HOTELS AND RESORTS.

THE SEMINOLE,
WINTER PARK, FLORIDA.
W. F. Paige, Manager.
Opens for Season of 1891 January 7th.

GROVE HALL,
CRESCENT CITY, FLA.
Now Open.
H. R. VAUGHAN, Prop'r.

The Indian River Hotel
AT TITUSVILLE, FLA.
UNDER NEW MANAGEMENT, by W. B. PECK for 20 years proprietor of the Mt. Everett House, South Egremont, Berkshire county, Mass. Offers first-class accommodations, at moderate rates. Finest spot in Florida for sportsmen.

GRAND VIEW HOTEL
JACKSONVILLE, - FLORIDA.
Opened Nov. 20, 1890, for the Season.
G. W. SMITH. - Proprietor.

BETTELINI'S HOTEL.
—EUROPEAN PLAN.—
No. 16 E. Bay St., Jacksonville, Fla.
All Street Cars from Depots and Steamers Going East Pass the House.
Rooms for One............25c, 50c, 75c and $1.00.
For Two ....75c, $1.00 and $1.50.
Meals, 25. Lunch Counter. New York Prices.
F. BETTELINI, Proprietor.

THE GLENADA,
JACKSONVILLE, FLORIDA,
Opens December 11th.
W. TAETEROW, Proprietor.

SARATOGA HOTEL,
Palatka, Florida.
Open October 28, for the Sixth Season.
A. S. WASHBURNE.

Hotel Punta Gorda,
On Charlotte Harbor, Punta Gorda, Florida.
One of the most beautiful resorts in the South. Below the frost line. Will open January 1st, 1891.
HARRY B WARDEN, Manager.

"THE ST. GEORGE."
St. Augustine, Fla.
Corner of St. George Street and the Plaza.
The select and favorite family hotel of the city, thoroughly comfortable and homelike; unexcelled cuisine and service; within a moment's walk of the Ponce de Leon, Cathedral Bay, etc. C. D. TYLER, Proprietor.

OCEAN VIEW HOTEL,
ST. AUGUSTINE, - - FLA.
(Only House on the Bay.)
OPEN MONDAY, NOV. 10TH.
$2 and $2.50 per day. Special rates by week.
W. S. M. PICKHAM, Prop.

THE ABBEY.
St. George St., Near City Gates,
ST. AUGUSTINE, FLORIDA.
First-class in every respect. Rates $10 to $14 per week. MRS. A. B. ABBE.
Also of Pierce Villa, Cottage City, Mass.

THE ALCAZAR,
St. Augustine, Fla.
—) NOW OPEN. (—
AMERICAN PLAN.
Russian, Turkish and Roman Baths and Swimming Pool open daily.
B. W ANGELL, Superintendent. O. D. SEAVEY, Manager.

"THE CARLETON,"
St George-Treasury Street, St. Augustine, Fla.
Located in the center of the city. Less than sixty yards from Post Office, Plaza, New Park, Opera-House, Old Cathedral, and Bay. Only one hundred yards from Ponce de Leon, Alcazar, and Cordova. Verandas on East and South. Hotel newly furnished. Table first-class. Service unexcelled. Everything new, bright and clean. Rates, $2.00 per day.

GREENO HOUSE, Marine Street, ST. AUGUSTINE, FLA.
Overlooking bay and ocean. Open all the year. Terms, from $7 to $9 per week or $1.50 per day. WM. YOUNG, Proprietor.

BROWN'S COTTAGE, Charlotte Street, ST. AUGUSTINE.
Delightful place for parties desiring quietness, good rooms and table. $7 per week. Overlooking Bay and Old Fort. MRS. F. C. BROWN.

MRS. D. R. TODD.
Of Hotel Carpenter, Bartow, Fla., has refitted
"THE SAN CARLO,"
ST. AUGUSTINE, FLA. WRITE FOR TERMS

ACME HOTEL,
EUROPEAN PLAN.
No. 111 West Bay St.,
JACKSONVILLE, - - - - FLORIDA.
Reopened with finely furnished apartments, with clean nice beds, 50c to $1 per day, each person. Good dining room in same block with moderate prices. H. A. BURT.

CARLETON :-: HOTEL,
Cor. Bay and Market Streets, opposite Post Office.
American Plan, Terms $2.50 Per Day AND UPWARDS.
Elevator and all Modern Improvements.
Horse Cars Pass the Doors.
MAHON TOWNSHEND & AHERN, Prop's.

—NOW OPEN—
DUVAL—HOTEL,
W. S. McCLELLAND, Proprietor.
Jacksonville, - - Florida.
Handsomely papered throughout and thoroughly refitted during the past summer.
Centrally Located. Liberally Conducted.

VAILL'S FLOATING HOTEL,
JUPITER, DADE CO., FLA.
SEA :-: FOOD :-: A :-: SPECIALTY.
Best Fishing in Florida. Boats, Fishing Tackle and Bait on Board.
Take J., T. & K. W. R'y to Titusville and steamer St. Lucie or St. Sebastian from there to Jupiter. E. E. VAILL, Proprietor.

HOTEL SANTA FE,
MELROSE, Clay Co., Fla.
60 miles from Jacksonville, on Lake Santa Fe, in the HIGH LAKE REGION, the HIGHEST and HEALTHIEST point in the state. First-class accommodations for 150 guests—$8 to $10 per week.
I. F. GRAHAM, Proprietor.

HOTEL COQUINA,
Ormond-on-the-Halifax.
Rates $2.50 Per Day.
Send for Circulars.
SEISER & VINING, Proprietors.
ORMOND, FLA.

THE EGMONT,
Fernandina, Fla.
WM. M. STEWART.

THE LAKEVIEW!
A New Brick Hotel, with New Furniture and all Modern Improvements will open at Leesburg, Fla., November 1, 1890.
The Hotel is Supplied with Pure Artesian Well Water, entirely free from sulphurous taste or any impurity.
WM. M. GRAY, - - - MANAGER

An eight-hour fire on Friday, May 3, 1901, reduced 146 blocks—466 acres—of Jacksonville to ashes and rubble. A wooden shanty in the LaVilla section, at the western edge of the city, caught fire shortly before 12:30 p. m. Sparks ignited fibre laid out to dry on the platform of the nearby Cleveland Fibre Factory at Beaver and Davis Streets, and flames riding a fresh wind roared first east, then south, then east again through the business district and the most populous residential sections of the Old City. From the pine shanty suburb of Hansontown at the northwest, to Hogans Creek on the east, and the waterfront on the south, the speeding fire leveled the prospering city. Three buildings, at widely scattered points at the edge of the blaze, and the bronze statue of the Confederate soldier in Hemming Park were the only structures to survive in the stricken area. Through a shift in the wind and the valiant efforts of the Jacksonville Fire Department, a score of blocks south of Adams Street and east of Laura, plus a few to the north at the western edge of the city, were spared. The total property loss was estimated at $15,000,000. It was, according to T. Frederick Davis in his 1924 **History of Jacksonville, Florida, and Vicinity,** "the largest fire, both in area and property loss, ever experienced by any southern city of the United States." Incredibly, there were only seven deaths.

The house at the bottom of the picture stood at the corner of Adams and Hogan Streets. Hogan runs along the right-hand side of the photo. The next two streets beyond Adams are Monroe and Duval. In the block between those two streets, facing Hogan, was the site of the Windsor Hotel.

The Jacksonville Union Terminal Station was opened to the public on November 18, 1919.

Left—The Duval Hotel, c. 1906. Note the "gingerbread" below the second floor porch railing and at the eaves above the third floor.

Below—An electrical star on Jacksonville's skyline marked the location of the New Hotel Jefferson in the 1930s.

Two views of the Hotel Burbridge (later the Floridan), which opened in December, 1911. Above: The exterior featured an enclosed balcony above the entrance. Right: Potted palms decorated the dining room.

Rocking chairs on the "plaza" of the Hotel Aragon were popular with the guests.

The three-story Shamrock Hotel, shown here about 1915, was notable for its rounded corner, and roof ornaments resembling a picket fence.

The Windsor Hotel, rebuilt after the original building was destroyed by fire in 1901, is seen here about 1940. A corner of Hemming Park shows in the foreground. The Windsor was razed in 1950. The site is occupied in 1980 by a Penney's store and a Woolworth's, both fronting on Hogan Street.

quite popular but of brief duration, could be taken either up the St. Johns and Oklawaha Rivers, or to St. Augustine, *via* Tocoi.

Points to be visited along the St. Johns River trip included Mulberry Grove, Mandarin (Harriet Beecher Stowe's residence), Hibernia, Magnolia, Green Cove Springs, Hogarth's Wharf, Picolata, Tocoi, Federal Point, Orange Mills, Palatka, Welaka, Beecher, Mt. Royal, Georgetown, Volusia, Orange Bluff, Hawkinsville, Cabbage Bluff, Blue Spring, Sanford, Mellonville and Enterprise. Silver Springs was reached *via* the Oklawaha River, and Sand Point *via* the Indian River.

At several of these stops there were pleasant, small resort hotels. They were described in general by Branch Cabell and A. J. Hanna in *The St. Johns, a Parade of Diversities,* as "sprawling wooden structures, two or three stories in height, with wide verandas for those patrons who elected to take out-of-door exercise in a rocking chair. Decorations were limited to a half dozen or so mounted birds, one stuffed alligator, a meager collection of seashells, and a few lithographs.

"Serious elderly patrons interested themselves in a shared study of the neighboring birds and of the Negro problem, or else dozed in semitropical sunlight. The more energetic preferred croquet. The truly strenuous turned to fishing for bass, or to sailing upon the quiet waters of the St. Johns, or to hunting wild turkey, deer, and quail; but the heroic hunted alligators."

The beautiful Atlantic beaches, some eighteen miles to the east, were too remote to become popular until 1884. Pablo Beach was developed that year as a resort, and lots were sold in expectation that the Jacksonville & Atlantic Railway would soon furnish train service to that point. The railroad builders and resort promoters were largely the same group—which was the pattern of Florida's early development, especially its resort areas.

Jacksonville was travel headquarters—the Winter tourist capital.

Most of the visitors' dollars were spent on hotels and steamboat rides, but a surprising amount of money was spent on souvenir items such as alligators' teeth, coral, sea beans, sea shells (polished or not), wood carvings, canes, and "every other thing of strange and grotesque fashion," wrote Davis. It was the age of souvenirs, and tourists bought them freely from the stores and bazaars along Bay Street.

California had not yet made its bid for tourism, and Florida, even in the 1870s, was the nation's playground. The only drawback was getting here in reasonable comfort—and the railroad tycoons were soon to solve that problem.

A number of orange groves had been planted along the river as far back as the early 1830s, but they were devastated by the freeze of 1835. Interest was revived briefly between 1838 and 1840, but the trees were killed by a blight. Not until after the Civil War did the citrus industry in Florida get off the ground.

Prosperous northerners came and established estates along the river as Winter homes, usually setting out groves on their property. One of these planters was Frederick DeBary, who built a handsome mansion on the north side of Lake Monroe (a part of the St. Johns River). The mansion still stands, a century later. He also established the DeBary Steamship Line.

These growers had no satisfactory means of shipping their fruit out of the state.

Tourist and shipping needs together prompted Henry B. Plant in 1881 to build the first direct rail line from the North to Jacksonville—the Waycross Short Line. A spur line on a wharf was built at the riverfront landing, so that fruit could be loaded directly into the cars from the boats which had brought it from the prospering groves along the St. Johns and sent quickly on its way to northern markets. The Jacksonville & Fernandina Railroad was built the same year to connect Jacksonville with that deep-sea port.

This was the start of the competitive railroad construction that afterward made Jacksonville one of the most famous railroad terminals in the United States. Along with the coming of the railroads, the preliminary work for deeper water was started at St. Johns bar, when the jetty work began. Thus both rail and water transportation to Jacksonville grew side by side under the same compelling circumstances—trade and tourist travel.

Plant was destined to push his rails south to Tampa and Punta Gorda on Florida's west coast; and only a few years later that other giant of Florida's development, Henry Morrison Flagler, performed a similar service down the state's east coast as far, finally, as Key West.

The railroad age had come to Florida, and with it, the golden age of hotels—large and luxurious, smaller and less luxurious. Not surprisingly, Plant and Flagler built the biggest and most elaborate ones during the next several decades.

In the late 19th Century it was the practice of the local newspapers to compile the total number of Winter visitors to Jacksonville, from the registers of hotels and major transient boarding houses. Beginning with the 1882-83 season, these were the figures for five consecutive seasons: 39,810; 48,869; 60,011; 65,193, and 58,460. The 1886-87 slump was caused by California's bid for the tourist trade, and Jacksonville produced the Sub-Tropical Exposition to regain its popularity.

Guests at the large hotels were rarely seen on the streets before mid-morning. Breakfast over, they turned toward Bay Street for shopping and a promenade from the Everett to the Carleton, a distance of half a mile. During these morning hours of the Winter, one might meet on the streets of Jacksonville people from every northern and western state as well as many southerners, and titled personages from foreign countries.

"The bazaars, curio shops and stores which lined Bay Street were thronged with well-dressed people on pleasure bent," wrote Davis. "Representatives of the New York and London society clubs, money kings, literary celebrities, dowagers and their daughters, bridal couples, and Bohemians jostled one another in their round of pleasure. From three to five in the afternoon the scene was repeated.

"In the evening, life on the street was transferred to the hotels, where good music by bands and famous orchestras invited the dance. Life at large hotels during the Winter season was a round of pleasure and fascination, for every facility was provided for the enjoyment of the visitors. For the convenience of foreigners who did not understand English well the hotels, particularly the Carleton, employed a special corps of waiters who could speak the principal foreign languages."

Among the major early 20th Century hotels in Jacksonville, in addition to the rebuilt Windsor, were the Seminole, Mason, Burbridge, George Washington and Carling. Several of them were renamed.

The Seminole, at the southeast corner of Forsyth and Hogan Streets, built for the Florida Hotel Company (R. R. Meyer, president), was the city's first skyscraper hotel—ten stories, with 250 guest rooms. The doors were opened on New Year's Day, 1910. Its construction comprised "a pleasing combination of grey granite, grey cut stone, and buff pressed brick, with carved panel decorations typifying its Indian name." One of its two dining rooms was the Indian Room, opening off the rotunda. The Seminole had a popular role in the city's social and club life, as well as providing accommodations for visitors.

Jacksonville's first skyscraper hotel was the ten-story Seminole. It opened on January 1, 1910.

The Burbridge, its lobby adorned wth trophies of Ben Burbridge's hunting trips to Alaska and Africa, was particularly favored by traveling men and sportsmen. Seven stories in height, it had 175 guest rooms, with baths, and was opened in December, 1911, at the northeast corner of Forsyth and Clay Streets. It became the Floridan in 1942.

The eleven-story Mason, built in French Renaissance style, was located at the northwest corner of Bay and Julia Streets, and had 250 guest rooms, all with private baths. Built for George H. Mason in 1913, it cost $1,000,000, including furnishings, and its eleventh-floor dining room provided an unobstructed and beautiful view of the St. Johns for many miles. It became the Mayflower in 1929, and was razed in January, 1978.

Among the major resort hotels near Jacksonville in this period—the years shortly before and after the turn of the century—were Murray Hall at Pablo (Jacksonville) Beach, the Continental at Atlantic Beach, two farther north at Burnside Beach, and two on Fort George Island on the north side of the river at its mouth. One of these faced the beach and the other, the river inside the north jetty.

Murray Hall, built in 1886 by John G. Christopher at a cost of $150,000, was of most unusual architecture. The main section and wings were three stories in height, with a tower-like section in front, six stories high. Several secondary towers and lookouts gave it the appearance of an exhibition building, especially when all of its flags were flying. Fifteen-foot wide piazzas graced the front on all floors.

The hotel was completely lighted with electricity (rare in 1886), having its own generator and artesian well. In addition to steam heat, Murray Hall had no less than fifty-eight open fireplaces, since it was to be a year-round hotel.

With its rare profile, comfortable accommodations (for 200 guests), and its elaborately landscaped grounds, Murray Hall gained the reputation of being the most attractive seaside resort hotel on the south Atlantic coast. In August, 1890, after only four years of existence, this frame structure was totally destroyed by fire.

The Continental, built in 1901 a mile north along the Atlantic shore, was one of the H. M. Flagler chain of hotels, and the most northerly, though by no means the first. A long frame structure, 447 feet by forty-seven, it had a rotunda six stories high, with four-story wings at north and south, each wing terminating with a five-story T.

A detached, covered promenade, sixteen feet wide and 1,100 feet long, paralleled the hotel on its east (ocean front), south and west exposures. The hotel had 186 guest rooms—later 220—and fifty-six baths. The dining room could accommodate 350 people at one time. The Continental was painted in Flagler's favorite colors, yellow with green trim. Its name was changed in 1913 to the Atlantic Beach Hotel. Being of wood construction, it, too, met its end by fire, in 1919.

Burnside Beach, several miles north of Pablo, was promoted in 1886 by the Jacksonville, Mayport & Pablo Railway. The four-story Palmetto Hotel was built about this time, a neighbor to the old Burnside House, an ante-bellum inn. Both hotels and the Burnside Beach pavilion were destroyed by fire on November 28, 1889.

The Fort George Island hotels met the same fate—but not before they enjoyed a time of much popularity. They were reached by water—first the side-wheel steamer *Water Lily* and later, to handle the crowds of visitors, the *Kate Spencer*, built especially for this service. She made two trips daily in the Winters of the early 1880s.

As Flagler extended his railroad farther to the south, the popularity of Fort George Island began to wane, the crest of tourist travel moving on to the new frontier of easy transportation.

The year 1926 saw the erection of two major hotels in downtown Jacksonville—the George

The Fort George flourished in the 1880s.

The Continental Hotel at Atlantic Beach was built by the H. M. Flagler interests in 1901.

A six-story central tower surmounted the three-story Murray Hall Hotel built at Pablo (Jacksonville) Beach in 1886 by John G. Christopher.

A more modest Pablo Beach hotel was the Ocean View, seen here about 1920.

The million-dollar Mason Hotel, built in 1913, was renamed the Mayflower in 1929.

Named the Osceola Hotel, 1911-29, this hostelry at 307 Cedar Street later became the San Carlos.

Washington and the Carling. The George Washington, at the northwest corner of Adams and Julia Streets, was built by Robert Kloeppel. It was fourteen stories high and had "the innovation of a radio in each room," according to the *History of Duval County, Florida,* by Pleasant Daniel Gold, published in 1928. The George Washington was opened on December 15, 1926. In 1937, air conditioning was installed throughout the building, and it became the first hotel in the United States to be completely air conditioned.

The Carling, twelve stories high, was built on the north side of Adams Street, between Laura and Main, and opened on September 1, 1926. Soon after Franklin D. Roosevelt was elected President in 1932, the Carling was renamed the Roosevelt.

Kloeppel entered the hotel business in 1912 when he bought the Flagler Hotel building, in which he had a law office. The hotel, under an earlier name, had been purchased in New York and moved, piece by piece, to Jacksonville, where it was reassembled near the railway station as the Flagler. Kloeppel renamed it the Jefferson.

After building the George Washington in 1926, he purchased the Mayflower and with his son, Robert Kloeppel, Jr., operated all three until his death in 1961. The younger Kloeppel sold the George Washington in 1963 to William O. Johnson, who also owned the Roosevelt Hotel, and sold the Mayflower in 1974 to the Charter Company.

The Roosevelt has become a retirement hotel. The George Washington and Mayflower sites became parking lots, the Jefferson a vacant lot. Another large Jacksonville hotel, the Robert Meyer, built in 1959, has become the luxurious Holiday Inn City Center.

The Hilton, on the south side of the St. Johns, was the only large transient hotel open in the city in 1979, according to Mr. and Mrs. Kloeppel, Jr. Dozens of motels dot the suburbs.

The senior Kloeppel, one of the receivers of the Collier Coast Hotels, and his son also owned two hotels in West Palm Beach—the El Verano, bought in the early 1930s, restored, and renamed the George Washington; and the Royal Worth, purchased in 1943 and renamed the Pennsylvania. Both of these became retirement homes.

To the list of Jacksonville's early hotels, Gold added the Pennington House, at the corner of Forsyth and Cedar Streets, the Grand Hotel on Forsyth between Clay and Bridge (Broad), and the Oxford, one of the first apartment houses, at the corner of Laura and Duval Streets, all three of which opened in 1863; the St. Mark's, a three-story brick structure on Newnan Street, in 1870; the Tremont, on the corner of Pine (Main) and Forsyth Streets, 1871; the Mattair House on West Forsyth, 1872; and the Rosalind, the city's first suburban hotel, in the Fairfield section, 1876.

Any such list of Jacksonville hotels can include only selected larger and better known ones

Four Jacksonville hotels, large and small. Clockwise from upper left: the George Washington, built in 1926; the Ambassador, boasting of being "100% Air Conditioned," formerly the Griner; the Carling, built in 1926 and renamed the Roosevelt; and the Westmoreland on Bay Street, seen in the early 1900s.

because, as early as the 1880s the city (of about 15,000) had no less than forty hotels, according to Cabell and Hanna.

A promotional publication entitled *Greater Jacksonville Illustrated—1905* lists also for that period the St. George at the corner of Forsyth and Julia, "thirty-eight sleeping rooms to let at 50 cents, 75 cents and $1 per day"; the Southern Hotel, corner of Bridge and Bay Streets, same rates; the Model, 619 West Bay Street, thirty rooms; the New Westmoreland, 335 West Bay, at Cedar, $2 per day and up, with meals; New Hotel Victoria, corner of Main and Adams, same rates as Westmoreland; the New Travelers Hotel, 407 West Bay Street, same rates; and the Manor (formerly Hotel Lenox), corner of Newnan and Adams.

Also advertised in 1905 were the Acme Quick Lunch at 305 West Bay Street, "A regular meal is served here at any hour of the night or day for twenty-five cents"; the elegant new ferryboat *Duval*, running from Jacksonville to South Jacksonville—trips made every fifteen minutes, fare only five cents for the half-mile river crossing; and the Florida Ostrich Farm, a popular tourist attraction "on the banks of the beautiful St. Johns River, in the pretty suburb of Fairfield."

A special attraction at the Ostrich Farm was Oliver W., Jr., "the famous racing ostrich, the only thoroughly harness broken ostrich in America."

"Railroad men only" proclaimed a sign on the door of the Terminal Hotel, seen here in the 1940s.

Not all of Florida's fabled inns have catered to traveling families and sun-seekers. Some of them, once identified by a discreet red light over the front door, have been sought out over the years by bachelors young and not-so-young, by men traveling alone, by husbands whose wives wished to avoid bearing children, and by teenage boys just discovering their new masculinity. In the present era of sexual permissiveness and contraception they have all but vanished from the scene.

But in earlier years they were a more or less accepted part of the social structure. Tampa had its "houses" in Ybor City: the Melville Club, the elegant Hilda Raymond's, and the disreputable "dollar houses." Pensacola had Molly McCoy and the whole "line," under discreet police surveillance.

Miami prior to World War II had, among others, Gertie Walsh, who began operating in a Victorian mansion on Flagler Street. She moved from there to a more modern place on the Miami River—a house known all over the United States as the bordello with a berth for yachts, according to Helen Muir in *Miami, U. S. A.*, published in 1953.

Gertie had a waiting list of fifty to one hundred girls, and when the Legislature was in session in Tallahassee it was her habit to bring her fairest to the state capital to make friends with the legislators. Several of her girls married men of position, Muir noted.

"It has been said that it took the Army, the Navy, the Air Corps and the Marines to close Gertie Walsh's. The military order in World War II was to close all bordellos, and Gertie's fell with the others."

As for Jacksonville, it had the legendary Cora Crane.

She appeared on the scene there in 1895, calling herself Cora Taylor, thirty years old, with two husbands in her past—neither of them named Taylor.

Cora owned two houses in Jacksonville at different times. The first was the Hotel de Dreme, listed in the City Directory as a "furnished boarding house" on the southwest corner of the intersection of Ashley and Hawk (Jefferson) Streets in the LaVilla district. Cora renamed it the Hotel de Dream, and lost no time in transforming the place after the famed sporting houses in New Orleans.

"Resorts like the Hotel de Dream and the pleasure palaces of the Vieux Carré belonged to an era when men led a life apart from their womenfolk," wrote Lillian Gilkes in *Cora Crane—A Biography of Mrs. Stephen Crane.*

"To comprehend the place that such resorts filled in the separate masculine world, one must journey back to a time long antedating the Kinsey reports and the dissemination of Freudian ideas. Outside the domestic circle, men had their clubs and barrooms which excluded women . . . Night spots thrived on the social and religious prohibitions on drinking, gambling or card playing in the home, as well as on the banishment of sex from the bedroom except for reproductive purposes; and the new mistress of the Hotel de Dream was in these things a student of human nature."

As the smartest night spot in the city, the place was given a Class-A rating by the clerk of the St.

The Talleyrand Hotel, listed in Jacksonville City Directories since 1927 at 720 Talleyrand Avenue.

The Court, Cora Crane's elegant bordello at Ward and Davis Streets, was tastefully landscaped outside; lavishly furnished in its multi-mirrored bedrooms. Note the round stained glass windows on either side of the arched main entrance.

James Hotel, who kept "a list of the better houses of ill fame for the intelligent guidance of guests of the hotel."

Cora, knowing that her guests came to see her in person, stayed in the parlor during the early part of the evenings. She would pass among the tables, smiling her luminous smile and occasionally joining in a conversation, before retiring to her suite, alone but for her companion-chaperone, Mrs. Charlotte Ruedy. No hard liquor was served—only champagne or beer, the latter at $1 a bottle.

Here at the Hotel de Dream Cora met Stephen Crane, age twenty-five, the brilliant author of *The Red Badge of Courage.* He was a correspondent for the *New York Press,* trying to get to Cuba to send reports of the war between Cuba and Spain, when he reached Jacksonville in November, 1896. Cora was thirty-one, and fitted perfectly into Crane's preference for beautiful older women.

It was a *grand amour,* lasting until 1902 when Stephen died abroad. He and Cora had lived in England together in a romantic manor house—Brede Place—entertaining as close friends such social and literary figures as Mr. and Mrs. Joseph Conrad, Mr. and Mrs. H. G. Wells, Lady Randolph Churchill, and Henry James.

Cora arrived back in Jacksonville in May, 1902, when the new metropolis of brick and concrete was rising from the ashes of the old wooden city, decimated by the fire of May 3, 1901.

During the next twelve months Cora was occupied with borrowing money and buying property, located at the southwest corner of Ward and Davis Streets. There she erected the Court—the most elegant bordello the city had ever seen.

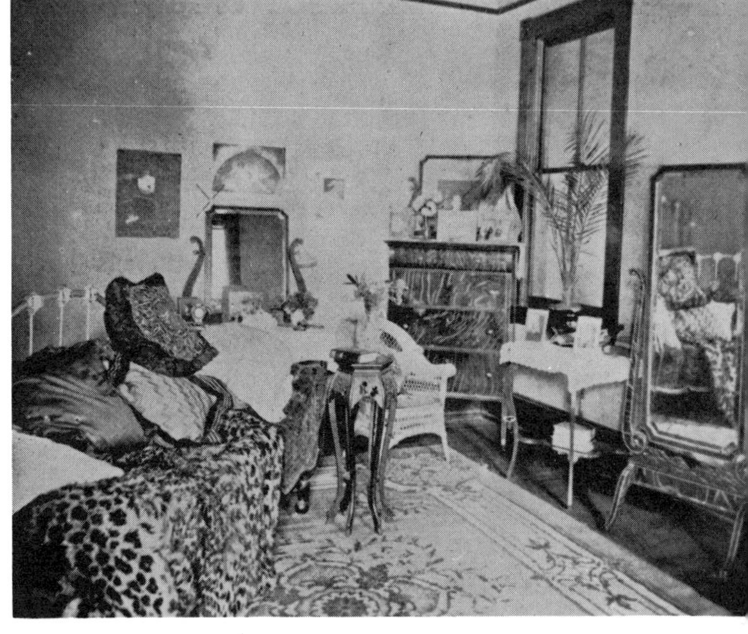

It was a handsome building of red glazed brick and smooth stone trim, containing fourteen bedrooms in the main structure, also parlor rooms, ballroom, kitchens, dining room, and an annex with eight additional bedrooms. The staff averaged thirteen in number.

The Court opened early in 1903, and prospered from the start. By 1906 Cora was financially secure; in 1904 she had purchased for $750 two ocean-front lots at Pablo Beach, the seaside Summer resort of Jacksonville's working-class population. To the north was Atlantic Beach, where the city's elite had their Summer homes.

In 1905 Cora built on her beach lots Palmetto Lodge, a vacation annex of the Court.

In 1908, after several suicides among the girls within a short time, her theory that life in a well-run house of prostitution "was to be preferred to the miseries of sweatshop labor, or existence behind a store counter" was demolished.

She was alone at Palmetto Lodge on Sunday, September 4, 1910, and had just helped a carload of strangers push their vehicle from the soft beach sand in front of the lodge.

It was very hot. Cora felt dizzy, went inside to lie down, and breathed her last. Her age—forty-five.

After Cora's death, the Court fell on hard times. It was reopened in 1911 as the Whitehouse Hotel.

"Gone then were the carefully tended grass plots, the umbrella tree and privet hedge, with every visible trace of the personality of its original owner and creator," wrote Gilkes. "The octagonal bay window had been supplanted by a door giving access to the street, and another door cut through on the Ward Street side, thus providing two additional exits for quick getaways in the event of a police raid.

"These doorways, and the Davis Street main entrance, were hideously daubed with white paint; the stone trim too was painted white. The place was, indeed, nakedly transformed into that which it had never been in Cora Taylor's lifetime—a bawdy house."

After 1917 the building stood unoccupied, "a forlorn shell, the hang-out of thieves and vagrants," until it was demolished in 1928.

The site became a parking lot for railroad employees.

Many large transient hotels in Florida's major cities suffered the same fate as the businesses which once occupied this downtown Jacksonville block, bounded by Julia, Monroe, Hogan and Adams Streets. One of the buildings facing Hogan Street was the modest Gilbert Hotel. This photo shows the George Washington, at left, and the Robert Meyer Hotel in the distance. In the early 1970s the George Washington was torn down and its site, too, became a parking lot.

2
Henry Morrison Flagler and His Hotels

NO NOTICE WAS TAKEN in the far-away frontier territory of Florida when on January 2, 1830, a son was born to the Reverend Isaac Flagler and his wife, Elizabeth Caldwell Flagler, in Hopewell, New York. But this child, Henry Morrison Flagler, was destined to write a very important chapter in Florida's history, beginning fifty-five years later.

The ready-made Flagler family consisted at first of the husband and wife, a daughter of Isaac by a former marriage—Ann Caroline—and a son of Elizabeth, whose name was Daniel Harkness, likewise born of an earlier marriage. The fact that young Henry had a Harkness for a half-brother (and another later for a wife) determined the course of his life. The Harknesses were numerous, more or less wealthy, and fond of Henry Flagler.

When Henry left the Flagler household at age fourteen to escape its poverty and seek prosperity, he knew exactly where he was going—to the Republic, Ohio, general store of L. G. Harkness and Company. There he joined Dan Harkness in the employ of the latter's uncle, Lamon G. Harkness. In time he succeeded Dan as manager of the Republic store, was given a better job in a similar Harkness store in Bellevue, Ohio (later expanded into the grain and distillery business), and in 1852, at age twenty-two, he became a partner in this firm with Dan and Lamon Harkness. A year later, on November 9, he married Lamon's daughter, Mary Harkness.

Although Flagler disliked dealing in liquor, he was bent on making money, so he "tucked his convictions in his pocket and hurried on in the making of a small fortune," wrote Sidney Walter Martin in his 1949 book, *Florida's Flagler.*

Flagler and John D. Rockefeller became partners in 1867, when another kinsman of Mary Flagler, Stephen V. Harkness, invested $100,000 on Flagler's behalf in the partnership of Rockefeller, Andrews and Flagler. The famous Standard Oil Company was formed by Rockefeller, Flagler and others early in 1870, followed in 1882 by establishment of the Standard Oil Trust.

Mary Flagler's health steadily declined. Only temporary relief was afforded her during a few weeks' stay in the relatively mild climate of Jacksonville, Florida, with her family during the Winter of 1878.

Flagler, although he was a devoted husband and father, was deeply involved in making that fortune he had resolved on at age fourteen; and the methods he and his partners, principally John Rockefeller, used in promoting the rapidly expanding oil industry must have taxed that Puritan Flagler conscience. They were in a highly competitive business from the start, and one which was interdependent with the mass transportation facilities then available. They resorted to rebates.

"Flagler would offer a railroad a guaranteed quantity of oil shipments if the carrier would rebate part of the freight charge," wrote Charles E. Harner in his 1973 book, *Florida's Promoters—The Men Who Made It Big.*

"The railroads were hungry for business and Flagler got his discounts. The lines which gave the biggest rebates got the most business, and he had them bidding against one another."

At one time the firm was known to be getting rebates of fifteen cents a barrel while paying thirty-five cents a barrel in freight.

"The other refiners couldn't meet that kind of competition. One after another they sold out to Rockefeller and Flagler—and it was Flagler who determined how much the former competitor would get for his property."

The partners were not breaking any laws, for none existed in this area until the Sherman Anti-

Trust Act of 1890. By that time the Standard Oil Trust had become the biggest monopoly the world had ever seen.

Mary Harkness Flagler died in New York in 1881.

Flagler, at fifty-two, had amassed an immense fortune, and gradually withdrew from active management of Standard Oil. In 1883 he married Ida Alice Shourds.

The Flaglers' honeymoon began in December, and they went to Florida. After ninety hours of traveling on rails of different gauges, they arrived in Jacksonville and stayed for a few days at the elegant St. James Hotel. They went on to St. Augustine by way of river steamer to Tocoi, some thirty miles south of Jacksonville, then aboard the St. Johns River Railroad, a fifteen-mile line built by John Westcott in 1858.

Although the ancient village had a population of about 2,000 at this time, it had no modern hotel, a fact that impressed itself strongly upon this man who was about to retire from the oil industry, who had millions (which would multiply throughout his lifetime), and who had became accustomed to a luxurious life style.

"The (St. Augustine) streets were unpaved, the buildings were shabby," wrote Harner, "but the little village had a very big thing going for it: the Winter of 1883-84." It was one of the North's most bitterly cold.

By the start of the Civil War, Florida had 416 miles of railroad, none of it south of Cedar Key. From that time until 1880, rail mileage increased only seventy-one miles, all but two of which were built during the Civil War. By 1883, the South was emerging finally from the clutch of carpetbag rule. Florida had the forward-looking William D. Bloxham as Governor, and Hamilton Disston had begun his miracles in draining vast acres of land, making his headquarters in "a cow camp called Kissimmee."

H. H. DeLand of New York settled in central Florida, and laid out the town which bears his name. Henry Bradley Plant was pushing his railway ever southward toward Florida's west coast.

The state was a sleeping giant, a virgin paradise which, not many years before, had been the lush domain of the free-roaming Indians, the deer, turkey, panther and alligator, and the ever-present scrawny range cattle. The time was right for Florida to begin realizing its enormous promise, and Henry Flagler was ready to help.

The Flaglers returned to St. Augustine in February, 1885. The trip from New York to

Hotel San Marco at St. Augustine was only a year old when Henry M. Flagler in 1885 first conferred there with its builders, James A. McGuire and Joseph E. McDonald. They became Flagler's Florida contractors.

Hotel Granada, St. Augustine, about the turn of the century.

Jacksonville took only two days in Flagler's newly-acquired private railroad car. They went on to St. Augustine *via* the newly-constructed Jacksonville, St. Augustine & Halifax River Railway.

This was the visit during which Flagler decided to invest several million dollars of his fortune in improvements at St. Augustine, principally by construction of the Ponce de Leon Hotel.

The momentous meeting of Henry Flagler, James A. McGuire and Joseph E. McDonald took place that year at the new San Marco Hotel. Both McGuire and McDonald had been prominent contractors in New England, had recently arrived in Florida, and had jointly supervised the building of this hotel for Isaac Croof, a well-to-do merchant, and some other investors.

Flagler liked their work, and employed them to construct his Ponce de Leon Hotel. Just before coming to St. Augustine, McGuire had built for Croof and his associates the beautiful Magnolia Hotel at Magnolia Springs, near Green Cove Springs. He and McDonald worked together for the first time on the San Marco, then became Flagler's Florida contractors.

The San Marco was financed by the same group of New Englanders and ably managed by Osborn D. Seavey, who also had come to the San Marco *via* the Magnolia at Magnolia Springs. His reputation as a manager led many New Englanders to visit St. Augustine.

The Ponce de Leon Hotel cost $2,500,000, and was opened to the public on January 12, 1888. Two days earlier, the first dinner was served at the hotel to Mr. and Mrs. Flagler and their invited guests—an exclusive group which included the hotel's architects and builders, some artists, and a few railroad executives.

An account of this event, and other facts about the hotel, are contained in an article by Thomas Graham of the Flagler College faculty, entitled "Flagler's Magnificent Hotel Ponce de Leon," in the *Florida Historical Quarterly* for July, 1975.

The menu for that first dinner consisted of nine courses: blue points; cream soup a la reine, consommé printanière; hors d'oeuvres variés, croquettes of shrimp Robert; broiled shad maître d'hôtel, Parisienne potatoes; roast ribs of beef, with mashed potatoes and stewed tomatoes, turkey and cranberry sauce, with sweet potatoes and onion (sauce Béchamel), ham (Madeira sauce), with cauliflower and canned corn, lamb chops with peas and baked macaroni; chicken sauté a l'Espagnole, with rice; Rack punch; broiled golden plover on toast, currant jelly, celery, lettuce; pudding, soufflé a la vanille, apple pie, cocoanut pie, chocolate éclairs, calf's-foot jelly, assorted cake, fruit cake, vanilla ice cream, fruit, cheese and coffee.

Hundreds of guests attended the first Grand Ball, viewing perhaps the most beautiful decorations ever introduced in any hotel in the world, wrote Martin. Two orchestras alternated in providing music for dancing.

The architects had faithfully preserved the spirit of Old Spain, with the theme of the sea apparent at all of the entrances. They had envisioned "not merely a big hotel, but a pleasure palace, embodying the characteristics of Spanish Renaissance architecture, with sunny courts and cool retreats, fountains, and towers, and decorations suggestive of the history of the city."

Their design of the Ponce de Leon launched its two young architects, Thomas Hastings and John M. Carrère, in careers of marked success. They

Horse-drawn carriages are shown lined up beneath the shed covering the passenger platform, waiting for new arrivals at the St. Augustine railroad station, c. 1903. The building beyond and to the left of the station is the Florida East Coast Hospital, which was built in 1902 after the first hospital burned in November, 1901.

Bird's-eye view of the Hotels Cordova (left) and Alcazar, from the Hotel Ponce de Leon, about 1895. All three were Flagler hotels.

Hotel Ponce de Leon, the grandeur, furnishings, and landscaping of which reflected the artistry of its architects and the touch of the Flagler millions.

Below—A corner of the court of the Ponce de Leon, pictured in 1905.

Five St. Augustine hotels, of varied vintage. From the top: Palmetto House, located near the City Gate, shown here in 1901; Hotels Bennett, Castle Warden, Gilbert (second floor) and Plaza (ground floor), all of a more recent time. The Plaza is still in operation in 1980. The Castle Warden has become Ripley's Believe-It-or-Not Museum.

later designed the Senate and House office buildings in Washington, D. C., among others.

The hotel grounds were handsomely landscaped, as was the inner court, surrounded by vine-clad verandas. The great rotunda and dining hall were decorated with murals by George W. Maynard. Louis Tiffany of New York was the hotel's decorator and supplied its elegant stained glass. Rich carvings, paintings, columns and arches, furnishings, chandeliers—all reflected exquisite taste and unlimited funds. The hotel contained 450 sleeping apartments, including single rooms, suites, and bridal chambers.

The furnishings in each room were worth about $1,000—which was a great deal of money in the 1880s. Also there were various private parlors, game rooms, reading rooms, and refreshment rooms. Each was luxurious with rich draperies, furniture of rosewood, mahogany and walnut, and Brussels carpet.

The hotel had two miles of corridors and covered most of a five-acre lot. However, it contained only one private bath—the one in Flagler's suite. Public bathrooms had been considered adequate prior to the time of its building; but hotel guests had come to expect this convenience, and the Ponce de Leon soon provided it.

The exterior walls of the hotel, four feet thick, were made of poured concrete. The mixture consisted of five parts coquina shell (obtained from quarries on nearby Anastasia Island), two parts sand, and one part cement.

Franklin W. Smith built a resort hotel, the Casa Monica, in St. Augustine in 1886-88. He operated it only for a year, selling it in 1889 to Flagler, who renamed it the Cordova.

Meanwhile, early in 1887 Flagler realized that the Ponce de Leon would be out of reach to travelers of ordinary means, and began planning for the Alcazar, facing the Ponce across King Street. It was smaller, but was considered as beautiful as the Ponce de Leon.

In 1885, while the Ponce de Leon was under construction, Flagler had bought the rail line from South Jacksonville to St. Augustine. In 1888 he bought and improved several other short railroads leading from St. Augustine to East Palatka and from there southeastward *via* Ormond to Daytona. In 1889 he built a steel railroad bridge over the St. Johns at Jacksonville, making possible through service from the North.

He next bought an interest in the small hotel at Ormond, built by John Anderson of Maine and Joseph D. Price of Kentucky. The hotel did not prosper until Flagler bought out his partners in 1890 and applied his magic touch. He enlarged the building and beautified the grounds, wrote Martin.

The hotel was well located, between the Halifax River and the ocean, but not far from either. Devotees of automobile racing filled the hotel to enjoy that sport, which soon made Ormond and Daytona beaches famous. Bicycling and water sports, for both of which special equipment was supplied, also became popular there.

Flagler subsequently entered first-hand into railroad building, constructing his rails southward to Palm Beach (1894) and Miami (1896). In each of these cities he provided fine hotel facilities and civic improvements.

For several years beginning in 1894, Flagler's personal life was chaotic. His second wife Alice developed paranoia, which in 1899 was legally declared incurable. Flagler settled some $2,400,000 on her, which by the time of her death in 1930 had increased to more than $15,000,000.

In 1901 he divorced her and married Mary Lily Kenan (age thirty-four) at Kenansville, North Carolina.

The "marble palace" the bride wanted was begun even before they were married. It was Whitehall, built in Palm Beach at a cost of $2,500,000. A lengthy article about the structure published in the *New York Herald* of March 30, 1902, begins:

"More wonderful than any palace in Europe, grander and more magnificent than any other private dwelling in the world is Whitehall, the new home Henry M. Flagler has built in the land of flowers for his bride. The Vatican, the forests, the quarries, the old salons, the art shops and the looms have contributed some of their choicest treasures to deck this marvelous structure . . . Men have been working day and night for a year in this country, in Italy and France, making and collecting the decorations . . . When the doors are opened to guests Mrs. Flagler can bid her friends welcome to a home which, in point of grandeur, queen or princess never knew."

The building contained a main hall 110 feet long, a library, music room, billiard room, French salon, dining room, breakfast room, pantry and kitchen, ballroom (ninety-one by thirty-seven feet), second floor hall and sixteen front bedrooms, plus eighteen bedrooms for servants, and a total of twenty-two baths and lavatories. A dormitory over the separate laundry house was occupied by Negro servants.

Mrs. Flagler did welcome many guests to Whitehall during the remaining years of her husband's life—and so did he. There were stag

Until Flagler purchased full ownership in 1890, the Ormond Beach Hotel was a small and struggling inn. It became a tourist mecca after Flagler enlarged the building and landscaped the grounds, as shown in this photo of the early 1900s.

Above—Rose Villa, also at Ormond, with accommodations for twenty guests, was open from November 1 to May 1. It is shown here in 1901.

Above—The Inn at Ormond, shown here in 1908, had been known earlier as the Hotel Coquina. Below and below right—Two views of the Ormond Beach Hotel with the Halifax River in the foreground.

dinners, bridge parties, teas and banquets; and music from the great pipe organ, said to be the largest ever placed in a private home in this country.

The pace of entertaining at Whitehall lasted only a few years. Flagler was feeling his age—and at seventy-five, he was contemplating the most ambitious and expensive of his Florida projects—extension of his railway out over the sea to Key West, a distance of 156 miles. It took seven years to build, and required the labor of an average of 3,000 men, a total of perhaps 400,000 during those years; it cost $35,000,000 and the lives of some 300 workmen.

The first train over the new line reached Key West on January 22, 1912, with Flagler among the dignitaries aboard, and a big celebration was held. He purchased a hotel in Key West, previously known as the Russell House, and renamed it the Key West Hotel; but it was not to be compared with his earlier hostelries.

Following the custom he had established at each of the coastal towns in which he invested, of furnishing elegant hotel accommodations for those who traveled on his railroads, Flagler immediately announced that he would build a luxury hotel in Key West.

Key West did not become the bustling port of international commerce that Flagler had expected, but it did become a favorite watering-spot for wealthy northern sun-seekers.

Although Flagler died sixteen months after the Key West extension was completed, and thus was not to see his hotel plans materialize in that city, the Florida East Coast Hotel Company carried out his plan. Property for the Casa Marina Hotel on South Beach was bought for $1,000 and construction was begun in 1918. The hotel was completed in 1921 and formally opened on December 31. Tourists poured in to occupy its 200 rooms each season during the prosperous 1920s and the Casa Marina flourished until 1931, when the Florida East Coast Railway went into receivership and trains ran on curtailed schedules. The following Spring, 1932, the Casa Marina finished a very poor season and was closed indefinitely. Only a skeleton staff was retained to care for the building and grounds.

In 1934 the hotel was opened again with a Christmas Eve ball. The Federal Emergency

Relief Administration was credited with getting the Casa Marina back into operation as part of the task of rehabilitating Key West from the depths of the Depression by promoting tourism, according to a chronology of the hotel compiled in 1979 by Joan Langley of Key West. Although the Labor Day hurricane of 1935 washed away Flagler's Overseas Railroad, Key West and the Casa Marina were untouched.

Between 1935 and 1941 the hotel opened each season with either a Christmas Eve or New Year's Eve ball, increasing in popularity and prosperity each year. From 1942 to 1945 the Casa Marina was a haven reserved for Navy officers and their immediate families.

In 1946 it was sold by the Florida East Coast Hotel Company to private interests. Between 1947 and 1962 it was opened to the public by a series of owners, with varying degrees of success. During the Cuban Missile Crisis in 1962, troops poured into Key West and the Casa Marina, closed for the season in October, reopened for the Army. For the next three years, under lease, it was home to the Sixth Missile Battalion.

The hotel was occupied again in the Summer and Fall of 1966 as a dormitory and training school for 320 Peace Corps members preparing for service in the Pacific islands of Micronesia. It was then vacant again for eleven years.

In April, 1977, the venerable hostelry was purchased by the firm of Cayo Hueso Limited. Renovation of the building and grounds began in January, 1978, and on December 22 of that year it was informally opened as Marriott's Casa Marina Resort. Extensive interior and exterior restoration, modernization and enlargement of rooms, plus construction of a new wing, swimming pool, fishing facilities, dining and convention rooms and other improvements, represent an investment of some $10,000,000. This does not include the $3,500,000 which the new owners paid when they bought the building from the John Spottswood estate.

By the time of Flagler's third marriage in 1901, his railroad reached from Jacksonville to Miami; his Florida hotel system included three at St. Augustine—the Ponce de Leon, the Alcazar, and the Cordova; the Ormond Beach Hotel; the Royal Poinciana and the Breakers at Palm Beach, and the Royal Palm in Miami. The Continental at Atlantic Beach was added to the list in 1901.

The great chain of hotels stretching along the east coast of Florida formed one of the most popular resort areas in the country, wrote Martin. It apparently was Flagler's plan to make his hotels the finest in the world. He chose some of the most beautiful spots in Florida on which to construct them, and engaged top-flight landscape artists, architects and builders to create them.

The hotels offered wide variety. The Ormond Beach and the Breakers had special appeal for

Built by Flagler's Florida East Coast Hotel Company after his death, the Casa Marina Hotel at Key West was opened in 1921. It had various ups and downs before being renovated and reopened in 1978 as Marriott's Casa Marina Resort. This was the front entrance in the 1920s.

those who enjoyed sports. The Ponce de Leon, Royal Poinciana and Royal Palm attracted the wealthy and discriminating, and catered to the most fastidious tastes.

The Royal Poinciana, largest hotel in the world at that time, was said to be the largest wooden structure ever built anywhere. Carpenters and other workmen on the hotel earned from $1.50 to $2.25 a day. When first completed in 1894, it had only 540 rooms; it was expanded in 1899 and again in 1901. It could then accommodate 1,750 guests and employed some 1,400 workers, housed in a dormitory which was itself a hotel. Many of its guests came in private railroad cars; sometimes the owners occupied suites in the hotel, while their servants were housed in those palatial cars.

Specific records of prices paid for those suites evidently were not preserved for posterity. One writer (Theodore Pratt: *That Was Palm Beach*) cited a top figure of $100 a day.

Charles Simmons, executive director of the Henry Morrison Flagler Museum in Palm Beach, said in 1979 that perhaps an apartment in the hotel, or a VIP suite, might have cost that much. The base rate, however, as shown on a diagram of the first floor plan included in an 1894 booklet entitled "Souvenir of the Royal Poinciana," was $5 a day and up per person, and a surprising $21 per week "and upward."

That floor plan shows rooms constructed so that they could be occupied separately or in any combination up to ten rooms. This ten-room suite would include two baths. Room 103, nine by seventeen feet in size, without a private bath, may have been one of the rooms rented at the base price.

One of the other Flagler hotels, the Cordova in St. Augustine, offered "suites, three to ten rooms each." Presumably the Poinciana had similar offerings. If a family or group was large enough to require eight or ten rooms, and meals for all in the party, the tab would have to be pretty high—especially in turn-of-the-century dollars.

The prestigious Hotel Escambia in Pensacola, for example, in 1898 charged $2 a day, which was about average for first class hotels at that time.

The Royal Poinciana had some very modern features, however; one bathroom for three to four bedrooms (plus an elegantly painted and gilded chamber pot inside the night stand in each room); a three-bulb brass light fixture in the ceiling of each private room, plus another bulb on a drop cord for reading, and an ingenious fire escape system.

Most hotels of the period provided for each guest only a knotted rope with a hook on one end which was to be fastened to the window sill, so that the guest could slide down the rope to safety in case of fire. At the Royal Poinciana, the same principle was used; but there was a galvanized fixture near the hook which would work against friction. The guest could put the loop around his waist, hold on to the rope, and the device would lower him to the

The Styx, shown here in 1895, was the Palm Beach area settled by workers who came there to build the Royal Poinciana Hotel and the railroad. When the projects were completed, the workers and their families, regarded as a health hazard and squatters on private property, refused to move, according to Mrs. Maxine Banash, librarian for the Historical Society of Palm Beach County. A group of businessmen, including Henry Flagler, had new houses built on the mainland at West Palm Beach, and gave a three-day carnival there. While the workers were at the carnival, their belongings were gathered up, tagged, and installed in the new houses, and the Styx was burned, The migration from the Styx to West Palm Beach, Boynton and Pleasant City was completed in 1912.

Looking west on Sunrise Avenue at County Road.

Looking north on County Road at Sunrise Avenue.

ground, "slowly, safely and majestically," wrote Pratt.

A special feature of the Poinciana was the greeting offered to new arrivals as they got off the train at the "jolly little special station" at the north end of the hotel. The hotel orchestra was there to provide a musical welcome; one of the dozens of Negro bellmen would take each guest's hand luggage and "execute a few dance steps" before escorting the new arrivals to their rooms or suites. Each bellman had to be able to handle his own size in luggage; trunks, however, were taken immediately from the baggage car, transferred on a mule-drawn cart to the hotel baggage room, then delivered by the freight elevator to the individual rooms by the time the guests arrived there. Bellmen were tipped at least a dollar—in an era when that sum would pay for three or four complete dinners in many places.

The customary daily round at this elegant hotel was vigorous, beginning with breakfast in the huge dining room (or in one's room for a dollar extra), then a visit to "the sands." For this, guests took their bathing costumes and rode a little mule-drawn car from the Poinciana on Lake Worth to the bathing casino at the Breakers, sister to the Poinciana but facing the Atlantic Ocean. This might be followed by a swim in the pool or the surf, or both, then by a lounge on the beach, with the orchestras from both hotels serenading those assembled. Rules of the resort decreed that all ladies must wear black stockings with their bathing attire, and that they should reach the suit, with no skin showing between suit and stockings.

Next would come another change of clothes in the Breakers dressing rooms, followed by an eight-course lunch at the Poinciana and perhaps a little time spent on the veranda, rocking in the shade. Then the men might be off to play golf (first changing to golf clothes), while the ladies visited the branches of Fifth Avenue shops in the corridors off the rotunda. Another afternoon diversion might be a visit to the nearby domain of "Alligator Joe" Frazier, with his sea-lions and turtles, to watch him wrestle one of the alligators.

Then came still another change, to casual afternoon clothes, and groups of friends gathered for tea in the Coconut Grove Tea Garden at the south end of the Royal Poinciana. There they enjoyed the orchestra again, and some of Mrs. Roche's famous coconut cake. The music ended at 7:45 and guests returned to their rooms to dress for dinner, which could be had in the dining room or the select Grill Room (extra cost). Or guests might ride in

This group on the lawn of the Royal Poinciana Hotel on March 14, 1896, included several Vanderbilts and other socially prominent people of the period.

Afromobiles to dine at the nearby Beach Club, Colonel Edward Reilly Bradley's gambling casino, which was "more exclusive than Monte Carlo," and which also housed one of the best and most expensive restaurants in the world, according to Pratt.

About those Afromobiles: No vehicles were permitted by Flagler in his island paradise except the trains, the little mule-drawn car, and these unique padded wicker chairs set on wheels, attached to the rear half of a bicycle. They were propelled by Negro attendants who would sit on the bicycle seat and pedal. The odd-looking chariots were painted white. The first ones were designed so that the driver was out in front, but this was changed later so that the riders had a better view of their surroundings. The rolling chairs were for hire at $2 an hour or $10 a day.

The Poinciana (six stories high, plus two attic dormer window floors) had an open elevator, raised and lowered by an operator pulling on a rope. The Poinciana was described by Cleveland Amory in his 1948 book entitled *The Last Resorts,* as looking like a skyscraper lying down.

A special attraction in the Royal Poinciana dining room, and later in the Coconut Grove Tea Garden, was the regular performance of the cake walk. Tables were moved after dinner to one end of the huge room and chairs lined up as in a theatre, to accommodate the many guests who attended. They wore their most glittering jewels and richest furs, the orchestra played popular tunes ("In the Good Old Summer Time" and "Bill Bailey," for example), and the Pinkerton plainclothes men kept a sharp eye for the lightfingered.

Four guests would serve as judges, seated before a table on which rested a huge white cake—the first prize, together with a sum of cash. Six Negro couples would march from the kitchen as the drum rolled; they were flamboyantly dressed, the men perhaps in red satin trousers and green coats, the women in vivid chiffons, with heavy make-up. They were the "cakeists," ready to dance to the ragtime music of the orchestra. The couples first would circle the room in a grand march.

The cake walk consisted of "strutting and striking extravagant postures in time with the music." The couples in turn would perform these

Kermit Roosevelt, son of President Theodore Roosevelt, is the man in white knickers looking at the camera. The picture was taken in the mid-1920s at the ocean front of the Breakers Hotel.

gyrations, each trying to outdo the others—stimulated by the applause of the audience, and perhaps also by the champagne and cash bonuses given by guests to their favorites. The judges would decide which couple was the most entertaining, and that couple would dance around the hall again, to thunderous music from the orchestra. That pair "took the cake."

The highlight of the season was the Washington's Birthday Ball—"the grand hop." For this brilliant event, some devotees came all the way from New York in their private railroad cars. Guests from the Breakers joined those at the Poinciana, making a total of some 2,000 or more dancers and observers. Again, Pinkerton men mingled with the guests.

"It was a gala, full dress affair," wrote Pratt, "with both hotel orchestras playing alternately for dancing, offering continuous music. Each year the hotel's decorations for the event were extravagantly different." A stand-up supper or buffet was served at these events at one o'clock in the morning, featuring such delicacies as roast squab, boned capon with jelly, and broiled quail. Champagne flowed freely, and stronger drink was plentiful.

"Suddenly in 1917 the character of the ball changed—possibly reflecting the attitudes and anxieties of a privileged people living in what they feared could be the last of a Golden Era," wrote Judge James R. Knott in an article for the *Florida History Newsletter* (March, 1979) entitled "The Biggest Party of All." Within a few days the United States declared war on Germany.

"The theme of the ball that year was 'The Feast of Lanterns in the Garden of the Gods,' and it had all the magnificence and opulence of Oriental splendor. It was said that lavish decorations outdid all former efforts, from a standpoint of expenditure as well as artistic beauty. Hundreds of thousands of dollars worth of Oriental rugs, ancient treasures of Turkey lent by the Turkish government, were set off by theatrical lighting.

"Huge Chinese and Algerian lanterns, some six feet in diameter, were suspended from a ceiling of solid smilax. At the entrance to the ballroom a pair of crouching lions on pedestals held in their paws large glass balls which shed a glow of moonbeams over the scene. Skins of rare Bengal tigers, Numidian lions and other beasts of the jungle were hung as a background for these statues, and subdued lighting emphasized the effect of an Oriental court."

The Breakers Hotel at Palm Beach, 1904-1925.

Two years later the war was over and jubilation reigned in Palm Beach. The ball that year was a Red Cross benefit, planned as a victory celebration, wrote Knott. "Decorations emphasized the jubilant mood by depicting a victory arch symbolizing the Triumph of Justice. Silken banners displayed the name and seal of each of the Allied nations. Above all the banners perched an American eagle with a halo of silver stars, and golden lights gleamed softly and glamorously. During the third dance the room was reduced to semi-darkness while the orchestra played 'The Rose of No Man's Land,' and a myriad of stars flashed into light.

"Another feature of the 1919 ball was a scene of Flanders Field with poppies, dismantled guns overgrown with creeping vines, and birds nesting in the muzzles. The orchestra crashed into Sousa's Victory March and a shadowy figure appeared—Victory bearing aloft a golden wreath of triumph to crown the Allies."

The Royal Poinciana continued to operate until 1931 and was finally dismantled in 1934, damaged by severe weather and fire. People came from far and near to buy mementos of the once-elegant hostelry. The lumber, still sound, was bought and used to construct private homes along the coast—perhaps as many as forty. The stained glass windows of the stairways leading from the rotunda went to the Driftwood Inn at Vero Beach.

Many years later, the Palm Beach Towers Apartment Hotel, the Royal Poinciana Shopping Plaza and the Palm Beach Playhouse were constructed on the site.

The Breakers burned to the ground in a two-day fire in March, 1925. This was the third time that the hotel had been ravaged by fire, according to *Palm Beach Entertains, Then and Now,* compiled by The Junior League of the Palm Beaches, Inc.

Originally built as the Palm Beach Inn in 1895, the hotel was being enlarged in 1903 when a disastrous fire destroyed it. Flagler ordered it rebuilt immediately, and the new structure was almost completed when it was destroyed again by fire. It finally reopened in 1904 as the Breakers Hotel.

Approximately 450 guests were in residence that day the 1925 fire broke out. Hotel employees tried to contain the blaze, but it was soon out of control.

The prestigious Palm Beach Hotel, northwest of the Breakers and facing Lake Worth, burned at the same time. This fire was caused by embers from the Breakers blaze.

"The new Breakers was opened for guests on December 29, 1926," according to the Junior League book. "Its architectural style is modified Spanish with Italian Renaissance accents, with twin towers and graceful arches inspired by the Villa Medici in Italy. It stands today as a bastion of past elegance which cost $6,000,000 to build.

"The present hotel contains much of the grace and charm of the Old World. The spacious lobby with its vaulted ceilings and frescos, the elaborate ceiling in the Gold Room, and the hand-painted beamed ceiling in the Florentine dining room

Billowing clouds of smoke poured from the original Breakers Hotel when it burned in 1903, as it was being enlarged.

reflect the artistry of the Italian Renaissance. Even the fountain in front of the hotel is patterned after the one in the Boboli Gardens in Florence.

"During the twenties and thirties the Venetian Lounge was the scene of many luncheons and bridge parties, and the seaside terrace was a favorite spot for tea-dancing at the sunset hour . . . Its Grand Loggia was the site of a yearly costume party for children.

"The reputation of the old Breakers brought back many of the guests who had enjoyed the hotel before the fire, and the beauty of the new hotel attracted many new visitors. The register of the Breakers during those years shows such names as John D. and William Rockefeller, Stephen Harkness, John Jacob Astor, J. P. Morgan, President Harding, William Randolph Hearst, Nellie Melba, William K. Vanderbilt, the Duchess of Marlborough and Andrew Mellon."

It served as a hospital for servicemen during World War II.

Renovated and expanded in 1969, the hotel now is open year around, and is a splendid reminder of the hotel boom of the 1920s. The Breakers now has 600 rooms, including suites. Double-room rates during the Winter of 1979 ranged from $110 to $155 a day, modified American plan (including breakfast and dinner). A parlor could be included for an extra $70 to $130 a day. A service charge of $10 a day was added.

Whitehall, when Mary Lily Flagler died in 1917, was left to her niece, Louise Clisby Wise.

In 1924 it was sold, and the new owners made it into a luxury hotel by erecting an eleven-story tower containing 300 rooms attached to the mansion. It was opened as Whitehall Hotel in January of 1926.

Whitehall was unique as a hotel; it offered both the grandeur of the Flagler mansion and the convenience of the new tower. The hotel dining room could seat 500 comfortably, and Flagler's original dining room was available for private entertaining. Dinner dances were held twice a week during the season.

Whitehall served as a hotel from that time until 1959, when it was bought by the Henry Morrison Flagler Museum. The tower was removed and the mansion restored to its original form. Jean Flagler Matthews, granddaughter of its builder, played a leading role in establishing the museum as a memorial to the man who caused the east coast of Florida to bloom, where previously there had been wilderness.

Flagler died in Palm Beach on May 20, 1913, after a fall at Whitehall in January of that year. He was eighty-three years old. His body was taken to St. Augustine for entombment.

The other Flagler hotels met with a variety of fates. The three in St. Augustine were preserved, after their usefulness as hotels declined, and converted to serve other purposes. The grand Ponce de Leon (used from 1942 to 1945 as a training center by the Coast Guard) closed in the Spring of 1967, after eighty seasons—some of them very lean indeed—to emerge in the Fall of 1968 as Flagler College. The success of the college, wrote Graham, "augurs well for the future of the great building whose walls were built to last through the centuries."

The Cordova, renovated, became the St. Johns County Court House in 1968. The other in this historic trio, the Alcazar, remodeled, began service as a city building in January, 1972. The Alcazar

The elegant ballroom of the Royal Poinciana Hotel at the turn of the century.

also houses the Lightner Museum of Hobbies. The Royal Palm in Miami was torn down in 1930 because it was considered a fire trap. The Continental at Atlantic Beach (renamed the Atlantic Beach Hotel in 1913) burned in 1919.

The Ormond Hotel at Ormond Beach is still in use, billing itself as "Providing Gracious Living for Nearly a Century." It has 300 accommodations, available by the day, week or month. Double room rates in 1979 began at a modest $14 a day, without meals, and ranged up to $640 a month, with three cafeteria meals daily. All rates were increased ten per cent during the months of December through April. The hotel is under "second generation family management."

In 1898 a five-week round trip excursion to Florida from New York, with stops at any of the Flagler hotels (meals included), cost only $350 per person.

A book entitled *A Guide to Florida* by Harrison Rhodes and Mary Wolfe Dumont, published in 1912 by Dodd, Meade and Company, lists daily rates at the Royal Poinciana, the Breakers and the Royal Palm as "$6 up." This figure is the highest listed for any hotel in Florida at that time.

Other hotels which charged a minimum of more than $3 a day in 1912 were the Clearwater Inn at Clearwater, the Ormond Beach, the Ponce de Leon at St. Augustine, the Royal Palm at Fort Myers, and the Clarendon at Seabreeze, each of which charged $5 a day and up; the Qui-Si-Sana at Green Cove Springs, the Magnolia Springs at that village, the Continental at Atlantic Beach, and the Nautilus at Seabreeze, $4 up; Useppa Inn at Useppa Island, and the Windsor at Jacksonville, $3.50. The Tampa Bay Hotel listed daily rates of $3.50 to $5.

All of these were American plan hotels, supplying meals as well as rooms, plus the elegance of those luxurious caravanseries.

A few more of the 493 Florida hotels and boarding houses listed in this directory charged as much as $3 minimum; most were in the $1.50 to $2.50 range, and a few charged only $1.

"Hotels may now be said to be generally good in the state," wrote Rhodes and Dumont in 1912, "though in the towns which are not definitely tourist resorts, there might yet be great improvements. Few except the newest are adequately provided with private bathrooms, but this want is being rapidly remedied.

"Hotels vary with accommodations provided; but broadly speaking, it may be said that Florida, more than many resort regions, provides for every purse. It is amply supplied with small hotels and boarding houses, and no one need be deterred from a visit by a fear of being forced into the excessively fashionable and dear hotels. It is as enormously democratic and simple on one side as it is gay and expensive on the other."

A grove of palm trees shaded the audience during the daily afternoon concerts at the Royal Poinciana Hotel. Big, elaborate hats were favored by the ladies. All of the photos on pages 50 through 54 represent Palm Beach in the early years of the 20th Century.

Stretching between the Royal Poinciana and Breakers Hotels was the Palm Beach Florida East Coast Golf Club links, as shown in this 1901 diagram. Similar courses were established at other Florida resort hotels about this time. Note that the longest hole was only 341 yards.

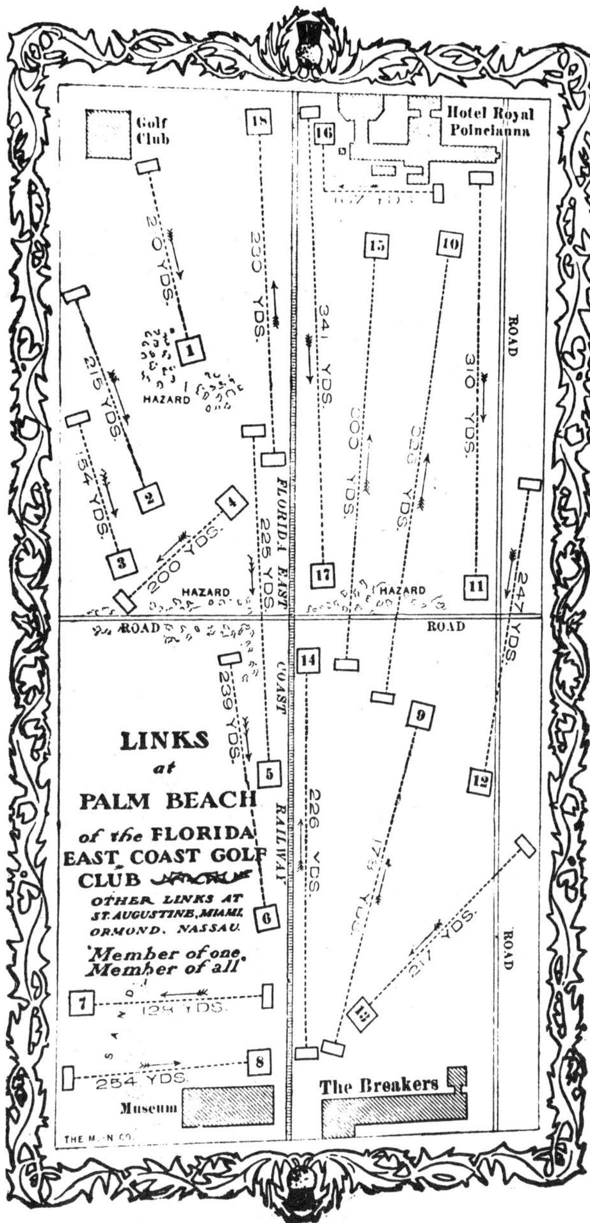

Rickshas as well as Afromobiles provided a popular means of transportation for patrons of the big hotels at Palm Beach.

The Golf Club house.

Alligator Joe's pavilion.

A crowd enjoys a sunny day and mild surf at the Palm Beach bathing casino.

Tennis stars of today would find it difficult to manage these ladies' tennis costumes. The photo w
taken at the Royal Poinciana tennis courts.

Swimming was both an active and a spectator sport at the Palm Beach bathing casino.

Clockwise from top left: mule car line at the Breakers; an Afromobile on the walk in front of the Palm Beach Hotel; a lady guest sharing the Palm Beach golf course with several male golfers; the piazza of the Royal Poinciana; walk and gardens of the Royal Poinciana; spectators at a sporting event at the Royal Poinciana grand stand, where even the roof provided seating for the athletic.

Bird's-eye view of Palm Beach, with the Royal Poinciana in the foreground, Breakers Hotel in the distance.

Afromobiles and their drivers, waiting for new guests arriving by train.

Sun and surf bathing at the Breakers Hotel.

More Afromobiles at the Breakers casino. The second Breakers Hotel is seen in the distance.

Hotel Ardma, 215 Brazilian Avenue, Palm Beach.

Palm Beach Hotel as it looked in 1906. It was burned to the ground in 1925, in the same fire which destroyed the second Breakers Hotel.

Colonel E. R. Bradley's exclusive Beach Club, a gambling casino at Palm Beach, where thousands of dollars were won and lost on a single turn of the wheel or throw of the dice. The most approved kind of patron was one who possessed a solid fortune and a listing in the Social Register. The club was in operation from 1899 until Bradley's death in 1946. In the middle distance is a wing of the Royal Poinciana; farther back, near the center, Whitehall Hotel.

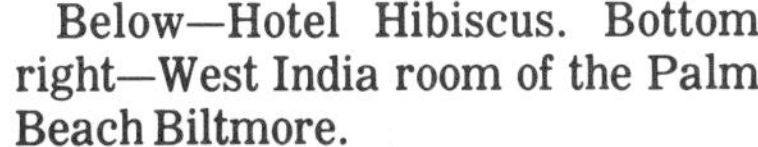

Below—Hotel Hibiscus. Bottom right—West India room of the Palm Beach Biltmore.

Only an aerial view could depict the full sweep of the Royal Poinciana Hotel, largest in the world in its day. It could accommodate 1,750 guests, who were served by some 1,400 employees, who in the early days were paid an average of about $1.25 a day. The Royal Poinciana was first completed in 1894, was expanded in 1899 and again in 1901, as shown here. It was dismantled in 1934.

Towering over the Flagler mansion is the Whitehall Hotel, which was in existence from 1926 to 1959.

The elegant Palm Beach Biltmore, seen here from the west, originally named the Hotel Alba, was opened in 1927, with 543 rooms. It reputedly cost $7,000,000.

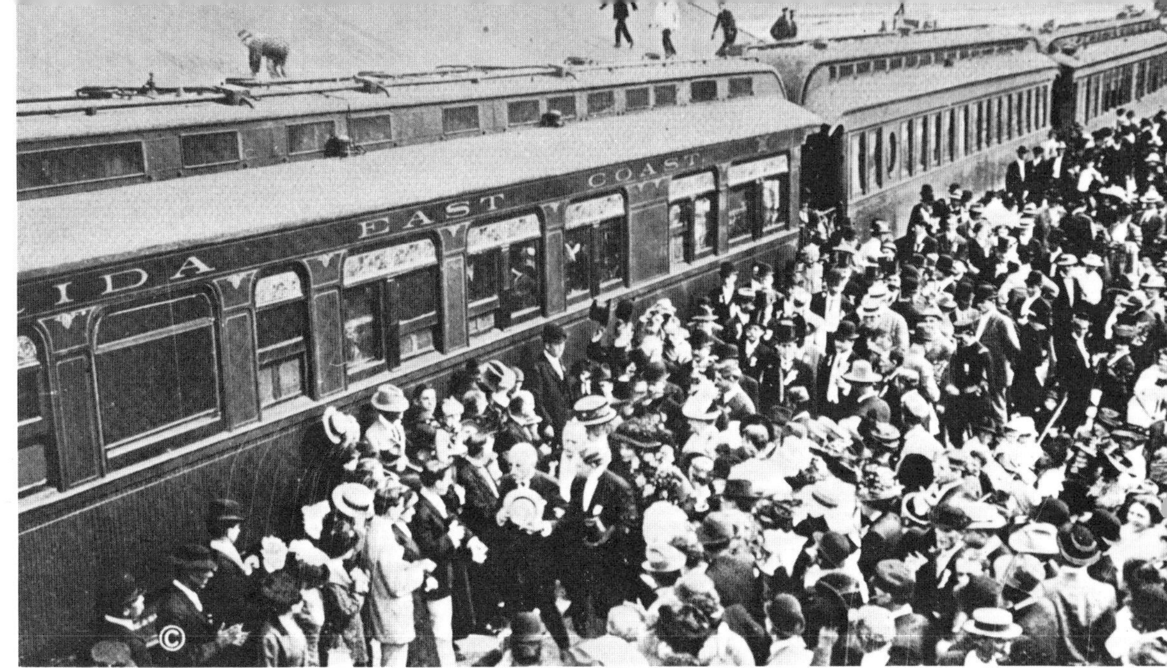

H. M. Flagler (holding straw hat at his chest) is greeted by local officials and admirers when he rode the first train over the water into Key West on January 22, 1912.

The sightseeing boat Princess Issena rounds into a landing on the Upper Tomoka River in 1906.

The colonnade of the Royal Poinciana was favored by the rocking chair brigade in the early years.

The extent of Flagler's transportation empire is shown in this map, published at the turn of the century by the Florida East Coast Railway. The rail line ran from Jacksonville (with a branch to Pablo Beach and Mayport) to Miami. From Miami steamship lines connected with Nassau, Key West and Havana. (Flagler's rail extension to Key West was made later, in 1912.) The names of principal Flagler hotels also are shown on the map at Atlantic Beach, St. Augustine, Ormond, Palm Beach, Miami and Nassau.

Railroads through the interior to several points on the west coast, mostly those of the Plant System, are indicated only by light lines.

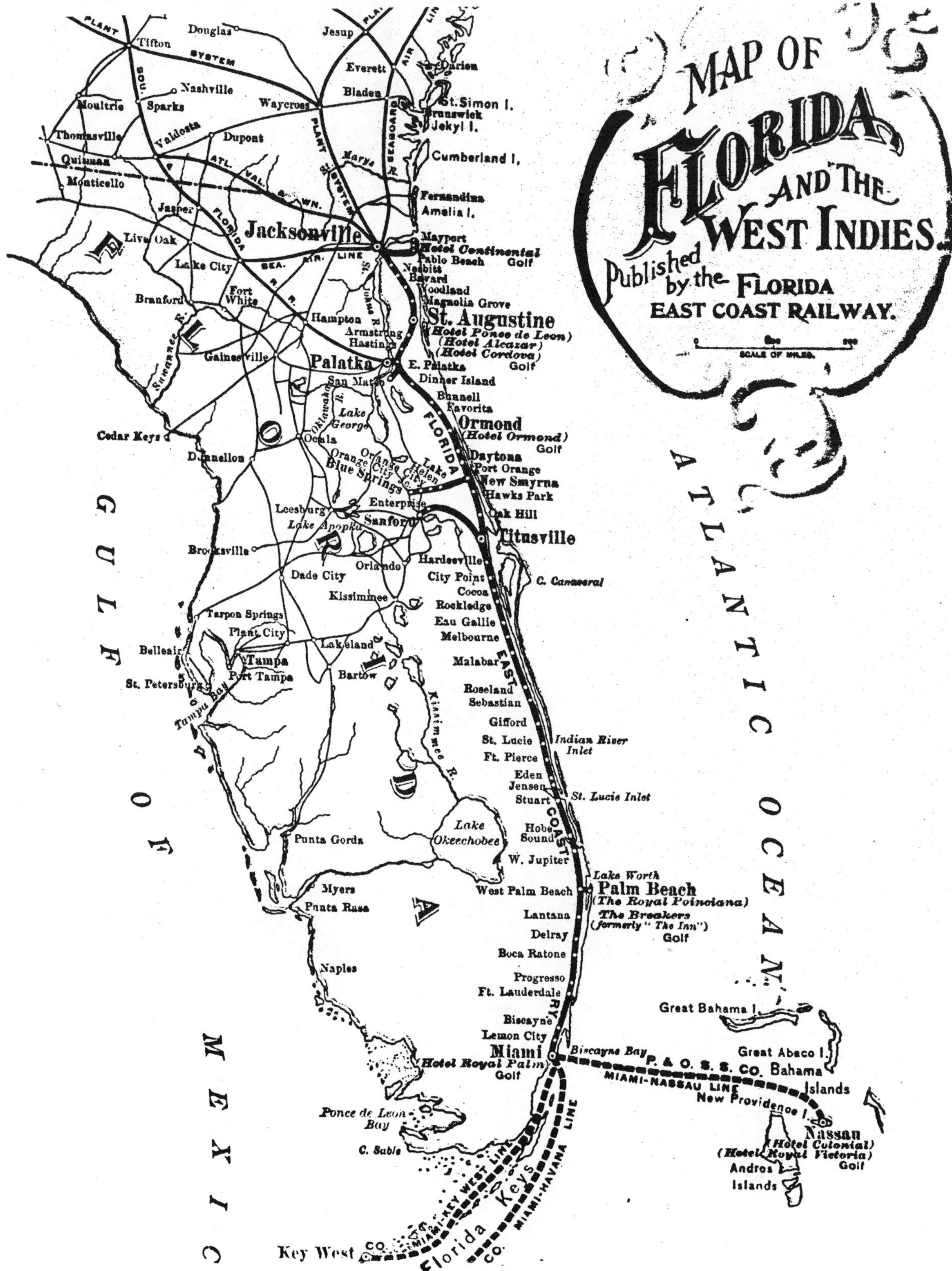

3
The Panhandle

ROADS HARDLY EXISTED, and trails were few, when in 1824 the territorial government descended upon Tallahassee, wrote Charles T. Thrift, Jr., in *The Trail of the Florida Circuit Rider.* Congress had appropriated money that year with which to build a road from Pensacola to St. Augustine, *via* Tallahassee. The western half was built largely by the Army and came to be known as the Military Road; the section eastward from near Tallahassee, constructed by a private contractor named John Bellamy, soon came to be known as the Bellamy Road. They were built between 1824 and 1826.

Only a matter of months after Tallahassee was approved as the site for territorial Florida's capital, its first hotel was in operation. The *Pensacola Gazette* on September 24, 1825, noted that more than fifty houses, a church, a school house and a hotel were built in Tallahassee within a short time. Slowly the wilderness was transformed into an organized community.

Elaborate balls were held in Tallahassee in the late 1820s and thereafter.

The renowned hospitality of the southern planter was brought to Florida, where the guest or traveler was always welcome at the home in town or country, wrote J. E. Dovell in *Florida: Historic, Dramatic, Contemporary.* In Middle Florida, the hospitality of the plantation houses caused one guest to write about "the cordial welcome, the patriarchal simplicity, the frank hospitality, and the surrender of time, slaves and everything the house affords to his comfort."

The late 1820s saw quite an influx of young men and women into the still-raw town of Tallahassee from some of the great plantation homes of Virginia, Maryland, the Carolinas and Georgia.

They brought their slaves, their agricultural implements and methods, their fine household furnishings, and the traditions of a gracious though fragile civilization, Karl Bickel noted in *The Mangrove Coast.*

The broad and fertile acres of Leon and Jefferson Counties welcomed the Bellamys, Brevards. Chaireses, Craigs, Calls, Duvals, DuPonts, Gadsdens, Turnbulls, Parkhills, Nuttals, Waltons and Wirts, among others.

These young bluebloods came to the Tallahassee area to create there the good life they had known in their former homes—plantation society, with slaves and overseers to do the work while the owners grappled with the economic facts of life, and socialized.

Many of their names are written across the map of Florida, wrote Bickel, and all of them had a determining hand in the political and social structure of the state.

One of the earliest inns in the new village of Tallahassee was an unnamed tavern containing "two or three large rooms which you would not deign to call barns," wrote A. J. Hanna in *A Prince in Their Midst.*

"It receives in a dozen beds twice that number of occupants. Those who cannot find better room extend themselves in their bed-clothes on the floor. No places are reserved for dining or sleeping. We are too democratic for that. Every one pays his dollar, and has a right to sleep where he pleases, provided he does not disturb a former occupant. It is understood that a bed contains two individuals, and nobody is so ridiculous as to trouble himself about who is next to him any more than in the pit of a theatre."

The annual session of the Territorial Council was the social, commercial and, of course, political climax of the year, wrote Bickel. "There were few commercial establishments and even fewer places of entertainment, yet visitors seemed to like the place. Whisky was sold in every store or inn as a matter of course. Ten cents a gallon was the standard price. It was good corn whisky, clear and unadulterated, and everybody—almost—drank freely of it. Ministers drank it; laborers drank it. All politicians drank it. Most of the ladies took it straight, sipping it delicately, with a small glass of water as a chaser."

There were four hotels in the capital city by 1828, according to Bertram H. Groene's *Ante-Bellum Tallahassee.* The hotels were "at the very center of the city's public life. Forerunners were the crude taverns of 1825 and 1826 where mess pork, cornbread, game, and rum or wine could be had, as well as a night's lodging on the floor or in a crowded bed."

The four were the Eagle Tavern (Josiah Everett), the Florida Hotel (Colonel Pindar), Washington Hall (J. R. Betton), and the Planters Hotel (William Wyatt). The first three faced Capitol Square, while the Planters was at the corner of Pensacola, looking south toward the new wing of the Capitol.

Colonel Pindar in 1828 advertised that the table of his Florida Hotel was furnished with as good food as the country could afford, his bar provided choice liquors, and his stables good provender.

Rates at the Florida were $18 monthly for room and meals, $15 for meals only; $1.50 a day for a man and his horse; 37½ cents for breakfast, 50 cents for dinner and 37½ cents for supper; and 18¾ cents for a room "most likely shared."

The Planters Hotel was the most prestigious. It was the principal temporary home of legislators, speculators, planters, national officials and foreign visitors, wrote Groene. Thus it was a center of political activity and was as important in the formation of local and territorial policy as the Capitol itself. Visiting dentists and other professionals stayed at the Planters. Its saloon doubled as a cultural center, where traveling theatrical troupes and others held their entertainments.

"Here, then, was the social hub of the village. Here the most widely celebrated balls were held, honorary dinners given, and national celebrations performed," wrote Groene.

Royalty also came to Tallahassee, in the person of Prince Achille Murat, nephew of Napoleon Bonaparte. Murat's father, Joachim Murat, King of Naples, was executed when the Napoleonic regime collapsed, and his mother, Caroline, took refuge in Vienna.

Achille, aged 22, came to America to join his uncle, Joseph Bonaparte, in New Jersey. He soon met R. K. Call, Florida's representative in Congress, and Call directed his attention to the little-developed territory of Florida.

Murat came, settling first at St. Augustine and moving in 1825 to the Tallahassee area. In anticipation of his marriage in 1826, he developed a 1,060-acre plantation, which he named Lipona. The bride was a widowed Virginia belle and great-grand-niece of George Washington, Catharine Grey.

In November, 1830, when the Murats were about to leave for an extended stay in Europe, they were honor guests at an elaborate ball at the Planters Hotel in Tallahassee. The ballroom was decorated with transparencies of the banner of France and of several American heroes, also "masses of laurel and myrtle, relieved by wreaths

The Lanark Inn, with a steepled lookout tower, was located at Lanark, southwest of Tallahassee on the Gulf of Mexico. It is pictured here in 1898.

The Florida Hotel, expanded by Thomas Brown after he bought it in 1833, became the Brown Hotel, later the City Hotel and the Morgan Hotel. It was Tallahassee's finest for many years. It is seen here about 1870, and was destroyed by fire in 1886.

and bouquets of roses and jasmine," according to Hanna.

The ball was "an occasion marking the ultimate achievement of Tallahassee in social refinements, on foundations which, six years before, had been at most the hogpens of an Indian camp." As a link between the United States and international society, the Murat ball was "an occasion for an unusual display of beauty and fashion."

In 1839, through financial reverses, Murat lost Lipona and his 108 slaves. He and Kate moved to a smaller plantation, Econchatti, with sixty slaves. There he lived out his life.

About 1830 Thomas Brown leased and took over the "genteel" management of the Planters. In 1833 he bought the Florida Hotel, expanded the old building by brick additions until it took in most of the block between Pensacola and Lafayette, facing the square. The enlarged Brown, or City Hotel was the finest, most expensive and successful hotel in the capital, and was to remain so until after the Civil War.

Brown, who later was to serve as Governor (1849-53), came to Tallahassee from Virginia in 1828 with no less than 140 slaves, planning to produce sugar. The venture did not succeed because of severe weather, and Brown brought his slaves with him into the village. He used many of them as hotel servants—waiters, hostelers, cooks and chambermaids—while others tended a small vegetable and dairy farm that supplied his new and popular hotel with vegetables, milk and butter.

Brown's City Hotel had almost one hundred rooms, including parlors, sitting rooms, suites for private families with a fireplace in each ($10 per month to keep burning), large stables, and "what must have been a large and spacious dining room."

There was no mention of bathrooms in these early years, for there was no indoor plumbing.

When the foundation of the Planters was dug up in the 1960s, as part of the excavation for the House office building on the north side of the new (1978) Capitol complex, two large privy pits were found. Both contained bottles, buttons and other artifacts dating from the late 1820s and early 1830s.

"One of the items they found in the privy pits was a dime dated, I believe, 1828," noted Malcolm

Originally the St. James Hotel, this 19th Century Tallahassee inn was renamed the Bloxham Hotel in honor of Governor William D. Bloxham. Popular with politicians and traveling men, it was known for good food. It was located at the northeast corner of the Monroe-Jefferson intersection.

The elegant Leon Hotel in Tallahassee was built in 1882 by the Tallahassee Hotel Company, of which Leroy D. Ball was president, on the site later occupied by the Post Office. For forty-three years it was host to many Floridians in public life, visitors of national renown, and to Tallahasseeans attending club meetings, parties and balls. A 1911 article about the hotel noted that "next to the State Capitol, the Leon has been the scene of the most stirring events in the political history of Florida." It burned in 1925.

Johnson, erudite editor (until his 1978 retirement) of the *Tallahassee Democrat*. "This gave rise to the story that archeologists had located Florida's first pay toilet."

A few boarding houses were in operation during the years before and after 1850, notably J. L. DeMilly's Georgia House.

Only two hotels remained in Tallahassee in 1850—Brown's (which went downhill after he sold it) and the faded Planters. Though much needed, no more were to be constructed until after the Civil War. Plans were made in 1858 by a "desperate" City Council to build a $20,000 hotel to be owned and operated by the city, but nothing came of this.

The port city of St. Marks, some twenty miles south of Tallahassee, had known its times of glory in the past, but by the late 1820s it was the capital's "poor sister"—shipping point for vast fortunes in cotton, and receiving point for the planters' staples and luxuries.

In 1829 it was said by a visitor to consist of "a few scattered huts half buried in the mud, and a hotel of sorts built in the center of the old Spanish fort."

The Cherokee Hotel, on the south side of Park Street between Monroe and Calhoun, was built in 1921-22.

The situation in St. Marks improved somewhat in later years, for in 1858 its Railroad Hotel was receiving travelers. A few pages of the hotel register for that year miraculously survived for 108 years, and were found in an abandoned house in the town. Also salvaged were records of a trading post operated in conjunction with the hotel.

The register indicates that sailors and gentry alike stopped at the Railroad Hotel (probably *en route* to other points), and its trading post offered many items the early settlers needed. Visitors passing through the village came from as far as New York, Texas and Virginia, as well as from Tallahassee, Pensacola, and other points in Florida.

On May 17, 1858, Richard Keith Call registered, still using the title of Governor. John Branch, another territorial Governor, also visited the hotel. The Chaires family stopped on May 27—G. B. Chaires and Lady, two children and servant; F. Chaires, and others. General William Bailey and Lady of Jefferson County were there on May 30, 1858.

However, this was not a resort hotel. "Its distinguished clientele probably was forced to patronize it more by necessity and through accustomed hardship than by choice," according to Malcolm Johnson. "It was a cotton port, then—and a port of entry for travelers by boat from the Gulf coast and up and down the Mississippi River."

The register was used also as a ledger to record trading post purchases. One of these included two barrels of coffee sugar, Reo coffee, a case of washing compound, candy, mustard, Holland gin, rice, butter, cider, vinegar, lard, oil, burning fluid, linseed oil and crackers. The bill came to $469.63. One drug order included calomel, adhesive plaster, paregoric, diarrhea cordial, Mexican Mustang liniment, and alum.

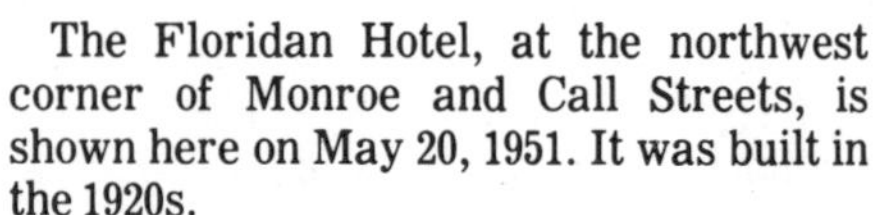

The Floridan Hotel, at the northwest corner of Monroe and Call Streets, is shown here on May 20, 1951. It was built in the 1920s.

Newcomers to the rich clay hills of the Tallahassee area from other southern states had brought "elegance and mannerly traditions" to soften the rudeness of the frontier capital. Governor Duval brought his family from Pensacola for its new social life, with its "pleasantly sophisticated. candlelit evening parties, dinner parties, dance parties," wrote Marjory Stoneman Douglas in *Florida: The Long Frontier.*

"Ladies wore silks, and gentlemen their well-cut nankins and flowered waistcoats. Many big comfortable log cabins were furnished with mahogany, silver, china, and portraits, among plain, slave-made pine furniture and bare floors."

Slips of Cherokee roses, camellia and wisteria were brought from their former homes and set out by the ladies, Douglas noted. Old recipes for eggnogs, syllabubs, sangarees and tipsy puddings were prepared by their Negro cooks. There was plenty of venison and turkey, quail, and lake fish; also red snapper, snook, bass and mackerel from the Gulf.

"Christmases, birthdays, weddings, house parties, the exciting horseback tournaments of the May Day party, when the winning knight crowned the Queen of Love and Beauty, were continuing festivities in a new land." Racing weeks were the height of the Tallahassee season, centered around the Marion track, to which gentlemen brought fine racing horses from as far away as Kentucky and Tennessee. Race days often ended in all-night balls.

The hotels in Tallahassee not only accommodated travelers but also served as social centers for local folk. The four best-known—the City, Planters and Florida Hotels and Washington Hall—all had notable reputations.

There was little social activity in the capital city during the period (1834-36) when John H. Eaton served as territorial Governor, by appointment of President Jackson. Eaton's wife, the former Peggy O'Neill, was *persona non grata* to the ladies of Tallahassee. She was, in fact, the "gorgeous hussy" of the Jackson administration, and her Washington reputation followed her to Florida. The Eatons spent little time in Tallahassee for this reason. They lived in Pensacola, largely in seclusion.

The average Florida citizen in 1845 "spoke English, claimed to believe the Bible, favored States' rights, opposed total abstinence, hated the Seminole Indians, took plenty of calomel, and, in spite of several years of financial depression, had faith in the future of Florida," according to a 1945 book entitled *Florida Becomes a State,* by W. T. Cash and Dorothy Dodd.

A retreat for Tallahasseeans at the turn of the century was the Panacea Hotel (above) at Panacea on the Gulf of Mexico. When this picture was taken in 1902, the Panacea advertised rates of $8 to $10 a week, $5 for children over ten and for servants.

The handsome twenty-five-room Wakulla Springs Hotel faces the springs across a broad lawn that is alive with birds and squirrels. The floors and stairs of the hotel are of Tennessee marble. Edward Ball, Florida financier, built the Wakulla Springs Hotel in the mid-1930s, according to Joe R. Wilkie, manager. The area of the springs is part of the 4,000-acre Edward Ball Wildlife Sanctuary.

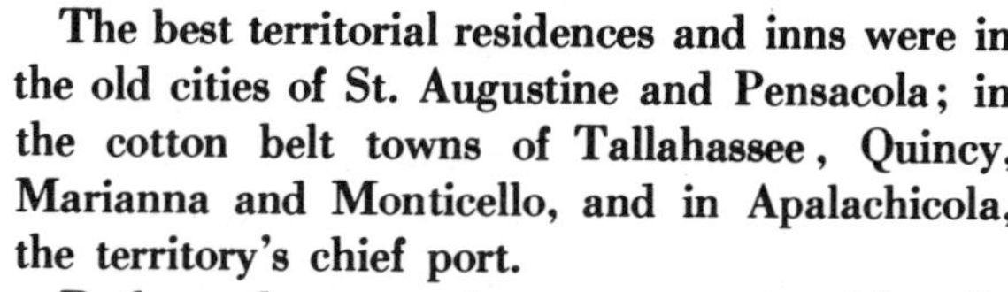

The best territorial residences and inns were in the old cities of St. Augustine and Pensacola; in the cotton belt towns of Tallahassee, Quincy, Marianna and Monticello, and in Apalachicola, the territory's chief port.

Rather than coming to terms with the Apalachicola Land Company regarding clouded titles, many of that town's inhabitants moved in 1835 about twenty-five miles away to the shore of St. Joseph's Bay and there established a town designed "to compete with and possibly wreck the enterprising town of Apalachicola," wrote Thrift.

For a while it appeared that St. Joseph would accomplish that purpose. It succeeded in 1836 in having the Legislative Council move the location of the county seat of Franklin there from Apalachicola, but Congress prohibited the change.

Top—The Raney House at Apalachicola, an impressive example of Greek Revival architecture, dates from 1838, when it was built for David G. Raney, a cotton merchant, and his family. It passed through several other ownerships until 1939, and was bought that year by Irene Tucker, who operated it as a boarding house until her death in 1972. During that year the house was placed on the National Register of Historic Places. In 1973 it was purchased by the city of Apalachicola. After six years of restoration to its former elegance, it was turned over in 1979 to the Apalachicola Area Historical Society. It is open to the public on a regular schedule.

Center—Apalachicola's Gibson Hotel was established as the Franklin Hotel in the early 1900s. It was built around a dwelling constructed before 1897.

Sailboats and a few steamers dotted the Apalachicola waterfront in 1837.

Frustrated in this effort, St. Joseph did succeed two years later in being named the county seat of the new county of Calhoun. Rivalry between the two towns was most acute from 1837 to 1839, as reported by their newspapers.

St. Joseph's greatest triumph, however, came when the Legislative Council chose that town as the seat of the Constitutional Convention. Here, on December 3, 1838, representatives from all parts of the territory came, by whatever means of transportation could be devised, to frame a Constitution preparatory to Florida's assuming the role of a state in the Union.

"One of the chief characters in the drama of the rise of St. Joseph was the son of a Methodist minister, Peter W. Gautier," wrote Thrift. "His son, named for him, was one of the most brilliant Florida newspapermen of this period." He moved in 1836 to St. Joseph, where he published the *St. Joseph Telegraph,* soon renamed the *St. Joseph Times,* from 1836 to 1841.

It was the younger Gautier who, as a member of the Legislative Council, was primarily responsible for having St. Joseph designated as the convention site.

In preparing to receive the influx of delegates and others expected to attend the Constitutional Convention, residents of St. Joseph not only constructed a convention hall and provided stepped-up boat service to the town, but also built several boarding houses and three hotels, the Pickwick, Byron and Shakespeare.

The decline of St. Joseph began shortly before 1840, for it could not compete with the natural advantages of the parent city. A yellow fever epidemic in the Summer of 1841, followed by a severe hurricane in September, virtually ended this most ambitious building scheme of territorial days, wrote Thrift.

One of the Methodist ministers who served at St. Joseph was Peter Haskew. Haskew noted in his diary for September 23, 1839, that he had gone to Apalachicola, stopping at a tavern "where they charged me six dollars for a day and a half for myself and horse, and this time there was so much cursing and noise that I could not rest well."

During the territorial period several short railroads were laid in middle Florida, the foremost of which reached from Tallahassee to St. Marks between 1834 and 1836, and was extended in 1839 to Port Leon. Large numbers of slaves were used in its construction. Locomotion for the line in the early years was provided by a mule team; not until 1837 was an engine acquired. The train carried passengers, mail, and a very substantial amount of cotton and produce. Its box-like passenger cars had rows of benches at either side.

This line was promoted by the Tallahassee Railroad Company. The segment between St. Marks and Port Leon was severely damaged by a

Sis Hopkins Inn, pre-World War I hostelry at Madison, was owned by Mrs. Ethel Hopkins. It catered to the elite, offering fine food, culture and charm, according to E. B. Browning, Sr., a present-day resident of Madison. Winter visitors included Sidney Smith, who drew "The Gumps" comic strip, and Edison Marshall, an English novelist.

great hurricane in 1843; since Port Leon was not rebuilt, neither was that portion of the railroad.

In an effort to make St. Joseph a major shipping port to compete with Apalachicola, investors built two short railroads in 1836. At stake was a share of the shipping of cotton and other products of middle Florida, Alabama and Georgia.

The first, the St. Joseph-Lake Wimico line, made its first run in September of that year, with twelve cars carrying some 300 passengers.

Another road was built to link St. Joseph with a point on the Apalachicola River known as Iola. This line was twenty-eight miles long, and made the distance from St. Joseph to Columbus, Georgia, fifty miles shorter than that from Apalachicola to the same city.

However, Apalachicola continued as the more popular port, and the newer line did not prosper. After the 1841 yellow fever epidemic and hurricane decimated St. Joseph, the line was sold and the rails incorporated into a later road elsewhere.

Apalachicola, established in 1821 and incorporated in 1827 as West Point, gained its permanent name in 1831. Six years later it had become the third largest cotton-shipping port on the Gulf of Mexico, handling increasing quantities of that product, brought down the Apalachicola River from Alabama, Georgia and Florida.

Apalachicola was a frontier town and a thriving port—with all the lively comings and goings which that status implied. But by 1865, it was clear that the wealthy days of King Cotton were over for that town, and commercial production of seafood could not match that prosperity.

Dr. John Gorrie settled there in 1833 and soon became its leading citizen, holding various municipal offices. He is best remembered for his discovery of a means of cooling the rooms of his fever patients—the forerunner of compression refrigeration.

In 1845 he built the first machine for making artificial ice, but found no backers to promote his discovery. He died in obscurity in 1855, unaware of his contribution to science—a discovery that affected the living patterns of the world through the development of refrigerators, freezers and air conditioners.

The Shivers Hotel in Chipley, which dated from the early 20th Century, was the center of much community activity during its heyday, according to E. W. Carswell, a present-day resident of Chipley. It was operated for many years by Olin G. Shivers, who served several terms in the Florida Senate and

Field stone pillars supported the porch roof of the Shivers Hotel at Chipley, built in the early 20th Century.

House of Representatives. The hotel was twice featured in Ripley's "Believe It or Not" cartoon—once for its sign which read "Steam Heat—Shivers Hotel," and again because its guest rooms had no locks, a condition that Ripley found unique among the hotels in his experience.

The Shivers continued in use as a hotel until the mid-1960s, when it was converted to a convalescent home. The building was razed in the early 1970s.

Paralleling the lifespan of the Shivers in Chipley was the Hotel Eureka in nearby Bonifay. It was a rambling wood-frame, two-story building with high ceilings. Downstairs there was a big community room with a large fireplace, around which guests gathered on Winter evenings. In Summer they spent a lot of time on its porches.

"Hotel Eureka had an unusual distinction during the 1920s and early 1930s, when it was operated by N. D. Miller," said Carswell. "He served chicken every day. Meals were served—into the 1960s—boarding house style.

"That chicken every day may not seem any great distinction, but it must be remembered that chicken in that era was a delicacy often reserved for Sunday dinner—and you couldn't get dressed chickens at the supermarket, not in Bonifay at any rate. Signs along U. S. Highway 90 advertised the 'Chicken Every Day' menu, and the hotel got a lot of trade because of it."

During the years before the dining car became a part of every passenger train, it was the custom for the trains to stop at certain points, where the hotel food was considered outstanding, so that the

Jackson County citizens had gathered in Marianna, in this 1909 photo, to discuss laying off and paving roads. In the right foreground is a hotel moved from Webbville in the early 1830s, after Marianna had become the county seat. At left: Citizens State Bank building.

This elegant lobby of the Valparaiso Inn of the 1920s, with its rich carpets and grand piano, was partitioned to form several private rooms after A. L. Harrell bought the building in 1957 and made it into an apartment house. The Inn is on the National Register of Historic Places.

Tall pines and a white sand beach formed a setting of beauty for the Valparaiso Inn.

passengers could get off and enjoy the local cuisine. Both the Shivers at Chipley and the Eureka at Bonifay were so honored.

Another Bonifay hotel was the Dixie, operated by Curt Miller, according to Shouppe Howell of that town, president of the Holmes County Chamber of Commerce.

The modest ($125,000) but once-elegant Valparaiso Inn at Valparaiso, listed on the National Register of Historic Places, figured largely in the development of Okaloosa County, the city of Valparaiso, and in the establishment of Eglin AFB, the country's largest Air Force base. Built in 1923-24 by James E. Plew, with Walker D. Willis of Pensacola as architect, the Inn "was painted Satsuma yellow with green borders and a red roof, making a happy color scheme," according to an article in the *Pensacola Journal* on August 8, 1924.

Plew, a Chicagoan of varied business interests, was an early promoter of aviation, owning a private plane prior to 1910. He came in 1922 to the land along Boggy Bayou where Frank Perrine, also of Chicago, had bought 16,000 acres of land in 1919 and attempted to develop the city of Valparaiso. Plew purchased the Perrine properties, built the Inn and a nearby golf course. The Inn was advertised heavily in golfing and real estate magazines, and soon became the site of regional golf tournaments as well as a vacation spot for Plew's Chicago business associates, a haven for prospective investors in real estate in the area, and a weekend retreat for aviators from the Air Corps Tactical School at Maxwell Field near Montgomery, Alabama. The Inn became the social center of that area of Florida.

When in 1931 Army Air Corps officials looked for a site for a bombing and gunnery range, Lieutenant Arnold Rich of Maxwell Field, who had spent many weekends at the Valparaiso Inn, suggested that area. Plew and the Valparaiso Realty Company offered to donate 1,460 acres to the War Department, and the offer was accepted.

The golf course which Plew had built in 1924, and named the Chicago Country Club for his former home, became the Eglin golf course.

The Inn continued as a center for local social activities until the 1950s. It was purchased in 1957 by A. L. Harrell and converted to apartments.

Bacon's By-the-Sea was located "where spreading oaks stood guard along the sandy shores of a crystal sound and looked across a narrow strip of romantic isle to the chameleon waters of the Gulf of Mexico," according to a brochure which advertised the Inn.

The property in the town of Mary Esther on which Bacon's By-the-Sea was built was purchased by Mabel Bacon and her son Page in 1935, according to Mrs. James N. LaRoche, museum director for the Historical Society of Okaloosa & Walton Counties, Inc., at Valparaiso.

The first building was constructed and the Inn

Rustic was the word for Bacon's By-the-Sea at Mary Esther. Shown here is "Captain's Roost" guest cottage, one of several on the hotel grounds. Lieutenant Colonel James Doolittle stayed in one of them (and also at the Valparaiso Inn) while he was in training to lead America's first air strike against Tokyo on April 18, 1942.

The Merchants Hotel in Madison was built in 1883, and wa later known as the Commercial Hotel and the Madison Hot When the original frame building burned in 1907, the hot was rebuilt of brick the same year. It catered especially traveling salesmen, then known as drummers. The structu served for a time in more recent years as the uptown stude center and alumni office for North Florida Junior College Madison. It has been converted by Mrs. Virginia Rowell in apartments and office space.

was in operation two years later, she said. It served as a leading hostelry during the World War II years, but did not come into its own until the 1950s when nearby Hurlburt Field (an auxiliary field of Eglin AFB) was active.

Page's wife, Nina, continued as an active partner, taking care of much of the business aspect of the enterprise until her death in 1972. The property then changed hands several times. In 1979 it was owned by a group of Fort Walton Beach men who were engaged in restoring it to its original charm.

Though the Inn was described in the brochure as being as modern and comfortable as the homes of the well-to-do, great pains were taken to keep the "modernistic touch" from appearing anywhere. "Accommodations are comfortably spacious," it was noted. "The architecture is rustic, with logs and hand-hewn timbers appearing in many places. We have tried to keep the air of the country estate where one may loaf, play, sunbathe, go boating, play tennis, swim, fish, and generally enjoy good living without being pestered by bellboys and extra charges.

"Those who like to vacation by lavish dressing, rounds of parties, splurging or carousing won't like it here. Those who enjoy relaxing, outdoor sports, interesting people and simple dress love it. We maintain a very close control on our class of clientele, as we do very little advertising except with the very best of the travel bureaus."

Jackson County, the state's third, was established on August 12, 1822, and during the next five years several small settlements served as the county seat. Webbville, with its post office, school, four stores and two hotels, had that honor in 1827, but not for long. Marianna was established later in 1827, was incorporated the next year, and by 1829 its politically ambitious founders succeeded in having it designated the new and permanent county seat.

A number of frame houses were moved from Webbville to the new town in the early 1830s, including a two-story building which was placed directly north of the new court house. This structure served as a hotel in the 1830s, according to Miss Clara Farley and Mrs. John C. Packard, present-day residents of Marianna.

"In the late 1830s a prince of hotel keepers in Marianna was William Nichols," wrote Samuel D. Irvin in his memoirs.

"Marianna was a lively place then, both Summer and Winter. Many persons from Apalachicola, then an important shipping port, spent their Summers in Marianna and its vicinity. The holidays of July 4, February 22 and others

An important structure in Jackson County's history was the Chipola Hotel, built in 1883 at Marianna. Vine-shaded verandas provided cool retreats in Summer; fireplaces warmed the interior in Winter.

never went by without a ball at the hotel, with such suppers and accompaniments as only Mr. and Mrs. Nichols could provide.

"No little town ever had such a fiddler as Tom Wynn, a person of color. Cotillions, and now and then a Virginia reel, were the rule, and Tom made his figures and his music accord with the most perfect harmony."

The old Chipola Hotel, a long rambling building with vine-festooned galleries, was built in Marianna when the trains came in 1883 on a line of the Louisville & Nashville (known as the Pensacola & Atlantic), from Pensacola to River Junction (Chattahoochee). With the trains came an influx of civil engineers and railroad personnel, and a corresponding need for a "modern" hotel.

The Chipola played a significant role in the early development of Jackson County and northwest Florida; it became popular not only with local residents but also with railroad people, some of whom settled permanently in Marianna, according to Mrs. Packard. The towns of Chipley, Bonifay and DeFuniak Springs carry the names of Louisville & Nashville officials.

Frank Edwards and his wife Agnes owned and operated the old Chipola from 1916 until 1925, according to their grandson, Gary Lloyd of Tallahassee. It was a popular resort with hunting and fishing parties. When the new Chipola was constructed, this building was moved to a nearby site and served as the Chipola Annex until it was razed in 1963.

The "new" five-story brick Chipola Hotel, built in the 1920s, stands on the site of the former one of the same name—at the corner of Main (Lafayette) Street and Caledonia. The latter Chipola, Spanish in architecture, was converted to an office building.

Another hotel in that historic town was the Marianne, built in 1925-26 as a hospital by Dr. N. A. Baltzell, prominent in Florida medical circles. After his death in 1940, the two-story brick building was sold and made into a hotel. It served as such for twenty-odd years before being razed.

A large three-story frame building of Victorian architecture was built on Marianna's Caledonia Street near the railroad station shortly before the turn of the century by the Solomon family, and was operated for a few years as the Solomon Hotel. After some time during which it passed from its original status, the Frank Stone family bought it in the 1930s and restored it as the Stone Hotel. In 1980 it is owned and operated by a daughter, Mabel Stone Cushing.

Mr. and Mrs. Edwards, upon leaving the Chipola in 1925, leased the Cove Hotel in Panama City and operated it until 1928. They then bought the Hotel Quincy at Quincy, northwest of Tallahassee, and continued to operate it until their deaths in 1931 and 1943, respectively. Their daughter Evelyn (Mrs. Frank W.) Lloyd continued operation of the Quincy until 1949.

The three-story, fifty-five room Quincy was a resort for local representatives of the American Sumatra Tobacco Company, also for Governors and other discriminating diners from Tallahassee and elsewhere. They came for "a first-class meal served in elegant surroundings with candlelight and soft background music," according to a

The cuisine of the Hotel Quincy at Quincy, seen here about 1940, drew discriminating diners from a wide area.

The picturesque Pines Hotel in Panama City, first built as a club house, was remodeled in 1919 into a forty-eight-room hotel. Facing St. Andrews Bay, it was a favorite meeting place for the community. It burned in November, 1932.

The Bagdad Inn took its name from the ante-bellum town of Bagdad, in Santa Rosa County. It was owned by the Bagdad Land and Timber Company, and is shown here about the time of World War I.

The boom-time Dixie Sherman Hotel, anama City's first large hostelry, was ened with an elaborate dinner dance on ne 29, 1927. Eight stories high, the hotel ntained 102 rooms and a roof garden. It as demolished by dynamite in 1970.

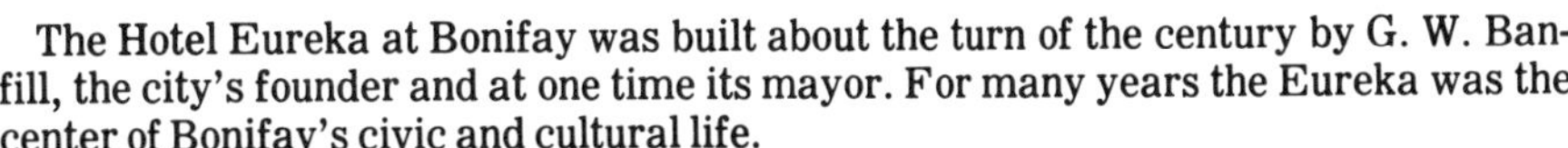

The Hotel Eureka at Bonifay was built about the turn of the century by G. W. Banfill, the city's founder and at one time its mayor. For many years the Eureka was the center of Bonifay's civic and cultural life.

feature story in the *Tallahassee Democrat* on April 14, 1972.

General George S. Patton spent a week's leave there in the early 1940s, with several other officers, to fish at the Dead Lakes near Wewahitchka, or at Lakes Talquin or Jackson. Their day's catch would then comprise the main course for dinner for the party. Meals were the main attraction at the Quincy, featuring not only traditional southern dishes, but specialties such as roast duck, oysters Rockefeller, fig ice cream, and biscuits (with mayhaw jelly), made by Agnes Edwards personally.

Like other Florida hotels of the era, the Quincy attracted its share of notables from the entertainment, sports, literary and financial worlds, who would have their itineraries planned so that they could stop there overnight. The town was then on major rail and highway routes. The tobacco companies closed, traffic routes were changed, and the pace of life in Quincy declined. Mrs. Lloyd sold the hotel in 1951, and it was demolished about ten years later.

Built in 1883, the Hotel Chautauqua was a large frame building facing Lake DeFuniak Springs. Constructed to house visitors and performing artists attending the local Chautauqua programs, it advertised rooms that were "large and airy" and provided with fireplaces. A wide porch faced the lake.

The dining room provided "excellent cuisine" and drinking water from the nearby Alpine Spring, noted for its health-giving qualities and billed as the "Poland of the South."

Rates at the hotel ranged from $10 to $15 per person weekly, with special rates for January and also for the entire season.

Years later and under new management, the Chautauqua became the Walton Hotel. After about seventy-five years as the leading hotel in Walton County, it was torn down.

Built in 1906 by Charles B. and Alice Shipley on Santa Rosa Sound in Mary Esther, the Cedars Hotel was named for the many cedar trees on the grounds. It was built on six acres of land owned by Mary Watson Rogers. Small cottages soon were constructed to accommodate the growing tourist trade.

It is said that Charles Lindbergh was a guest at the Cedars when he was forced to land on the Narrows because of an oil line break.

The last of the buildings was torn down in the 1960s and condominiums constructed on the site perpetuate the name, the Cedars.

Built on the Sound at Camp Walton (now Fort Walton Beach) by a northerner named Faircloth, about the same time as the Cedars, was the Gulf View Hotel. This frame building with wide verandas facing the water is still in operation in 1980. It was purchased in 1913 by Adam J. Gerlach of Crown Point, Indiana, and members of his family, who have continued to own and operate it.

The Indianola Inn was built by Sarah Frances and Willie Pryor atop an Indian mound in the center of Fort Walton Beach about 1912. The property on which it was located was given to Mrs. Pryor by her father, Tom Brooks, founder of Fort Walton Beach.

The Indianola was designed to accommodate the overflow from Brooks House, the Pryor home which was used for rooming and boarding guests. The Inn burned in 1962.

In 1922, William B. Harbeson took over the Brooks Hotel at Camp Walton and changed the name to the Harbeson Hotel. The Harbeson did so well that a new wing was soon constructed to serve the growing clientele. In the 1920s a private boat, the *Harbeson*, brought guests from Pensacola to spend a few days or the entire Summer. The rate was $23 a week per person, including a room, bath and three meals a day.

Electricity for the hotel was produced by a diesel engine, and water came from an artesian well. To entertain its guests, the hotel maintained a pavilion over the water for dancing, and a six-piece orchestra played nightly. During World War II this pavilion was divided into additional rooms for guests. The hotel was later enlarged and its name changed to the Miramar.

After Harbeson's death Mrs. Harbeson married Brownlow Jackson and continued as manager of the hotel for more than thirty years. The original structure is gone and a motel, the Sheraton Marina Inn, stands on the site.

Built in 1926 by R. L. Sudduth, the Cove Hotel in Panama City was sold in 1928 to Mrs. Ruby Harris and Robert Sealy, and later to Hamilton Kenner. It was destroyed by fire on January 3, 1976.

In an article which appeared in the *Panama City News Herald* on May 5, 1968, the Cove was said to "retain the splendor of the Old South."

Still another, of earlier vintage (1909), was the towered, two-story Hotel Panama City at the foot of Harrison Avenue, according to Jane Patton,

A popular resort in Lynn Haven, called "Florida's Indian Summerland," was the forty-room Lynn Haven Hotel, built in 1920 by Minor C. Keith. Two four-room cottages were erected on the grounds six years later to accommodate the growing number of guests. The hotel catered especially to sportsmen, and had its own wharf (left) in St. Andrews Bay, which it faced. It was ultra-modern, heated by electricity brought from Millville, seven miles distant.

Facing Lake Defuniak Springs, the Hotel Chautauqua was built in 1883, and served Walton County as its leading hotel for some seventy-five years, the latter part of that time under the name of Walton Hotel. This picture was taken in 1908.

director of the Northwest Regional Library System, with headquarters at Panama City. Its architecture featured an abundance of Victorian "gingerbread."

The Northwest Florida Official Guide for June, 1937, described the Andrew Jackson Hotel at Floridatown as "one of the delightful resorts of Santa Rosa County," offering in addition to splendid hotel accommodations, well furnished cottages, a large casino, restaurant, and a swimming pool. It was located on a beautiful point reaching out into Escambia Bay.

Pensacola, permanently settled in 1698, is the second oldest city in Florida. Panfilo de Narvaez, as early as 1528, "sailed into its harbor and promptly declared it the world's finest of natural deep-water ports," wrote T. T. Wentworth, Jr., in an article published in 1970. Other explorers came and went until 1698, when the Spanish succeeded in founding a colony at Pensacola under the governorship of Admiral Andres de Arriola.

During the next 123 years Pensacola, like its sister city on the Atlantic coast, St. Augustine, was the pawn of European powers which occupied it at various times. The island village of Pensacola was raked by a hurricane in 1752, when many lives were lost and houses leveled.

Pensacola's three-story City Hotel, with Ed Sexauer as proprietor, was serving guests at least as early as 1885, when it was listed in that town's first City Directory.

"For over 200 years, Chumuckla Springs have been sought by the white man, following the lead of the Indian, and thousands have gone their different ways, bodily ills forgotten after taking the waters, singing praises in honor of Chumuckla," according to a booklet published in 1914 by the Chumuckla Mineral Springs & Hotel Company. The water was recommended for treatment of dyspepsia, indigestion, acute or chronic dysentery, "and every form of stomach or blood and skin disease, including rheumatism and pellagra." This was the Chumuckla (Chuckmuckla) Springs Hotel, located in northeastern Santa Rosa County. It burned in 1917, according to Richard C. Mancini of the Santa Rosa Historical Society at Milton.

Those who survived moved from Santa Rosa Island to the mainland, settling in the Seville Square area, and built new homes.

The methodical English, who were the new occupants in 1763, laid out the present-day city, wrote Wentworth. The lots south of Garden Street were reserved for dwellings, while the section north of it was set aside for the vegetable gardens of the thrifty villagers.

Another noteworthy event was the establishment in the 1780s of the Panton-Leslie Indian trading post. It was enormously successful, made a wealthy man of William Panton and, with the aid of Chief Alexander McGillivray, part-Creek, kept that tribe of Indians loyal to the British at that time. The trading post maintained, among other facilities, campgrounds for visiting tribesmen.

While the settlers to the north were fighting the Revolutionary War, the Spanish recaptured Pensacola (in 1781), occupied and controlled West Florida until the state became a permanent part of the United States. Andrew Jackson, who had made forays of dubious legality into West Florida in 1814 and 1818 to quell recurrent troubles with hostile Indians, became Florida's first provisional Governor in 1821, with George Walton as Secretary of State.

After a few months Jackson left, with his wife Rachel (who deplored the city's "wicked ways") before a civilian Governor, William R. DuVal, was appointed. Walton served during the interim.

The first Territorial Legislature met in 1822 in Pensacola, the temporary capital. Construction was begun at the Navy Yard in 1825, and Forts Pickens, McRee, Barrancas and Redoubt were built, the first begun in 1829, the others in the following fifteen years. The battleship *U. S. S. Pensacola* was launched in 1859 from the Navy Yard.

Pensacola was a prize plum in the Civil War. After several battles, the city was abandoned in May of 1862, the municipal government was moved to Greenville, Alabama, and Federal troops held Pensacola until the end of the war. Pensacolians then returned to rebuild their lives and their town. Railroads were built, and the port was busy with lumber and naval stores.

The city played a key role in the Spanish-American War as well.

Ship construction slowed in the decades which followed. Just as it appeared that Pensacola's Navy Yard was no longer important in America's defense, along came the Wright brothers and the flying machines. The Yard was reopened as the Naval Air Station.

You are cordially invited to attend a
Grand Opening Ball
at the
New Continental Hotel
Pensacola, Fla.

Greatly enlarged by erection of a three-story addition, the New Continental Hotel at Pensacola was the scene of a "Grand Opening Ball" on February 16, 1885.

George Catlin, Indian explorer, described Pensacola in 1835 as "the only place I have found in the southern country to which northern people can repair with safety in the Summer season; and I know not a place in the world where they can go with better guarantee of good health, and a reasonable share of the luxuries of life. The town of Pensacola . . . contains about 1,500 inhabitants, most of them Spanish Creoles . . .

"The Navy officers' houses are eleven in number, neat and handsome buildings, two stories high, with balconies around each—a true comfort and luxury in this warm climate to which to retire, and there repose during the heat of the midday sun." The town contained a bank, three churches, and "three or four hotels, of which at present Allin's carries off the palm," Catlin noted.

Among the early places of entertainment and accommodation in Pensacola was the Eagle Tavern, constructed between 1810 and 1820, according to Sidney Martin in *Florida During the Territorial Days.* Catering particularly to travelers, it boasted "a good bath house in connection with the tavern where either hot or cold baths may be taken at any time." The Collins House later superseded the Eagle Tavern in popularity.

"In 1824 a public dinner was tendered Richard Keith Call at the Collins House, after which thirty or forty toasts were drunk," wrote Dovell.

Pensacola's first modern hotel, the Continental, originally was the ante-bellum home of General William Henry Chase, who graduated from the United States Military Academy in 1815. Between 1828 and 1854 he was in charge of fort construction and defenses in Pensacola; he was appointed by President Franklin Pierce as superintendent of the Academy, but resigned from the Army and became president of the Alabama and Florida Railroad Company. He lived in Pensacola and was prominent in the development of that region. He fought with the Confederacy in the Civil War, and died in Pensacola in 1870.

His spacious two-story home, known as the Chase House, was used as a hotel during the early 1870s.

In an advertisement on December 1, 1875, Proprietor H. E. Palmer announced with pleasure to the traveling public that Pensacola "now boasts of her long needed First Class Hotel, the Continental."

It was, he pointed out, in a desirable location, not far from the railroad depot and within ten minutes' walk of "the most beautiful bay on this continent"—Pensacola Bay. It offered large and airy rooms, the best of foods, a first-class news room furnished with newspapers and other periodicals, and an extensive lawn for croquet and other outdoor sports.

By the Fall of 1884 it was tripled in size by the erection of a large three-story addition directly behind and south of the older structure. On February 16, 1885, an elegant Grand Opening Ball was given there for the New Continental Hotel. Hugh Bellas was chairman of the committee in charge, other members of which were W. D. Chipley, Louis P. Knowles, F. O. Howe, S. S. Harvey, B. R. Pitt, W. H. Knowles, J. C. Avery, J. B. Guttmann, H. Baars, J. F. Simpson and L. Hilton Green.

By the year 1892 the hotel was known as the Escambia, under which name it served the public until a short time after the San Carlos Hotel was in full operation. The Escambia, with one hundred rooms, had steam heat, many bathrooms, handsome chandeliers, lace curtains, prompt bell service, a beautiful Japanese tea room, and a billiard room with four open fireplaces. Its large north-south hall was sixteen feet wide and 130 feet long. The hotel was located on Palafox Street between Gregory and Wright Streets.

Other hotels in 1885, listed in Pensacola's first City Directory, were the City Hotel, on Government Street opposite the Opera House, with Ed Sexauer as proprietor; the Commercial, at the corner of Government and North Tarragona, with William Blumer as proprietor, and the Merchants Hotel at Palafox and Government, operated by

This photograph of the Continental Hotel shows details of the original building at right, known in the early 1870s as the Chase House. The larger addition at left dated from 1884.

Jacob Kryger. The European, adjoining the depot, in 1882 charged $1.50 a day.

The Merchants building, later becoming the DeSoto office building, stood until 1970. In its heyday the Merchants was favored by traveling actors, such as Sarah Bernhardt and John Drew, when they came to perform at the nearby Opera House. Guests paid $2.50 a day. The *a la carte* price of a bowl of soup was 10 cents; for a full plate of raw oysters, 25 cents; a whole fried Spring chicken, 50; sirloin steak, 30; pie, five cents per serving.

Mrs. A. Sexauer was proprietress in 1893 of the Plaza Hotel on Government Street, rates $2 to $2.50. The National, at 120-122 East Government Street, charged $1.50 to $2. Mrs. C. Pfefferle was manager. Others of the late 19th Century were the Santa Rosa and Central Hotels and Winter Rest.

The year 1905 saw the Old Mill Inn in operation, built on the foundations of an old sawmill on what is now Bayshore Drive, close to the water near Cary Lane. A ceiling fan in the dining room was activated during mealtimes by ropes in the hands of two small black boys. The Inn had a large screened front porch, used during the daytime for relaxing, during the evenings for dances or impromptu parties. It had also two bathrooms, one for ladies, one for men.

In 1910 a large once-private residence at Palafox and Gregory was being operated as the Magnolia Hotel.

As the 20th Century dawned, the city of Pensacola had a lot of catching up to do. James R. McGovern in *The Emergence of a City in the Modern South: Pensacola 1900-1945* described the city in 1900 as "basically drab and unattractive," with unpaved streets, uneven wood sidewalks, inadequate water, drainage and sewage facilities. Few houses had private baths, and bath houses on Pensacola Bay (a nickel to swim and a nickel for a towel) were popular during the Summer months.

The San Carlos Hotel was begun in 1909 and occupied in February, 1910. The spacious ballroom was the scene of many colorful Mardi Gras celebrations between 1910 and 1930.

The San Carlos was a principal social center for the city for half a century. The elegant white marble lobby, the handsome curving grand stairway leading to the mezzanine, and the splendid stained-glass dome over the mezzanine contributed to an aura of elegance and space which made its numerous public rooms ideal for fashionable entertaining.

George H. Hervey was in charge of the hotel during those early years. It originally had only 156 guest rooms.

During the building boom of the mid-1920s a million dollar addition was built onto the San Carlos, more than tripling the number of private rooms and suites. The key figure in this project was William B. Harbeson, who had bought the San Carlos a few years earlier.

Harbeson's first hotel in Florida was the old Walton at DeFuniak Springs, which he renamed the New Walton; next came the Harbeson at Camp Walton.

One of the major factors in the growth of Pensacola's social life was the San Carlos Hotel, shown here soon after its completion in 1910.

This was the 1912 Mardi Gras Court in Pensacola. From the left, seated: Pearl Sheppard, George H. Hervey; standing: Sue Dishman, Phillip Yonge, Ruth Withnell, Filo Turner, Anderson Leonard, Ruth Hull, Clarence Avery, Marguerite Finch. This was one of many Mardi Gras coronations held in the San Carlos grand ballroom.

The Paradise Beach Hotel, on the Lillian Bridge Road near Perdido Bay in Escambia County, was completed, with adjoining cottages, in 1932. Its ballroom was cooled by eight fifty-two-inch ceiling fans. It also was known to have gambling tables. In its later years, it was known more as a supper club than as a place to stay overnight. It was torn down in the mid-1960s.

Harbeson also was the owner at that time of the Cherokee Hotel at Tallahassee, and had owned another Tallahassee hotel, the Leon, which burned in 1925.

The San Carlos was operated on the European plan, with rooms and meals priced separately. In 1927 the cost of a four-course *carte du jour* lunch or dinner (same menu) was $1. *A la carte* items included a dozen fried oysters, 70 cents; choice sirloin steak, $1.25; vegetables, 15 to 35 cents; a slice of layer cake, lemon or apple pie, 15 cents.

Rooms were equipped with ceiling fans, and heated by steam. The hotel had its own power plant.

The San Carlos became a retirement hotel.

After remodeling in the 1920s, the San Carlos Hotel—more than triple its original size—was an imposing part of the Pensacola scene and a prominent center of the city's social life.

4
The Peninsula and Upper East Coast

SOUTH FROM St. Mary's River is the island of Amelia, well known in the early 19th Century both to commercial men and to politicians, wrote James Grant Forbes in 1821. Forbes was born in St. Augustine in 1769. During the War of 1812 there were generally in port at Fernandina "upwards of 150 sail of shipping of all nations and flags, carrying on an immense transit trade." Also, because it was contiguous to the United States, it served as "a resort for adventurers of every kind, and for every purpose."

From those circumstances arose the town of Fernandina, consisting in 1821 of about forty houses, built of wood, in six streets, regularly intersecting one another at right angles. Several of the houses were two stories high, with galleries, presenting a handsome appearance. Some of them undoubtedly furnished shelter and food for travelers; and the seamen aboard those "150 sail" no doubt taxed the brothels to capacity.

Fernandina continued to prosper during the next decades. In 1878 the associates of the Florida Railroad took over its Egmont Hotel to capitalize on the ever-increasing crowds of Winter visitors, wrote Dovell. With the new Egmont, in addition to the Strathmore, Fernandina was heralded as "the Newport of the South" and welcomed such patrons as the Goulds and the Tiffanys.

Traveling southward on the St. Johns, Forbes noted in passing the "Cow Ford" (then sparsely settled), and several handsome plantation homes, where travelers might find lodging.

Forbes reported that there were nearly 1,000 houses of all descriptions in St. Augustine, which was about three quarters of a mile in length, and one quarter in breadth.

From the time of its establishment in 1565 by the Spanish, until the English occupation in 1763, the most remarkable fact about St. Augustine is that it continued to exist—a European colony clinging to the Atlantic coast, while the interior of the peninsula was peopled with aborigines, potentially hostile.

The St. Augustine of those two centuries left two structures, however, which are still sturdy. One is the many-sided Castillo de San Marcos (later known as Fort Marion), built in the late 17th Century. Earlier wooden forts either were burned by attackers or rotted in the humidity.

The Castillo was probably the first building constructed of coquina, a natural blending of donax shells (a little half-inch butterfly clam) and the sand on the beach of Anastasia Island, which lies between the town and the ocean. The coquina shell had been in the making for thousands of years. It was soft enough to be cut into blocks by a saw or ax, but when exposed to the air it became rock-hard. Quarrymen were imported from Havana to chop grooves into the soft yellow stone and crack out slabs which were hauled by oxcart to Escolta Creek, wrote Virginia Edwards in *Stories of Old St. Augustine.*

"First a labor gang of peons and convicts, as well as 150 unfortunate Indians who were dragooned into service, had to clear the palmetto and live-oak thickets from the deposits on Anastasia," she wrote. "No one knows how many fell victim to snakebite."

Building the Castillo required fifteen years and a great deal of money, but because of it, Spain remained dominant in St. Augustine until 1763. It has been a popular tourist attraction during the 20th Century.

The other notable structure of that period (besides a number of private buildings) was the Franciscan Monastery, converted by the British in 1773 into a military barracks.

The United States improved the property after

The Cleveland House, in the mid-19th Century.

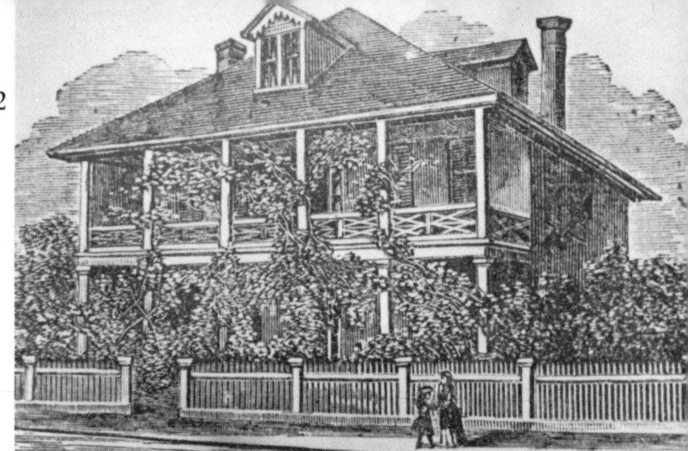

Miss Hasseltine's Boarding House, wreathed in shrubs and vine: was advertised as "one of the most attractive family boardin houses in St. Augustine." It faced the Magnolia House across S George Street.

A baker's dozen early St. Augustine hotels are seen on these two pages, some of them dating far back into the 19th Century. Several of the photos were taken from "Chapin's Hand-Book of St. Augustine," published in 1884.

Pictured in 1848, the Magnolia House was built by B. E. Carr, who had received his hotel training in New York. Although it had been opened only recently, Carr already planned to enlarge it by adding seventeen rooms and a bigger dining hall.

Rolleston's, opening on St. George, Treasury and Spanish Streets.

The St. Augustine Hotel, built in 1869 by F. H. Palmer and Captain E. E. Vail, was situated on the Plaza. It was lighted with gas, and furnished "with all the modern improvements."

The Florida House was described in 1848 as "a large well-kept establishment belonging to Mr. Cole."

Clockwise from the top: St. George Hotel; Barcelona Hotel; the Buckingham; the original Monson House; Valencia Hotel (later the Alencia); Hotel Marion; Spear Mansion.

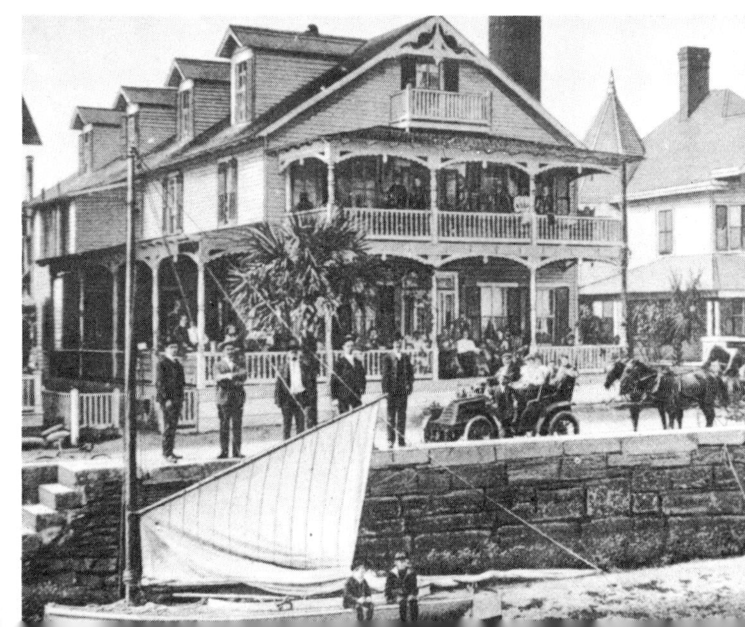

Florida became a territory, and St. Francis Barracks, as it is popularly known, remains to the present day a military site, serving as headquarters for the Florida National Guard.

During the two centuries of the first Spanish period, little effort was made to induce new settlers to the isolated peninsula. However, Pensacola was established by the Spanish in 1698.

Neither of the two villages had much to offer when Bernard Romans visited them in his travels in the early 1770s and wrote *A Concise Natural History of East and West Florida,* (1775). St. Augustine then had a population of about 1,000, living in less than 300 houses. At Pensacola, Romans found 180 houses, "built in general, in good taste, but of timber."

When the Revolution broke out to the north of Florida a few years later, St. Augustine became a stronghold for the British Crown, to which it remained loyal. Relocated British soldiers, Scotsmen in kilts, mercenary Germans and a dozen other elements strove for space on its tiny streets and in its taverns.

The first printed reference to accommodations for travelers in Florida may be in an advertisement in the *East-Florida Gazette* dated "From Saturday, February 22, to Saturday, March 1, 1783" (Vol. 1, No. 3), published in St. Augustine.

The advertisement, under the caption, POLICE OFFICE, notes that "frequent riots and other disorders have happened in this province, and particularly in the town of St. Augustine, for want of regulations and restrictions in keeping taverns, watch-houses, and retailing of spiritous liquors, whereby the peace and good government of the province have been disturbed, and the morals of many of the people have been corrupted . . ."

The General Assembly had passed an act that no "beer, cyder, brandy, rum punch, shrub, or other liquors whatsoever" could be sold in quantities of less than two gallons at one time. An exception was wine, when a license had been issued.

Terms for obtaining licenses to keep "a tavern, victualing house, or house of accommodation for the entertainment of strangers," and also to keep "a skittle alley, shuffle board, billiard table, or any other gaming place" were set forth.

License fees ranged upward to thirty pounds.

Women were scarce, and much in demand—whether as wives, mistresses, keepers of taverns and inns, or whatever.

The industrious English lost little time, after acquiring the Floridas, in building a "highway" leading to and from St. Augustine. It began at New Smyrna, where Dr. Andrew Turnbull's indigo plantation was to die ingloriously in 1777, and went northward through St. Augustine, then on to the Cow Ford, to the St. Mary's River at Colerain, and into Georgia. The state provided a ferry and ferryman at the Cow Ford.

In 1824, when Tallahassee was made the state capital, Methodist ministers were assigned to Pensacola, Amelia Island (Fernandina) and St. Augustine—which indicated the state's population centers at that time.

Prior to the Second Seminole War, which began in 1835, Newnansville was a sizable village, the seat of Alachua County. The area was noted for growing corn, sugar cane, indigo and cattle. (Newnansville vanished after the cross-state railway by-passed it in favor of Gainesville.)

Early Newnansville had only one block house, designated as a court house, and one tavern, built "in the same primitive style of architecture."

In May, 1837, the village had "two rival hotels, a fort, shops in abundance," and numerous

The Keystone Hotel at Fernandina, shown about 1915.

The Hotel Blanche, a 19th Century hostelry facing on Marion Street at Lake City, had a spring-fed pool, lined with cypress logs, behind the building. The spring provided water for the hotel and for its boiler—and was sometimes used for swimming. The hotel is seen here about 1900.

dwellings, wrote Jacob Rhett Motte, an Army surgeon who left a journal covering his years in Florida, 1836-38, entitled *Journey Into Wilderness.* Growth of the village during the early months of the war came about when small farmers and their families took refuge from the threat of Indian attack.

Dr. Motte and the men in his detachment were often invited to attend "the balls that were nightly given by this fashionable community." He made it a point to attend, partly to show respect for the local people. Also the balls "afforded a fund of amusement after the monotonous routine of a day in camp, on account of the original style of dancing the *'double trouble'*, and the high tone of refinement which pervaded the conversation of the polished gentlemen and accomplished ladies.

"On the occasion of a dinner given by the inhabitants to Colonel William J. Mills, we were invited to attend. At the hour stated in the notes of invitation we presented ourselves at one of the rival hotels, the scene of operations upon this festive occasion. We found a long arbour erected in the yard, back of the house, and an equally long table extending under it, with all the appliances of the feast. All the inhabitants of the country, men, women, & children, were present.

"The ladies dined first; the children next; and after them, upon the remnants of the feast, the gentlemen and invited guests. This order was observed apparently, for want of a better reason, that the gentlemen might not be interrupted in the patriotic duty of drinking toasts."

In July of the same year—1837—Dr. Motte was sent to St. Augustine and recorded an eyewitness account of the town at that time.

He found the houses to be built "in a peculiar

The Telford Hotel at White Springs at the turn of the century.

The Colonial Hotel, at the south entrance to the Stephen Foster Memorial at White Springs, offered "wonderful cooking, true to the traditions of the Old South." It stood until 1974.

These guests at the Travelers Home in Hastings were dubbed in 1907 as "spud hunters." Flagler invested in Hastings property and helped the town to gain a place in the world of potatoes.

The Hotel Granada at Eau Gallie in 1901, built by Willia Henry Gleason about twenty years earlier.

style, of a kind of stone, or tabbia, formed of a vast accumulation of marine shells. At a distance, the houses present the appearance of fancy work on a large scale." The streets were narrow, unpaved and dusty.

"We were favored with an invitation from the lady of Judge Joseph L. Smith to attend a party . . . The appointed festal hour found me properly attired for the presence of beauty; and with palpitating heart—for I had become rustified by my long exclusion from the influence of ladies' society—I made my bow amidst gladdening strains and chaste, bewitching smiles.

"As soon as I had sufficiently recovered from the effects of this operation, I ventured to look around upon the assembled company. The dance went joyously on; and figures of the most lovely proportions, fit models for sculptors and painters, and arrayed in dazzling beauty, were gliding through the labyrinthian mazes of the graceful Spanish dance. The moments flew, for I was in Elysium."

William Levingston, proprietor of the City Hotel in St. Augustine, advertised in the *Florida Herald* for February 6, 1836, modern accommodations, which included private apartments, a bar well furnished with wines and liquors, plenty of servants, stables, carriages, and "a cistern containing 3,000 gallons of rain water for washing, etc."

In January, 1839, C. M. Rowan advertised in the *Florida Herald & Southern Democrat* that he had leased the City Hotel which would in future be kept by him in a manner, he trusted, that would give satisfaction to all who might favor him with their patronage, and to entitle the House to retain the high reputation it had "so long sustained."

From St. Augustine to the keys, recovery from the effects of the Indian wars was slow until after the Civil War.

In 1867 a soldier of fortune named Henry T. Titus settled in a wartime camp, first known as Sand Point, and renamed it Titusville in 1874. He built a one-story hotel, the Titus House, with long wings and verandas, which was to become popular with visitors because of its bountiful table, featuring game and sea foods. Another hotel, the Dixie, was built there a few years later. By 1880,

Wrought iron railings guarded the second floor porch of the Hotel Hastings at Hastings, shown here in 1910.

Novel methods of transportation were enjoyed by visitors to Daytona's famous beach in 1902.

H. H. Deyarman of Wisconsin, who came to Orange City in the 1870s, built this hotel—which bore his name—in 1875-76 beside the road which was to become U. S. Highway 17-92. It served as a hotel for about seventy-five years, sometimes known as Orange City Hotel, then was used as a nursing home until 1970. In its heyday, the Deyarman included President Grover Cleveland among its guests. In its early days it also was used for "preaching services." The hotel is shown here about 1900.

Titusville had a population of 150, was the county seat, and was served by two stores and a circuit-riding minister.

In the late 1860s, the resettlement of New Smyrna began. The 1870s saw the beginnings of Daytona and Ormond on the Halifax River; also of Cocoa, Eau Gallie, Melbourne and Fort Pierce.

The 1895 census showed Jacksonville to be Florida's leading city, with a population of 25,130. The next seven were Key West, 16,502; Tampa, 15,634; Pensacola, 14,084; Ocala, 4,597; St. Augustine, 4,151; Tallahassee, 3,931; Apalachicola, 3,061. Next in order came Fernandina, Orlando, Palatka, Lake City, Bartow, Milton, DeLand, Sanford, Daytona, Jasper, Kissimmee and West Palm Beach.

Soon after the Civil War, Ledyard Bill wrote one of the state's first promotional booklets after traveling on the St. Johns River to Sanford, then to St. Augustine *via* Picolata.

Growth was noted at Green Cove Springs, Palatka and Enterprise, and especially at Jacksonville and St. Augustine.

"The number of strangers in St. Augustine greatly exceeded our expectations," wrote Bill, "and thronged in every street and public square. The fashionable belle of Newport and Saratoga, and the pale, thoughtful, and furrowed clergyman of New England were at all points encountered."

A strong caste system existed among the employees of the great American plan hotels in Florida during their heyday.

Karl P. Abbott, who was in the business nearly all his life, wrote a humorous account of his more colorful experiences entitled *Open for the Season,* which was published in 1950. As a boy he worked at miscellaneous chores for his father, Frank H. Abbott, himself a career hotel manager in Florida and in New Hampshire. Young Karl's first job on his own was that of "front clerk" at the Alcazar in St. Augustine, in 1912.

"A front clerk in those days 'fronted up' at the main desk—answered questions, sorted the mail, supervised the service in the lobby, and gave incoming guests their rooms when the room clerk was off duty," wrote Abbott. "My hours were from seven in the morning until eleven at night, with one hour off duty from eleven in the morning until twelve noon. I say that with qualifications, because there was a train due at eleven in the evening and if the damn thing was late, which it usually was, I had to stay on duty until the bus came and the incoming guests were registered and in their rooms."

The Hotel Suwannee at Live Oak, shown here in the 1930s, merited AAA approval.

"Old World charm with New World comfort" was the boast of the Riviera Hotel, built in 1924 on the Halifax River near Daytona Beach, in a section known as Rio Vista. In 1980 it is "a Christian organization," with rooms for rent. Plans are under way for a Christian school to be housed at the former hotel, a spokesman for the organization said. It is no longer a transient hotel.

He described the caste system prevalent among the staff at the Alcazar. Everything ran like a military regime; orders came through channels. The managing director headed the operation, had his private suite of rooms, his choice table in the dining room, and he entered the dining room by the main entrance.

Next came the department heads, known as "first officers": the assistant manager, room clerk, auditor, headwaiter, housekeeper, porter, steward, chief engineer, and secretary to the managing director. They all had unobtrusive seats in the rear of the main dining room, but they entered it by a side door. (That rule also extended to entering and leaving the hotel.)

The "second officers" were the cashiers, front clerk, assistant housekeeper, head bartender, dining room captains, assistant steward, and superintendent of service, among others. They had their private dining room with the main hall menu, but the choice, expensive items were crossed off.

The remainder of the staff ate in a cafeteria adjacent to the kitchen which they called the Zoo. They, like the second officers, roomed in the dormitory provided for the help—but the two groups occupied separate wings. The first officers had rooms at the top of the hotel itself.

Relationships between the first and second officers were cordial, but the line of demarkation between them was sharp. Each group had its

The Ridgewood Hotel at Daytona, about 1900. It was built in 1894 and torn down in October, 1975. In 1912, with accommodations for 150, it was operated by E. D. Langworthy.

An assortment of hotels in what is now the Daytona Beach area during the early years of the 20th Century is shown on pages 88 through 91. Prior to 1936 this section consisted of three separate communities—Daytona, Seabreeze and Daytona Beach. This "composite resort community" was described in a 1919 promotional booklet as having "all the charms of a seaside resort" while offering the accommodations of "a modern metropolis." Daytona was on a ridge skirting the Halifax River. Daytona Beach and Seabreeze, on the peninsula between the Halifax and the Atlantic Ocean, were connected with the mainland by four bridges. The thirty-five mile drive along the Ocean Beach Speedway, which at low tide was 500 feet wide, was "smooth and hard as a boulevard, famous among auto enthusiasts the world over."

The Prince George Hotel at Daytona Beach. In 1912 it offered accommodations for 125 guests, and was the property of Hilyard & Holroyd.

aytona's Palmetto House in 1901 charged $2 to $3 a day and open from November 15 to May 1.

Arched gateways greeted travelers at the Hotel Princess Issena, Daytona Beach, shown here in 1933.

The Despland Hotel at Daytona Beach was built in 1901 by Leon Despland, who named it the Despland, according to research by Walter Jubinsky of Daytona Beach. Later it was bought by Leon M. Waite, who added a number of rooms, so that by 1912 it had accommodations for 200 guests. When Waite left the city, the hotel was bought by T. F. Williams, who renamed it the Williams. It is seen here soon after its construction.

Above and to the right—Two of the many faces of the venerable Hotel Clarendon at Seabreeze: the beach side, showing guests enjoying the mild surf, about 1918; and the land approach on Ocean Boulevard, a picture taken not long after the brick structure was completed in 1910. The first Clarendon, built in 1899, had burned after ten years. In 1945 this hotel was purchased by the Sheraton Corporation and renamed the Sheraton Plaza.

At left—Approach to one of the early bridges leading from the mainland, across the Halifax River, to the Atlantic beaches about 1905.

"Bathing hour on the beach at Seabreeze" was the caption given this 1904 photograph.

The Colonnades at Seabreeze. In 1901 it was advertised as "a modern hotel, with electric lights, steam heat and private baths."

Schmidt's Hotel at Daytona in 1912 had accommodations for one hundred. Henry Schmidt was proprietor.

separate social functions. "The line of social prestige was drawn fine," wrote Abbott, "but it made for the respect and prestige of the 'first officers' and for the betterment of service throughout the hotel."

Among early settlements in the interior of the Florida peninsula are the towns of Bartow and Fort Meade, in Polk County on the Peace River. Fort Meade, established as a military fort toward the end of the Seminole Wars, dates from 1850.

Bartow's first permanent settlers, members of the Blount family and a small group of Negro slaves, came in 1851. Its first hotels were the Carpenter House and the Blount House. The former was built in 1878 in the midst of an orange grove in the 200 block of South Broadway. The Blount House was built as a residence by Gideon Zipprer, stepson of cattle baron Jacob Summerlin, in 1867, and converted to a hotel about 1880. It was located at 195 West Main Street.

Several early hotels offered transportation to and from the depot, after it was built, by horse-drawn bus. In 1881 the Blount House was owned and

Two 19th Century hotels at Melbourne. Both overlooked the Indian River. Above—The Belleview had a tennis lawn and rowboats free for the use of guests, and advertised "baths and good sanitary arrangements." Below—The Carleton offered bowling, tennis and trap shooting among its recreational facilities. Both are seen here about 1900.

Above—the Rio Vista Hotel; below—the Ocean House, both a New Smyrna. The Rio Vista was built early in the 20th Centur by land developer F. E. Lovejoy, according to research b Frances H. McGrath, columnist for the New Smyrna Beac News & Observer. It later was named the Gordon, and still late (in the 1930s), the New Smyrna Hotel, managed by Han Melgard. In 1980 it is the Indian River Lodge on South Riversid Drive, operating as a non-denominational Christian retrea center. The Ocean House, much older and located on the bank of the Indian River, is listed in an 1882 hotel directory wit Frank W. Sams in charge; and again in a 1912 directory, with ac commodations for one hundred, Sams & Sams, proprietors. I 1901 it had "sanitary plumbing, baths, etc.," and a large sulphu pool for those suffering from rheumatism. In 1980 the site of th hotel is occupied by the Southeast Volusia Annex of the Volusi County Court House.

Upper left—The Riverview on Merritt Island, shown in 1910, appears to be deserted; in 1901 it was in operation, with J. J. Wilkinson as manager. The other photos on this page date from the same era—the early years of the 20th Century. Upper right—Hotel Cassadaga at Lake Helen. Center right—Port Orange House at Port Orange, open December to May, accommodations for forty-five, $2 per day, $9 and up per week. Bottom photo—Camp Cassadaga, from Spirit Lake at Lake Helen, established as a "Winter retreat for Spiritualists" and for "all those who desired a quiet spot." Middle left—Thomas Cottage at Cocoa, with accommodations for fifteen and "new bath rooms."

892 Lake Helen, Fla.
Camp Cassadaga from Spirit Lake

operated by Georgia Eunice Mann, widow of Dr. Americus V. Mann. In that same year W. T. Carpenter offered accommodations not only to transients but to "pupils wishing to attend the Bartow school."

By 1891 an average of 400 guests a week registered at the several hotels in Bartow.

Farther south on the river was the Peace River Hotel at Wauchula, built in 1912 by Albert Carlton. It occupied the top two floors of a large building, the ground floor of which housed Earnest's department store. The building, which covered most of the block and faced south on Main Street, burned in the 1960s. The site became a shopping center, facing west on U. S. Highway 17.

A picturesque country inn on Marco Island, south of Naples on the Gulf, was the Marco Island Hotel. Built in 1883 by Captain W. D. Collier, it was favored by hunters and anglers. It had twenty bedrooms, a parlor, a dining room and one bathroom. During World War II the hotel was taken over for military use as an air-sea rescue base. Barracks and a dock were constructed nearby.

About 1970 the hotel became the Marco Island Inn, a large restaurant, still housed in the same 1883 building. Those twenty rooms are occupied by members of the restaurant staff, rather than by guests. The owner is William Blomier.

By 1878 the Ocean House at New Smyrna was receiving such patronage that it was enlarged.

Daytona, established in 1870 by Mathias Day of Ohio, soon had a hotel known as the Colony House, also known as the Palmetto House. To the north was Ormond, named for "that James Ormond and his progeny who hewed a plantation out of the wilderness in Spanish times," wrote Alfred and Kathryn Abbey Hanna in *Florida's Golden Sands.*

Rockledge in the 1870s was a real tourist mecca, with its Indian River Hotel, where 400 guests could rock on large piazzas; also the Hotel Plaza, with rooms for 300, and the White Cottage, which could accommodate forty.

The Park House at Maitland, later named Maitland Inn, was constructed in 1878 between Lake Catherine and Park Lake, on ground close to where the railroad ended, according to *Maitland Milestones,* published in 1976 by the Maitland Historical Society. This hotel became a vacation place for many of the prominent people of the day.

Senators, congressmen and Presidents were among those who came to this popular resort. When the hotel was full, guests often would park their private railroad cars on a siding and use them for sleeping accommodations. Water sports and bicycling through the pine forest were favorite recreations.

Melbourne to the south and east, settled in the early 1870s, soon had the Goode House and the Carleton Hotel catering to tourists.

"Cap" Dimick and his wife in 1880 built an eight-room addition to their home on Lake Worth, opened it as the Cocoanut Grove Hotel and advertised for "first class boarders." Dimick brought guests part way to it in a mule-and-wagon stage from Jupiter to Juno, seven miles. They continued southward down Lake Worth some thirteen miles to the Dimicks' hotel. Settlement at this time centered on the east shore of Lake Worth, or what is today Palm Beach. When the town received its own post office in 1887, it took the name Palm Beach.

Captain H. P. Dye was operating the Lake Worth Hotel, at the north end of present-day Palm Beach, by 1886.

Only a few isolated families lived between Lake Worth and the Miami River, on the north bank of which was the deserted Fort Dallas. W. B. Brickell's tract and store were situated on the south bank, and still farther south, most of the Biscayne Bay families were gathered in the community of Cocoanut Grove.

The Spanish-American War brought thousands of soldiers into the Tampa area and advertised the

Hotel Lake Worth, 1894. This was the first building in the Palm Beach area built specifically as a hotel.

The earliest social and political life of the Lake Worth (Palm each) section centered around the Cocoanut Grove Hotel bove), owned and operated by Mr. and Mrs. E. N. Dimick. It as originally the Dimick residence. The lakefront property on hich it was located, near present-day Clarke Avenue, cost ap'' Dimick a dollar per acre. It was here that the lakeside settlers had a Christmas party in 1880, each family bringing food for the feast held on the hotel grounds. The first dance was held that night in the hotel dining room, with members of the pioneer Brelsford family providing music. The hotel is shown here in 1891. It burned in 1895.

locality to hundreds of cities and towns over the United States, wrote Rembert W. Patrick in *Florida Under Five Flags.* St. Petersburg across the Bay, Tarpon Springs and Clearwater to the north, Sarasota and Fort Myers to the south became thriving settlements.

"On the east coast Fort Pierce, Palm Beach, Fort Lauderdale, Miami and Miami Beach came into existence. Orlando became the largest city in south-central Florida, and DeLand, Sanford, Kissimmee, Lakeland and Bartow grew rapidly."

When Napoleon B. Broward became Governor in 1905, he gave high priority to drainage. After drainage made much of the Everglades habitable, towns came into existence in the Lake Okeechobee region. Within two decades, many thousands of acres of land were reclaimed, and such towns as Canal Point, Pahokee, Belle Glade, South Bay, Clewiston, Moore Haven and Lakeport served that rich agricultural area.

When the community of Hillsborough Canal Settlement (on the south shore of Lake Okeechobee) sought in 1921 to obtain a post office, the residents were told that a more euphonious name for the town must be found.

F. M. Myer, proprietor of the Pioneer Hotel, placed a blackboard in the lobby and invited suggestions for a new name, wrote Allen Morris in *Florida Place Names* in 1974.

"One day a group of tourists came by way of the canal from West Palm Beach and stayed at the hotel after making a trip through the Everglades. One of them remarked that the Hillsborough Canal Settlement was the 'belle of the 'Glades.' Mrs. Elsie Myer, wife of the proprietor, quickly added Belle Glade to the list of names on the blackboard, and when an informal poll was later taken it was voted the favorite."

Duck Hunters are seen on the grounds of the Indian River Hotel at Rockledge.

Two Rockledge hotels, the elegant Indian River (above) and the Plaza (left), with its sweeping "steamboat" lines. Both contributed largely to the tourist boom which began in that area as early as the 1870s. By 1901 the Indian River offered electric lights, an elevator, and orchestra music, day and evening. Both offered optional private baths.

Titusville's second hotel, the Dixie, was built in the late 1870s and was later renamed the Indian River Hotel. This turn-of-the-century view shows it with porches running the full length of all three stories, and an observation tower.

Cocoa House at Cocoa, seen here about 1920.

In 1908 this was the Dade City Hotel in that town.

The Hotel Brevard at Cocoa in the 1920s.

Putnam Inn at DeLand, about the turn of the century.

Dating from 1882, the Lakeside Inn at Mount Dora is shown here about 1900. It has 110 rooms, including suites. The Inn sits on a hill above Lake Dora. The original inn, built by J. M. Alexander, was a two-story wooden structure (which comprises about a third of the present main building), with a windmill for pumping water. It was known first as the Alexander, then Lake House, Lakeview House and, finally, Lakeside Inn.

The Wachusett Hotel at Tangerine was opened in 1883 under the name of the Acme Hotel, advertised as "one of the largest hotels in this part of the state." It was renamed the following year. For several decades the hotel, later known as Lake Ola Lodge, was the center of the town's social life. Eventually it became a naturopathic clinic. Good hotel accommodations at that time could be found also at Astor, Altoona, Fort Mason, Eustis, Tavares and Leesburg, all served by the St. Johns & Eustis Railway.

Two other Mount Dora hotels: above, Robert Burns Inn, 1907; below, Else-Backus, c. 1890.

Built in the 1880s, the Longwood Hotel at Longwood is still sturdy. Its Victorian lobby and dining room are still open to the public.

Lake Catherine Inn, under construction in Chuluota, 1914; its guests in the early years included DuPonts, Dodges, Cabots and Rockefellers.

Above, College Arms Hotel at DeLand, which in 1912 offered accommodations for 125; in 1940 the figure was 150. Center, the Lakeview Hotel at Leesburg, built in the late 1890s, seen here in 1908; it was razed in 1957. (Another popular Leesburg hotel, not shown, was the Magnolia, built in 1908.) Below, the Mount Plymouth Hotel, built in 1926, had not only its own golf course, but its private landing field for guests, some of whom are shown here in 1928 after having taxied their planes up close to the hotel.

Pine-clad hills, lakes and the "famous spring of purest water" made the Altamonte Hotel at Altamonte Springs a delightful place for Winter residence, according to a 1919 travel brochure. Man-made attractions included a golf course and tennis courts at that time. A horse-drawn trolley transported guests from the railway station to the hotel. The Altamonte eventually consisted of five buildings for guests, plus garages and a barn housing horses and hunting dogs used to bring in quail for the guests' breakfast. E. C. Bates was the hotel's long-time owner, as was his father, George Bates, before him.

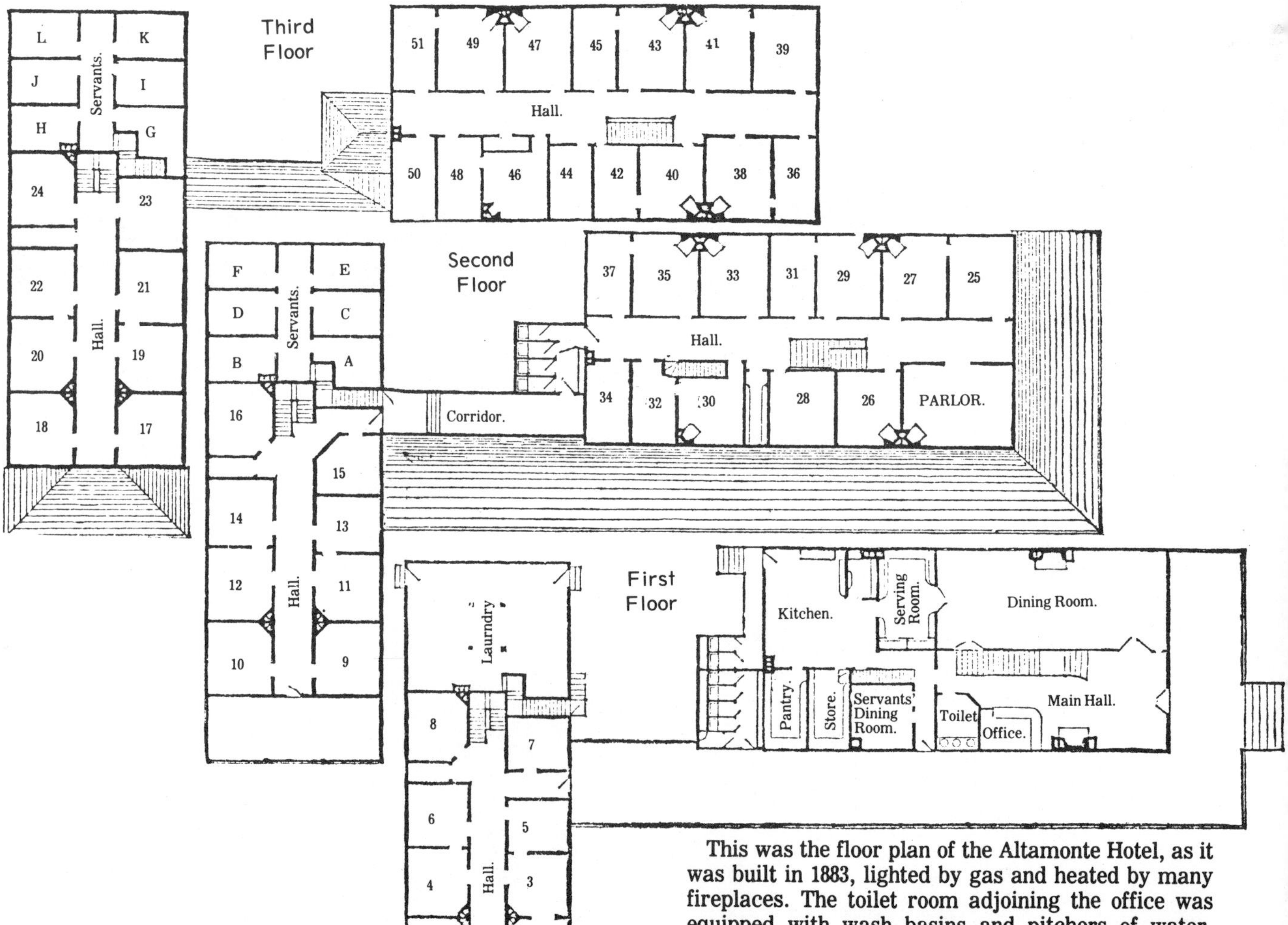

Third Floor

L K J I H G Servants. 24 23 22 21 20 19 18 17 Hall.

51 49 47 45 43 41 39 Hall. 50 48 46 44 42 40 38 36

Second Floor

F E D C B A Servants. 16 15 14 13 12 11 10 9 Hall.

37 35 33 31 29 27 25 Hall. 34 32 30 28 26 PARLOR. Corridor.

First Floor

Laundry 8 7 6 5 4 3 2 1 Hall.

Kitchen. Serving Room. Dining Room. Pantry. Store. Servants' Dining Room. Toilet Office. Main Hall.

This was the floor plan of the Altamonte Hotel, as it was built in 1883, lighted by gas and heated by many fireplaces. The toilet room adjoining the office was equipped with wash basins and pitchers of water. Years later, each floor had its own tin bathtub and a few private baths were available. Weekly rates for two persons in the 1920s began at $85 a week with private bath, $50 without bath. Golf, tennis and other sports were provided without extra cost. The building burned in 1953.

The Arlington Hotel was Gainesville's finest in the early 1880s. Located at the northwest corner of the University Avenue-Main Street intersection (later the site of Woolworth's), the hotel burned in 1884.

Two well-known 20th Century hotels in Gainesville were the Thomas (left) and the White House (below). The Thomas was especially favored by girls from Florida State College for Women (now Florida State University) when they came for weekend festivities at the University of Florida. It also was the frequent choice of visiting dignitaries, and was a popular local meeting place. Both of these hotels were often hosts to fans of the University of Florida Gators. The Thomas in 1980 houses Gainesville's Cultural Affairs Department. The White House was the girls' dormitory of the East Florida Seminary until the University was founded, and absorbed the Seminary, 1905-06. The White House, located across the street from the depot, was a favorite "dinner stop" for passengers riding the Atlantic Coast Line trains, before the advent of the dining car. This hotel was razed in 1962, and the Sun Bank occupies the site.

Guests gathered on the porch of the Arrowhead Hotel at Sebring for this picture early in the 20th Century. The Arrowhead, Sebring's first tourist hotel, was built in 1912 and was a social center of the town for a number of years.

Harder Hall on Lake Jackson at Sebring; in 1940 it fered accommodations for one hundred.

"No Sun, No Charge for Rooms" advertised the Hotel Nan-Ces-O-Wee at Sebring. American plan rates in 1923, when the hotel was built, were "$5 a day and down." Nan-Ces-O-Wee is the Creek name for an Indian girl mentioned in Sebring's history. George E. Sebring built the hotel.

Four-story wings flanked the two-story central portior the Hotel Sebring, seen here about 1940. It was built dur the boom of the mid-1920s by H. Orvel Sebring, son of Geo E. Sebring. The two men were founders of the town.

Three of these four historic Sebring hotels—the Nan-Ces Wee, Sebring and Harder Hall—are still in operation in 19 as is Kenilworth Lodge (not shown), built in 1915 as a res hotel. The site of the Arrowhead is now occupied by a c dominium.

At Avon Park the picturesque Jacaranda Hotel faced the main highway when it was built during the boom of the 1920s. When U. S. Highway 27-98 was constructed in 1956, its main route by-passed Avon Park, and so did the major traffic. It is now the Jacaranda Retirement Hotel, operated by E. F. Callaway. Its lobby still is graced by the crystal chandelier which characterized its elegance in the early years, when a five-piece orchestra furnished dinner music each night.

5
H. B. Plant and the West Coast

WITH THE OUTBREAK of the Second Seminole War in 1835, Fort Brooke (Tampa) gained a sudden importance. Soldiers poured in, and in 1837 the fort was designated by General Thomas H. Jesup as headquarters of the Army of the South. The pioneer French physician-grower Odet Philippe provided the soldiers billiard rooms and a ten-pin alley, according to Karl H. Grismer in his 1950 history of Tampa.

The first hotel was opened in 1837 by Captain Rufus D. Kilgore, who called it the Tampa Hotel. Located slightly north of the garrison on the river front, the frame structure had twelve rooms, which were rarely empty.

The hotel, sometimes referred to as the Kilgore, was leased in 1841 by Josiah Gates, who had come from South Carolina. The following year Gates moved southward to the Manatee River, planning to stake a claim under the Armed Occupation Act, soon to be enacted. He found a tract to his liking—especially since it previously had been an Indian camp site, and several acres of the land had been cleared by its former occupants.

Returning to Tampa, wrote Grismer, Gates loaded his belongings on the sloop *Margaret Ann*, owned by Captain Frederick Tresca, and went back to the Manatee, taking along his wife, two children, and eight Negro slaves. They quickly constructed a six-room log cabin, with a passage way and detached kitchen, and in a few weeks the Gates House, a lodging in the wilderness, was ready for travelers.

A New Yorker named Henry Clark established the first store in the Manatee area. Others who came in 1842 were Major Robert Gamble and Dr. Joseph Braden, wrote Charlton W. Tebeau in his 1971 *History of Florida*. They came from Leon County to undertake to restore the fortunes largely lost in the depression which followed the 1837 panic and failure of the Union Bank of Tallahassee.

Braden and his brother Hector acquired by grant and purchase 1,000 acres of land and erected the first buildings on the site of present-day Bradenton. Other refugees from the financial debacle soon joined them, among whom were the Wyatts, Wares, Ledwitts, Reeds, Snells, and the Craig brothers, wrote Tebeau.

The Tampa area continued to be dominated by hostilities with the Seminoles—scattered skirmishes, rounding up strays after the war and deporting them to a reservation in the West. The town suffered greatly, too, when Gates and other prosperous settlers on the Manatee formed their own county in 1855, and were no longer bound to Tampa, their former county seat. In 1858 a widespread yellow fever epidemic hit the town. As many as 275 cases were reported, with thirty deaths.

Nevertheless, by 1860 there were three hotels in town—the Palmer House, which had been in operation for some time and was then managed by one Reason Duke, the Washington House (Mrs. Ann M. Roberts), and the Florida House (Mr. and Mrs. R. B. Thomas). At the Florida House, board and lodging "of the finest" were offered at $1.50 a day, $8 a week or $30 a month. Built and owned by Captain James McKay, this hotel stood at the corner of Marion Street and Lafayette Street (later part of Kennedy Boulevard), according to the late Theodore Lesley, a Tampa historian.

Tampa's first "mansion-like" home was constructed by William B. Hooker, a well-to-do cattleman and veteran of the Seminole Wars, who disposed of his stock and moved into town in 1860. The home was built that year at the corner of East and Madison Streets, and was converted after the Civil War into the Orange Grove Hotel. Captain

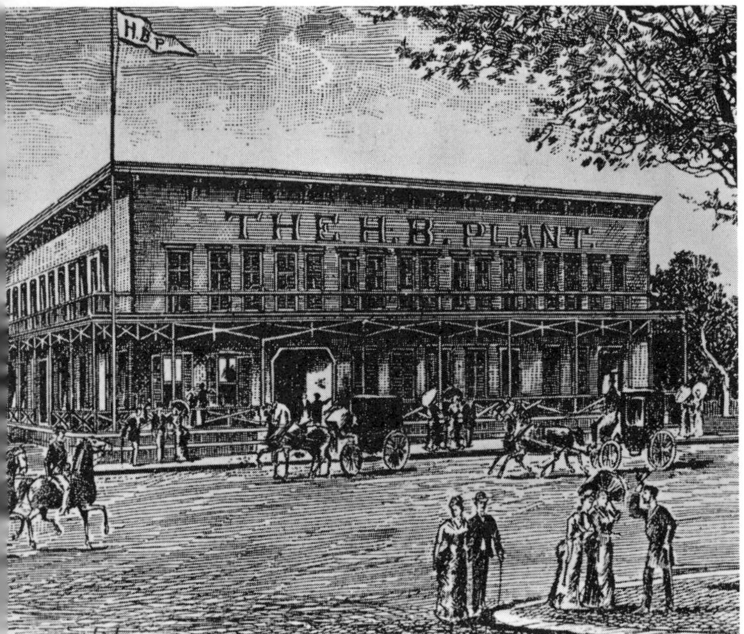

Sketches of the H. B. Plant Hotel (above) and the Palmetto Hotel, both built in Tampa in 1884.

Hooker's son-in-law and daughter, Mr. and Mrs. Henry L. Crane, were operating the hotel in 1876, when poet Sidney Lanier and his wife were there. Lanier described it as a "large three-story house with many odd nooks and corners, altogether clean and comfortable in appearance and surrounded by orange trees in full fruit." This was in late December.

Although Lanier had planned to remain in Tampa for only a short time, he stayed for three months, rhapsodizing in personal correspondence about "the glitter of great and tranquil waters, the liberal friendship of the sun . . ."

The highlight of the social season was the Knights of Hillsborough Ring Tournament, held annually during the Christmas and New Year holidays, beginning as early as January 2, 1877. Seventeen young men participated that year; judges were W. B. Henderson and W. W. Wall, and marshal was James E. Lipscomb. The "Knight of Reform" (first place winner) was Thomas E. Jackson, who named Miss Etta Warner as Queen. Other winners in order, and their maids of honor, were Dr. Thomas S. Daniel, Miss Ada McCarty; Wesley P. Henderson, Miss Mamie Parish.

This event had some similarity to the tournaments of medieval England; but instead of jousting each other off their horses, the gaily costumed knights tilted their lances at three rings suspended ten feet off the ground from horizontal bars.

The queen was crowned at a ball held a few days after the tournament. It was the big social event of the season and everyone socially prominent attended, wrote Grismer.

The railroad era began in Tampa on September 1, 1883, with the arrival (by schooner) of the first two locomotives, even though the rails had not been completed. Teams of workers were hastily laying the last of the narrow-gauge tracks of the South Florida Railroad between Tampa and Kissimmee, to meet the deadline by which owner Henry B. Plant would receive valuable grants of land from the state. The two teams met near present-day Lakeland on January 23, 1884.

When Plant came to Tampa first on December 1, 1883, accompanied by James E. Ingraham and Colonel H. S. Haines, ranking officials of the SFRR, the party had to journey eighteen miles over the uncompleted line (Auburndale to Plant City) by horse and buggy. The Plant party was royally entertained at the Orange Grove Hotel and taken on an excursion on Tampa Bay.

Plant City was platted and named for the railroad tycoon by H. L. Mitchell, then an attorney for Plant in his railroad ventures (later Governor of Florida, 1893-97). A prominent early settler of Plant City was J. T. Evers, who had owned a general store at Shiloh, a mile north of the railroad, and moved his store to the new station.

When the two segments of the road were joined and through rail service became a reality, a big celebration was held at the Orange Grove. It was a stag event, attended by prominent railroad officials (though not Plant himself) and by virtually every prominent man in Tampa. Many speeches were made, and the festivities lasted until almost daybreak. The committee in charge of the banquet included Judge James T. Magbee, Dr. Duff Post, Rev. T. A. Carruth, Henry L. Crane, John B. Spencer, Judge H. L. Mitchell, J. B. Wall, R. B. Thomas, John T. Lesley, Captain John Miller, G. B. Sparkman, S. A. Jones, Harry L. Branch and John N. C. Stockton.

Another early developer of Florida was Hamilton Disston of Philadelphia, who rescued the state from threatened bankruptcy when in 1881 he bought, for twenty-five cents per acre, 6,250 square miles of land and converted "a virtually worthless wilderness into one of the world's most desirable living places," according to Charles E. Harner. The price was $1,000,000—which was never paid in full, although the purpose of restoring the state's credit was by this transaction accomplished.

Harner quoted a writer in the *New York Herald* in 1864: "I am confident no sane man who knows what Florida is would give . . . a thousand dollars to gain possession of all the territory beyond the St. Johns. No decent man would think of living in the state outside of two or three points on the St. Johns and the Gulf."

Disston was a plunger, though, and had faith in Florida's future, despite the fact that heat, swamps, insects, Indians and outlaws made the interior and the southern part of the state virtually uninhabitable, wrote Harner.

In his heyday in Florida, Disston decided to build a city to perpetuate his name. He set aside 12,000 acres on Boca Ciega Bay, had it surveyed, with one-hundred-foot wide streets, decided it should have 50,000 inhabitants, and named it Disston City, wrote Harner. He built a wharf, a warehouse, several model homes, three retail stores, and a twenty-six-room hotel which he unabashedly named the Waldorf. Disston City eventually became Gulfport.

Disston dug canals, drained vast amounts of acreage and founded towns, serving the state's interest in numerous ways. Perhaps the most valuable contribution was his success in attracting outside capital, which started to flow into the state as "the moneyed titans, Henry Flagler and Henry Plant, constructed their own empires to the east and the west of the Disston domains."

As for Disston's personal fate: He was convinced that Florida's future development would rest on water transportation, rather than rail. To this end, he gambled all that he had—and more. He went broke. On April 30, 1896, Disston attended the theatre in Philadelphia. He then went home, filled the tub in his bathroom, sat down in the water and shot himself in the head.

Henry Bradley Plant fared better—very much

The Inn, built by Henry B. Plant on stilts over the water of Tampa Bay at Port Tampa, as part of Plant's development of the port, 1887-88.

Tampa Bay Hotel, Tampa, Fla.

One of America's most beautiful buildings is the Tampa Bay Hotel, with its thirteen Moorish towers, opened in 1891 on the shore of the Hillsborough River in Tampa. Electrically lighted inside and out, it contained 511 rooms. Its furnishings included a million dollars worth of carpets and art objects imported from Europe. The building in 1933 became home for the University of Tampa. The lower picture shows one of the bedrooms in April, 1926. Note the graceful, fluid lines of both the room and its furnishings. Sharp angles have been virtually eliminated.

better indeed, although his early life was unremarkable. Born October 27, 1819, in Branford, Connecticut, of poor but proper farm parents, he was an indifferent student and didn't finish high school. He did odd jobs, and at eighteen, became a deck hand on a steamer between New York and New Haven, Connecticut.

After four years he was put in charge of handling express packages—and this small promotion was to determine the direction of his life. At age twenty-three he was assigned to a land job with a major express company, and married a young lady of an old and wealthy family, Ellen Elizabeth Blackstone.

By age thirty-four (1853), Plant was a minor executive in the Adams Express Company, which was expanding. He had a son, Morton Freeman Plant, and a wife with "congestion of the lungs." A mild climate was prescribed, and since Plant could not afford the Mediterranean, he brought his family by steamship to Florida—an eight-day voyage.

They spent one night in Jacksonville in "a rickety hotel," then crossed the St. Johns in a dugout canoe and reached the hospitality of friends at Strawberry Mills, seven miles away. Mrs. Plant's health improved, but worsened again when the family returned to New York.

The Plants came back to Florida in 1854, and remained in the South because of Mrs. Plant's

Elaborate brickwork marks the foot-thick exterior walls of e Tampa Bay. The arch and keyhole motifs, repeated in th exterior and interior, reflect its Moorish design. This otograph was made in 1926.

Bronze statuary, carved mirrors from Italy, and fine cabinets were among lavish decorations of the Tampa Bay Hotel.

Street cars were the principal means of transportation in Tampa for many years, and bolder passengers rode the outside running boards. The building is El Pasaje Hotel and Restaurant in Ybor City, Tampa's Latin Quarter, pictured here in 1898.

The Orange Grove Hotel in the 800 block of Madison Street, Ta pa, photographed on May 7, 1924. It originally was the home William B. Hooker, built in 1860.

Franklin Street, Tampa, looking north from Zack Street, 1919. The Oglethorpe Hotel.

health. That year, Plant was made superintendent of the southern headquarters of the Adams company in Augusta, Georgia. From there he traveled to organize branch offices in several other southern cities, becoming quite well known.

Plant managed to weather the Civil War without antagonizing either his southern customers or his previous northern business friends.

Mrs. Plant died on February 28, 1862, and her husband, for a year, taxed his health with grief and overwork. A year spent in Europe brought him restored strength and vigor.

Returning *via* New York, Plant renewed acquaintance there with former associates and met a Philadelphian, Henry S. Sanford. These men had capital to invest, and Plant was persuasive.

Continuing on to Augusta with some of this capital and the promise of more, Plant hired Colonel Haines of Savannah, who had been rail chief for General Robert E. Lee, and together, wrote Harner, they wrapped up the bankrupt railroads of the Southeast into a neat package. They were canny, and the South was in great need of new money.

Plant's main office was now in New York. There he married (at age fifty-four) Miss Margaret Josephine Loughman, and they made their home in New York. Plant, however, spent much of his time thereafter traveling about his ever-increasing empire in "Private Car 100," which contained his office, as well as bedrooms and a dining room. By now he was head of the Southern Express Company.

With a group of wealthy stockholders (among them Sanford and Flagler), he organized the Plant Investment Company. By this time Sanford had acquired his acreage on the St. Johns and was president of the Adams Express Company.

The Plant Investment Company was the vehicle Plant used in opening the Florida west coast for settlement and profit, with a dependable rail-and-steamship line.

Tampa, with a history of yellow fever epidemics, was Plant's second choice for a coastal town to develop. He had first chosen Cedar Key, which had been a port for decades, and which was the western terminus of Florida's first cross-state railroad, originating at Fernandina.

But when Plant believed that he had acquired all the necessary properties at Cedar Key, he learned that the railway terminal at that village was not included, and was not for sale. Infuriated, Plant is said to have exploded: "I'll wipe Cedar Key off the map! Owls will hoot in your attics and hogs will wallow in your deserted streets!"

He then chose Tampa, its population diminished

Looking south down Franklin Street, Tampa, from the top of the Almeria Hotel in 1913. The Olive Hotel (later the Thomas Jefferson Hotel) is at left center. The Hillsborough River is in the background.

Towers on the Tampa Bay Hotel dominate the skyline in this view from the top of Tampa's City Hall. The dark building in center foreground is the Tremont Hotel. This photo, August 10, 1921.

The flag atop the Bay View Hotel in Tampa was "the largest electric sign in the South" when this night view was photographed in the early 1920s.

Tampa's tallest building for several decades was the eighteen-story Hotel Floridan, built during the land boom of the 1920s.

in twenty years from 885 to 720 because of recurrent fevers, and revised his plan. He bought the South Florida Railroad, which ran from Sanford to Kissimmee, *via* Orlando. It was facing bankruptcy and its president, Sanford, was happy to sell it to his friend and business associate.

One might wonder—why did Plant not choose Punta Gorda, with its magnificent Charlotte Harbor and its better health history?

Perhaps it was because he learned that another company, the Jacksonville, Tampa & Key West, held a franchise to extend its railroad from Kissimmee to Tampa in return for a state grant of 13,840 acres of land for each mile of rail constructed.

This figure compared more than favorably with the 3,840 acres per mile to be paid by the state to the South Florida's builder. The JT & KW had run out of funds, and Plant easily added this segment to his line on May 4, 1883. The shrewd tycoon

The massive DeSoto Hotel was Tampa's principal year-round hotel for twenty years. This picture was taken during remodeling in 1911.

thus was able to collect the land bonuses offered for both of the lines.

The Plant Steamship Line came next, providing dependable service to Key West and Havana.

Tampa became one of the nation's outstanding boom towns, and into it poured men from every walk of life, wrote Grismer. The population increased from 722 in 1880 to 2,376 on December 1, 1885.

Such was the power of the Iron Horse.

The editor of the *Ocala Banner* exclaimed: "How this railroad service kills time and space! Only a little while ago it took two days to go from Ocala to Tampa and four days to reach Jacksonville. Now we can speed over the route in a few hours in comfort. Because of the railroads, this entire country is being magically transformed."

So many newcomers flocked to Tampa during the Winter of 1883-84—the beginning of a golden era for the town—that its hotels and rooming houses were filled. During the Summer of 1884 three new hotels were built: the H. B. Plant, the St. James and the Palmetto, each of frame construction and each having about forty rooms.

The H. B. Plant was situated on the east side of Ashley Street between Lafayette and Madison. Jerry T. Anderson, the owner, opened it on December 4, 1884.

The St. James, on the northeast corner of Franklin and Harrison Streets, had a billiard room and 405 feet of verandas. It was built by Dr. H. M. Bruce.

The Palmetto, built by Judge N. G. Buff, was advertised as "one of the largest and most commodious hotels in South Florida." It was three stories high, with a five-story observatory.

Another boom-time hotel in Tampa was the Tampa Terrace, shown here on August 5, 1925. At left is a portion of the 1891 Hillsborough County Court House.

The Hillsboro Hotel, opened in July, 1912, served travelers in Tampa for more than half a century. This view is from the post office.

The Palmerin Hotel on Davis Island in Tampa Bay, seen here in 1926, was styled with a multi-level tile roof.

The Park-View Hotel, at the intersection of Lafayette and Park Streets, overlooked Plant Park. This view, from the northeast, w the scene on June 27, 1921.

The first high-rise building facing Tampa's bayshore was the Bayshore Royal Hotel, at Howard Avenue, shown here in 1926.

Another of Tampa's boom-time hotels was the Mirasol.

Tampa came alive, and gained Havana's cigar industry; Ybor City was born.

In 1886, when Ybor City was in its infancy, a forty-room hotel, the Habana, was built there and served until it burned in 1891, according to Anthony Pizzo, a Tampa historian. A smaller hotel in Ybor City in this period was the Victoria.

More durable and prestigious was the restaurant-hotel El Pasaje at Eighth Avenue and Twenty-First Street, which dated from the 1890s. For some forty years it welcomed guests, from Cuba's José Martí to Florida political leaders.

Tampa's first three-story brick building was the Almeria Hotel, built in 1886 by Dr. Howell T. Lykes at the northeast corner of the Franklin-Washington intersection.

Dr. Lykes, a prosperous physician and cattleman of Brooksville, named the hotel for his wife, Almeria McKay Lykes. For years it was one of Tampa's leading hotels, wrote Grismer. Later it was modernized and converted into office space for the Lykes brothers, sons of Dr. and Mrs. Lykes. The Lykes Brothers firm moved in 1968 to the Hillsboro Hotel.

By the latter part of September, 1886, all of the narrow (three-foot) gauge rails between Tampa and Sanford, and many others in Florida, had been converted to standard gauge (four feet, eight and one-half inches) like those of trunk lines to the north. This obviated the need for numerous transfers to rails of different gauge, resulting in greater convenience and less time consumed in traveling long distances.

One might wonder why the growth and improvement of railroads should merit such space in a volume on Florida's hotels. The answer is that the great hotels built by Plant and his opposite number on the east coast, Henry M. Flagler, and others after them, would not have been constructed without the existence of rail service. Florida was accessible previously only by water—its Atlantic and Gulf coasts, its system of inland rivers and lakes—or by slow and comfortless stage coach, or simply by trail-blazing with horse- or ox-drawn wagon.

One of the periodic epidemics of yellow fever struck in September, 1887, and people fled the city. Property values plummeted.

The epidemic over, Plant again waved his magic wand, announcing plans to invest millions in assorted improvements to the city. He built a railroad bridge across the Hillsborough River and extended his rail tracks southwestward six miles farther, to deep water, thus creating Port Tampa.

He constructed a wharf a mile long, and built Port Tampa Inn out over the water, on stilts. Guests at the Inn could enjoy the novelty of fishing from the windows of their rooms.

Port Tampa was fully operational by June, 1888. In July, Plant laid the cornerstone of the Tampa Bay Hotel, "undoubtedly one of the most fantastic buildings this nation has seen," wrote Harner.

Plant's offer to build a fine hotel—the Tampa Bay—was subject to extension of Lafayette Street a half-mile west of the Hillsborough River, and construction of a bridge over the river at that point, both of which improvements were made by city and county authorities.

The wooden bridge cost $15,000 and "put Jesse Hayden's ferry enterprise out of business," wrote Harris Mullen in 1966 in *A History of the Tampa Bay Hotel.*

Essentially Moorish in architecture, the hotel was designed by J. A. Wood of New York, who also supervised the construction. Hundreds of craftsmen were hired to build it, including a new breed—electricians.

All 511 rooms were lighted by electricity, as were its thirteen silvery domes and minarets, each bearing a crescent moon and each representing a month in the Mohammedan year. The exterior walls, twelve inches thick, were of concrete reinforced with railroad trackage which became surplus when the rails of the South Florida were widened in 1886.

The hotel covered six acres, a stroll completely around it was a mile long, and one of its main corridors was 1,200 feet from end to end. Its cost was close to $3,000,000. Mr. and Mrs. Plant toured Europe, where they and their agents spent about $1,000,000 on period furniture, statuary and the like, sending shiploads of these treasures to Tampa to be installed in the new hotel.

Floors were covered with 30,000 square yards of red carpeting with a pattern of blue dragons, and walls were adorned with 110 carved mirrors from Italy. All of the original glass for windows was imported from France.

"Entering the hotel through the main doors, guests found themselves in a rotunda, with its many chairs, divans and art objects," wrote James W. Covington in an article entitled "The Tampa Bay Hotel" in the 1966 edition of *Tequesta,* the journal of the Historical Association of Southern Florida. "From the great central hall, corridors led left and right to the interior wings of the building. The northern corridor led into the solarium and a beauty shop which offered hair styling and manicuring service."

Public rooms in the south wing included a waiting room for men and women visitors, several others reserved for women, and writing rooms. Here also was the ballroom, where dances were held at night and where tea was served in the afternoon.

On the level below the ground floor the men could visit a cafe, billiard room, barber shop and drug store, while the ladies could enjoy segregated shuffleboard, billiards and cafe facilities. Mineral baths, massages, and the services of a physician also were available there.

Thirteen polished marble columns supported the base of the circular two-story rotunda, and bronze figures were placed by each column. Groups of life-size bronze Indian girls served as light fixtures to illuminate the steps leading to the second floor.

Among the drawing room furnishings were a sofa and two chairs which had belonged to Marie Antoinette, four gilt chairs once owned by Louis Philippe, and a number of Spanish, French and Japanese cabinets. Along the hallways were antique carved Dutch chairs and others of rare onyx, and the beautiful art collection which decorated the walls included oil paintings, water colors and steel engravings.

A staff of 300 persons, including top-flight chefs, managers and other key personnel from outstanding hotels of the country, was hired and kept busy preparing for the new hotel's formal opening, wrote Covington.

Some 15,000 invitations were sent out, reading, "Tampa Bay Hotel will be open for guests Saturday, January 31, 1891, and the opening ball will take place Thursday, February 5, 1891, to which you are respectfully invited." About 2,000 guests arrived by train, in carriages and launches. Every room was filled. A New York orchestra played for dancing throughout the night. Champagne was abundant, while stronger drink was dispensed in the downstairs rathskeller.

(In that rathskeller seven years later, some young Army officers awaiting shipment to the Spanish-American War in Cuba discovered that Cuban rum, mixed with a new soft drink from Atlanta with the improbable name of Coca Cola, poured over cracked ice, prompted the imbiber to exclaim, *"Cuba libre!"*)

Opening festivities included operatic and popular music, and a tennis tournament in which Dr. Dwight Davis (of Davis Cup fame) was a contestant.

"It was like a fabulous house party," wrote Mullen. Not only were the private rooms and suites filled; guests slept in the public rooms, bunking on tapestried couches or on two chairs pulled together to make a bed.

Some of the finest food ever prepared in America was served at the Tampa Bay, on Wedgwood china. The hotel's pastry cook had been with Delmonico's for fifteen years.

Plant kept a fleet of rickshas for transporting guests, not only about the hotel grounds but also through its long interior hallways.

Outdoor sports provided for guests included golf and tennis.

For fees which ranged from $30 to $50 a day including food, transportation, guns and ammunition, Arthur Schleman, chief hunting guide, and his associate, John Gallie, took guests to the nearby forests in Hillsborough and Manatee Counties where game abounded.

The casino adjacent to the hotel contained a huge interior swimming pool. When not in use, the pool was covered by the movable casino floor.

Among artists who performed in the theatre were John Drew, Anna Pavlova, Sarah Bernhardt and Paderewski.

The grounds of the Tampa Bay were beautified, even before the hotel was begun, with more than 150 varieties of palm trees, ferns, and other tropical plants.

During the heyday of the hotel, guests paid up to $75 a day for suites. The base rate was $6 a day per person, with meals.

The Plant system grew steadily; by 1895 it employed 12,639 persons in its express, rail and steamship operations.

An editorial about Plant in the *Atlanta Constitution* on October 27, 1895, noted: "Above any other man living, he represents the great industrial revolution which has come over the face of the Southern States and which marks the success of free over slave labor."

When the U. S. battleship *Maine* was blown up in Havana harbor on February 15, 1898, the event that set off the Spanish-American War, Plant's ships rescued the survivors; his trains brought the troops to Tampa, the point of embarkation for Cuba; his hotel, the Tampa Bay, sheltered the general staff of the Expeditionary Force awaiting transportation to Cuba; his ships were converted to floating hospitals during the war, and his trains took the soldiers home again after the war if they had not been killed in combat or, more likely, died of yellow fever.

During the hostilities, men and war *materiel* were being moved *en masse,* "a good many officers gave a good many commands and things grew somewhat chaotic," wrote Harner. Plant, then seventy-nine years of age, decided to go from his New York home to Tampa and sort matters out.

"He knew what he was doing and he took no nonsense from anyone," wrote Harner. "It was a happy day for his subordinates when an aggressive young lieutenant colonel confronted him with the warning that unless there was more efficiency the War Department would seize the whole system.

" 'Seize it and be damned,' said Plant, and turned his back on the officer." So Theodore Roosevelt returned to his headquarters and concentrated on the Rough Riders he had recruited.

The old tycoon personally directed the work of winding down the system of military transportation. It was a herculean feat, and it used him up, wrote Harner. He died on June 23, 1899, at his Fifth Avenue home.

His holdings, at various times, totaled 4,297,368 acres of Florida real estate, in addition to his railroads, steamship lines and hotels—a monumental fortune.

The Tampa Bay Hotel was not destined to be just a hotel building where good food and drink were served, rest and relaxation provided for its guests, wrote Covington.

"As a direct result of the Spanish-American War it acquired a place in history as one of the great American hotels. The fame acquired from the dispatches and books written by famous guests who came to the hotel at that time caused Tampa to become known throughout the world."

Captain R. F. Webb in 1892-93 built the DeSoto, which was Tampa's major year-round hotel until July, 1912, when the Hillsboro was

The magnificent Hotel Belleview at Belleair, built in 1896, includes a number of family cottages on its expansive grounds. It is now the Belleview Biltmore, said to be the largest occupied wooden structure in the world.

completed. Built by a company headed by Lee B. Skinner, who had made a fortune in the citrus industry at Dunedin, the DeSoto was the largest commercial hotel in Florida at the time of its completion. Skinner's associates were Charles Wright, a well-known Tampan, and J. L. Tallivast, who had made money in naval stores in Manatee County.

The twelve-story Tampa Terrace Hotel and the eighteen-story Floridan were products of the land boom of the mid-1920s.

A group of forty citizens invested $1,000 each, late in 1924, and bought the northeast corner of Florida Avenue and Lafayette Street from Joe B. Johnson for the Tampa Terrace site. The hotel was financed by an Atlanta syndicate. After the boom collapsed, it was sold to Barron G. Collier of New York, who had made millions in street car ad-

Boasting Florida's first hotel golf course—a six-hole layout—when it opened, the Belleview Biltmore now offers its guests two eighteen-hole courses on the hotel grounds (designed in 1915 by Donald J. Ross) and another nearby. These are two views of the sixth hole on the No. 1 course, now known as the West Course. Above: The green. Right: A natural hazard guarding the approach to the green. The Belleview Biltmore courses were completely renovated in 1973-74.

vertising and was investing a good bit of his money in Florida properties.

The Tampa Bay Hotel was sold in 1905—the magnificent structure with all its treasures, plus 150 acres of land, to the City of Tampa for $125,000 cash, wrote Mullen. The hotel remained as the center of Tampa's social life until 1920 although it was not financially profitable, and by the time of the great Depression it had ceased to function as a hotel.

The University of Tampa, which in 1933 was operating as a junior college at Hillsborough High School, was offered the use of the Tampa Bay Hotel for $1 a year. "Through this move, a grand old building was saved from obscurity and a vital new university was created," wrote Mullen.

Another of the Plant hotels which has survived handsomely is the Hotel Belleview at Belleaire (facing Clearwater Harbor), still standing in all its glory, much enlarged, tended with care, still serving a wealthy clientele. It is now known as the Belleview Biltmore, and it looks as if it might still be going strong for many years to come.

Rates for 1979 at the Belleview Biltmore during the months of February and March were $48 per person, double room and bath, modified American plan (including breakfast and dinner). A parlor could be included for $46 a day extra, and a fifteen per cent service charge was added to relieve guests of all tipping except for beverage or other special services. Thus a couple could have a double bedroom, bath and parlor for $142 a day plus service charge and tax.

During January and April the comparable rates were $45 per person, $41 extra for a parlor.

Other hotels in the Plant System, in addition to the Inn at Port Tampa, were the Seminole at Winter Park, the Kissimmee Hotel in that city, the Ocala House at Ocala, the Punta Gorda Hotel at Punta Gorda, and the Fort Myers. Though not as grand as the Tampa Bay or the Belleview, all were worthy of the Plant tradition.

"The Floridan, then the tallest hotel in Florida," wrote Grismer, "was conceived in 1925 by A. J. Simms, a native of New Brunswick who had come to Tampa in 1907 and had been a leading developer for years. Forming the Tampa Commercial Hotel Company, which he served as general manager and secretary, Simms enlisted the support of prominent citizens to serve as company officials. They included W. E. Dorchester, L. C. Edwards, T. N. Henderson, C. H. Constans, Abe Maas, J. W. Warren, Clarence Holtsinger, G. C. Warren, J. C. Vinson, Ben Cosio, Webb Clarke and L. J. Efird.

"Bonds were sold by the Adair Realty & Trust Company. Work on the hotel was started February 4, 1926, and it was opened on January 15, 1927. The Floridan, like the Tampa Terrace, passed into Collier's hands after the crash. Both were operated by the Collier Florida Coast Hotels, Inc."

On May 11, 1943, the Floridan was bought by a group of twelve persons, among whom were children of Paul H. Smith and Julian L. Cone. This group organized the Floridan Hotel Operating Company, buyer in 1946 of the Thomas Jefferson Hotel (originally the Olive), which had been rebuilt and greatly enlarged in 1926 by Logan Brothers. Purchase price for the 162-room Thomas Jefferson was reported to be $250,000.

The Tampa Terrace Hotel was purchased on February 7, 1946, by a syndicate composed of Mrs. Angeles Corral, widow of Manuel Corral, and fifteen other persons, wrote Grismer. To operate the hotel, Overlord, Inc., was organized.

One Spring morning in Sarasota in 1886, Colonel Hamilton Gillespie carefully teed up his ball, let fly his driver, and watched the white dot slowly sink to the turf against the bright green of the scrub palmetto off the fairway, wrote Karl A. Bickel.

"Golf enthusiasts in Florida like to tell you that this was the first golf ball ever put in play in America. Maybe. Others make the same claim, and the debate grows acrimonious at times."

Within a few years there was a growing tendency on the part of wealthy Winter visitors to expect fine golf courses in connection with the fine hotels. The Belleview was the first to provide this sport when it offered its first (1896) guests "six sporty holes of golf, with shell greens." Others followed in the years around the turn of the century. Many of the courses were designed by Donald J. Ross, dean of American golf architects.

It may be surprising to learn that one section of the beaches on Florida's west coast along the Gulf of Mexico became an attraction for pleasure-seekers some ten years before the Gold Coast beaches on the Atlantic began to flower.

In 1883, a passage was hacked out of the wilderness which separated interior Pinellas County from the Bay at Indian Rocks. This back-breaking work was done by John H. Hendricks and his son Harvey, who had arrived there by sailboat earlier that year, to claim and occupy about half of a 106-acre tract for a homestead. The

Called the La Plaza Hotel when it was built in 1906, this is the Pass-a-Grille Hotel after it was renamed in 1913.

other half was promptly sold to L. W. Hamlin, who had "discovered" it that year on a schooner cruise with Hendricks and two other men, Jesse D. Green and Judge J. D. Bell, from Cedar Key to Disston City.

Hamlin had his work cut out for him in convincing the State Land Office and later the U. S. Government Land Office in Washington that St. Clement's Point (as the area was then designated) did in fact exist, since contemporary maps of the area were contradictory.

The first house at Indian Rocks Beach was Hamlin's, across the Bay from Indian Rocks, built in 1886 soon after his return there to settle, according to Frank T. Hurley, Jr., in his 1977 book about the lower Gulf Beaches, entitled *Surf, Sand & Post Card Sunsets.*

Zephaniah Phillips built his cabin at Pass-a-Grille about the same time. Thus the two pioneer beach settlements on Pinellas County's west coast had their beginnings in the same year, twenty miles apart.

A colorful Frenchman, George Lizotte, was the first to build a hotel at Pass-a-Grille, as early as 1901, "when there was nothing much there—just a handful of claptrap houses," wrote Hurley. It was the Bonhomie.

"Fifty cents bought a seven-course meal beginning with clam chowder and ending with dessert and a demi-tasse, plus all the stone crabs one could eat. Captains of industry, politicians, and everyday visitors rubbed elbows in the cramped dining room as the fame of Lizotte and Pass-a-Grille spread."

Lizotte's monopoly on accommodations and food lasted until 1906, when Mrs. Anna C. Hartley, a daughter of Zephaniah Phillips, built the Hotel La Plaza on a strip 400 feet wide ex-

The ornately landscaped grounds of the Pass-a-Grille included a three-leaf clover of shrubbery.

The Hotel Lizotte (right) and the Mason House at Pass-a-Grille, about 1910.

tending between 23rd and 25th Avenues from Little McPherson Bayou to the Gulf on land that was part of her father's estate, wrote Hurley.

Until the Don Ce-Sar was completed in 1928, the La Plaza (renamed in 1913 the Pass-a-Grille) was the beaches' grandest hostelry. It was a square frame building ornamented with Victorian "gingerbread" and surrounded by covered verandas. On those broad porches, guests could spend warm afternoons rocking while watching the changing patterns of water and the more adventurous guests who preferred to frolic in the surf.

Pass-a-Grille's third hotel, the Mason House, opened at 102 Eighth Avenue on Christmas Day, 1907. During the Summer of that year Captain and Mrs. James A. Mason had rented and operated the Bonhomie while Lizotte took a holiday. The Masons decided they liked innkeeping and built their own hotel.

The Masons and Lizotte alike offered shore dinners for fifty cents. Rooms at the Mason House cost $2.50 per day, or $10 and up by the week, with meals. Lizotte, who charged $9 per week, described the Bonhomie in his directory ad as the "hotel that made Pass-a-Grille famous."

In 1910 Lizotte razed his tiny Bonhomie and built the sumptuous Hotel Lizotte on the site. The Lizotte had sixty bedrooms, a dining room accommodating 300 persons (usually filled to capacity on weekends) and, Lizotte said, "It had one bath."

By early 1911 the area had several stores, a score of houses, and three hotels in the village, as well as the La Plaza "a mile up a sandy trail through the palmettos."

Pass-a-Grille began to look like a town.

The city of St. Petersburg owes its beginnings in part to a shrewd Russian immigrant named Piotr Alexevitch Demenscheff (Peter Demens) who owned and operated a sawmill at Longwood, in Seminole County, and in part to John C. Williams of Detroit, a health-seeker who first saw the area in 1875 and settled there in 1887. By the Spring of 1885, the supply of timber in the Longwood area was pretty well depleted, and Demens was casting about for a new enterprise to pursue, according to George W. Pettengill, Jr., in *The Story of the Florida Railroads.*

The Bloxham era was at its height and Florida's piney woods resounded to the clash of steel, for many promoters were building or trying to build railroads, encouraged by a friendly state administration and liberal land grants from the state's Internal Improvement Fund. It was natural for Demens to join the railroad builders because, in connection with his sawmill, he owned "a few miles of sixteen-pound rail and a couple of wheezing little teakettles, which passed for locomotives," used in hauling logs to his mill.

The Orange Belt Railway was organized by Demens, Josef Henschen, Henry Sweetapple and A. M. Taylor. Despite money troubles, delayed shipments of iron, heavy rains, and a demoralizing epidemic of yellow fever, it was pushed to completion in three years.

Built in 1888, about the time the railroad reached St. Petersburg, the Detroit Hotel was one of only two buildings which could be seen from the depot at that time. This photo was taken about 1890.

On June 8, 1888, the first regular train came into town, wrote Pettengill, and for a time, the "end of track" was at the location of the later Ninth Street Atlantic Coast Line crossing, where a small post office building was erected.

By December of 1888 the tracks were laid to what later became Second Street, where a depot was built, the architecture of which followed the Russian motif characteristic of several Orange Belt structures planned by Demens.

Two other buildings erected at that time, the company land office and the Detroit Hotel, were the only buildings in sight of the station.

"One of the first 'improvements' undertaken by the company was boxing in the underpinnings of the high station platform, in order to prevent the wild hogs from rooting and wallowing there," wrote Pettengill.

By 1912 St. Petersburg had thirty-seven hotels, the largest of which were the Hollenbeck, Huntington, Manhattan, Central, Ansonia, Belmont, Livingstone and Chautauqua, in addition to the Detroit. These contained from one hundred to 225 rooms each.

Later (boom-time) hotels included the Mason (Princess Martha), the Soreno, Rolyat (at Gulfport), Vinoy Park, Pheil, Suwannee, Pennsylvania, Dennis, Jungle, and the Don Ce-Sar out at Pass-a-Grille. The Rolyat in 1954 became the home of Stetson University's College of Law, and the Jungle Hotel became Admiral Farragut Academy, according to Dick Bothwell in *Sunrise 200: A Lively Look at St. Petersburg's Past.*

A luxury resort in the late 1920s and 1930s, the Don Ce-Sar Hotel at Pass-a-Grille was conceived by Thomas J. Rowe, a land developer, during the boom of the mid-1920s. The massive edifice of stuccoed Belgian concrete was not completed until 1928, after the boom had collapsed, but it remained open through the Depression of the 1930s. In 1942 the federal government purchased the Don Ce-Sar for use as a rest and rehabilitation center for troops during World War II. From 1945 to 1967 it served as a federal office building, then was vacated. Local citizens soon began to work for preservation of the huge pink building, and in 1972 hotel developer William Bowman, Jr., bought the property. He restored the Don to its former elegance and reopened it as a luxury hotel in 1973. Restoration was completed in 1975—the same year that the Don Ce-Sar was placed on the National Register of Historic Places.

Clockwise from top—Opened in 1911, the Hotel Poinsettia in the Roser block was one of St. Petersburg's first modern hotels. The Ponce de Leon Hotel at Central and Beach Drive was established in 1922. The Suwannee Hotel was built during the boom of the mid-1920s. The Mason Hotel, opened in 1924 at the northwest corner of Fourth Street and First Avenue, North, was later acquired by William Muir, who renamed it the Princess Martha to honor his wife.

The Soreno Hotel in St. Petersburg opened on January 1, 1924, and within a month was filled to capacity. The million-dollar hostelry was built by Soren Lund, a Danish immigrant who arrived in the U. S. in 1914 with only a few dollars in his pocket, and with neither relatives nor friends in his new homeland. This photo was taken on March 24, 1925.

The Vinoy Park Hotel at St. Petersburg was brand new when this picture was taken on January 18, 1926. The Vinoy was a luxury hotel, described by Karl Abbott, its first manager, as "one of the finest in the state."

The Rolyat Hotel at Gulfport, built by Jack Taylor, was designed around a courtyard. Constructed during the boom as a luxury hotel, it later housed the Florida Military Academy before becoming the home of the Stetson University College of Law in 1954.

The Wayside Inn (or Olds Tavern) at Oldsmar, a boomtime development between Tampa and St. Petersburg, was a popular dining place with local residents, as well as a haven for transients and would-be investors.

The Fenway Hotel at Dunedin had a spacious practice putting green for guests, as shown in this 1950 photo. The boom-time Fenway in 1960 became the new home of Trinity College, from which Evangelist Billy Graham graduated in 1940.

The Gasparilla Inn at Boca Grande was built in 1913 under the supervision of Karl Abbott, who was its first manager. It had a wide screened porch and featured dormer windows along the roof.

Built in six months at Sarasota, the Mira Mar Hotel was part of a pre-boom development rushed to completion in 1922-23 by Andrew McAnsh, a Scotsman from Chicago.

Clockwise from the top—One of the Collier Florida Coast Hotels was the Manatee River Hotel at Bradenton, shown here in 1936. The Manavista Hotel in 1918, when the city was still spelled Bradentown, had its own wharf on the river. The DeSoto Hotel at Sarasota, shown here in 1885, later was named the Belle Haven Inn. The Palms Hotel on Indian Beach at Sarasota is shown in 1900. A modern skyscraper at Sarasota was the Hotel Orange Blossom, pictured about 1935. It is now a retirement home, operating under the name of Orange Blossom Club.

Three Clearwater hotels. Upper left: Verona Inn in the early 1900s; above: the modern Fort Harrison Hotel with the causeway to Hillsborough County in the background (note radio broadcasting towers); left: the Gray Moss Inn which advertised in the 1920s, "Florida forever exempts state taxes on incomes and inheritances."

The prestigious Punta Gor Hotel, built in the 1880s, is sho (left) as it appeared in the ea years. It later became, in turn, Charlotte Harbor Inn and Charlotte Harbor Spa. The lov photo shows the building moderniz and streamlined, the grounds ha somely landscaped. The buildi burned in 1959.

.e three-story Oaks Hotel at Palmetto had wide covered ndas on the first two floors, as shown in this photo, taken .t 1920.

The Bradford Hotel at Fort Myers was built in 1905 at the intersection of First and Hendry Streets by Harvie E. Heitman, with money borrowed from Mrs. A. M. McGregor, a prominent Winter visitor to Fort Myers. The hotel was named in memory of Mrs. McGregor's only son.

The Royal Palm Hotel at Fort Myers, known in its early years as the "Queen of the Frontier," helped to transform that rustic town into a popular Winter resort. Built and furnished by Hugh O'Neill of New York, the Royal Palm opened (as the Fort Myers Hotel) on January 7, 1898. For a limited time at the turn of the century it was one of the Plant chain. The name was changed to the Royal Palm after O'Neill planted tropical shrubbery on the grounds. The hotel was said to be the first building in Fort Myers wired for electricity, and each of its floors contained a "ladies' retiring and bath room with two porcelain tubs." The hotel housed servicemen in training during World War II, and was dismantled in 1947-48.

Bottom right—Useppa Inn on Useppa Island off the mouth of Charlotte Harbor was developed by Barron Collier as a luxury resort from a twenty-room inn in 1912. It was a favorite of fishermen and the "beautiful people" of the era prior to World War II. It went downhill and passed through several ownerships until renovation was begun in 1977 under the direction of Garfield R. Beckstead. The expanded complex, a private club known as Useppa Island Club, includes this building—the original Collier residence—fully restored and renamed Collier Inn. Other island resorts nearby, which likewise have their roots in historic properties, include South Seas Plantation on Captiva Island (dating from 1900), and Casa Ybel Resort, Sanibel Island (from 1890).

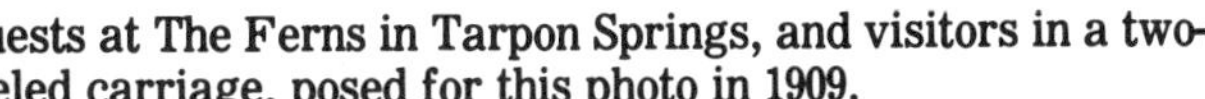

uests at The Ferns in Tarpon Springs, and visitors in a two-eled carriage, posed for this photo in 1909.

A huge, rambling frame building was the Naples Hotel at Naples, shown here in 1947.

Long a popular hotel in Fort Myers was the Frankl Arms, shown here about 1920. Remodeled in the 1970s, it now the Edison Regency Hotel, serving retirees and tra sients.

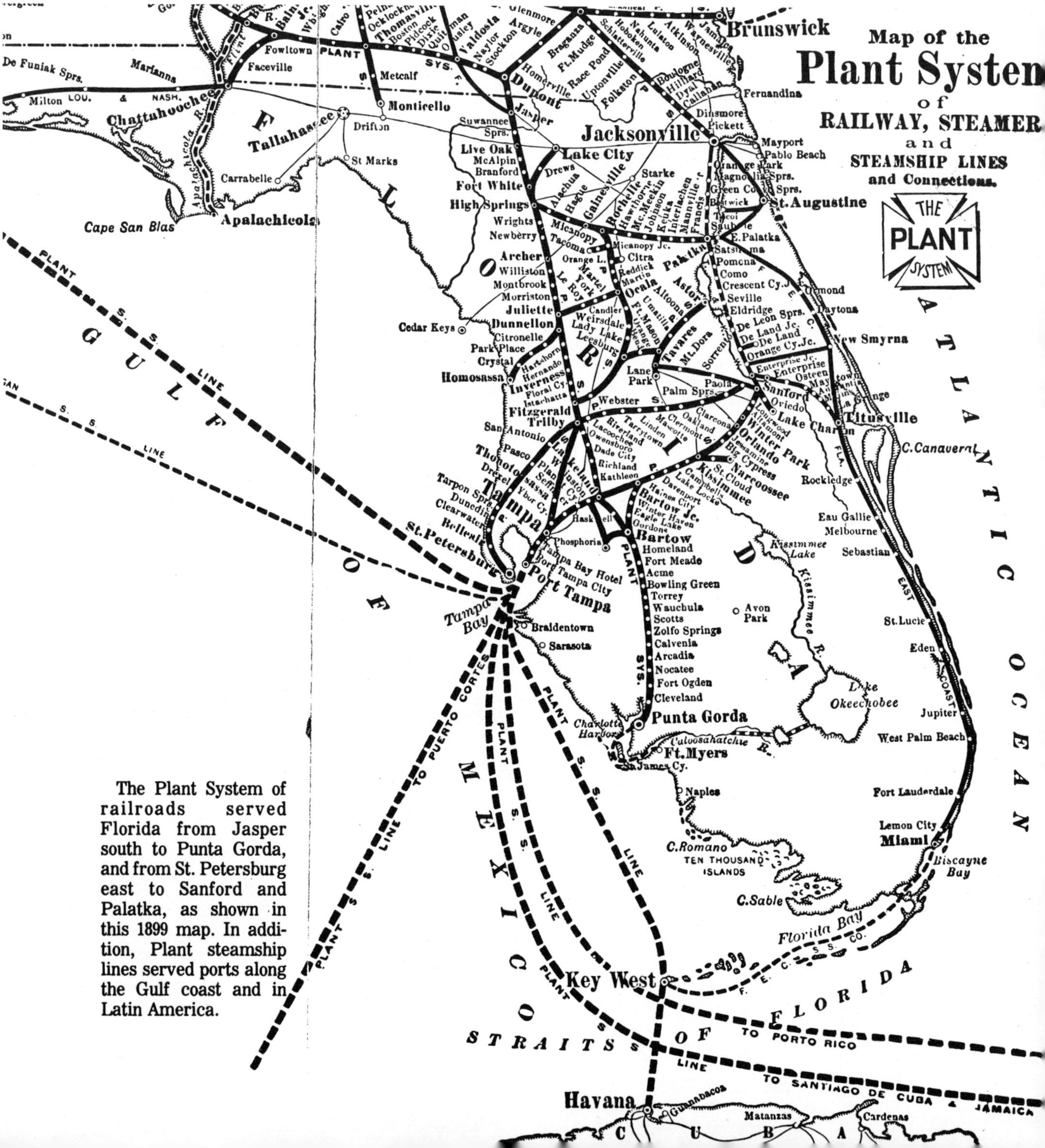

Map of the
Plant System
of
RAILWAY, STEAMER
and
STEAMSHIP LINES
and Connections.

THE PLANT SYSTEM

The Plant System of railroads served Florida from Jasper south to Punta Gorda, and from St. Petersburg east to Sanford and Palatka, as shown in this 1899 map. In addition, Plant steamship lines served ports along the Gulf coast and in Latin America.

6
Latter–Day Explorers

AS THE TERRITORY and state developed and the influx of settlers and tourists increased, the business of furnishing accommodations for transients attracted the time and investment of many persons to the profitable endeavor of providing bed and board for the public, wrote Dovell.

When Bishop Michael Portier traveled from Pensacola to St. Augustine in 1827, accommodations for transients usually were found in the homes of farmers and ferry tenders along the wilderness trail. Meals at these humble homes in the wildwood were scarcely worthy of the name. The bishop noted that for one breakfast he "was treated to a piece of stale bacon and some hot corn bread," and near the Aucilla River, he and his fellow-travelers had for dinner "broiled bear-steak that was really delicious, followed by watermelon for dessert" at the house of a man "who dwelt in a wretched hut in the midst of the desert . . ."

Francis, Comte de Castelnau, in his travels through the southern states in 1835-36, reported that "a traveler stops at all the homes he is fortunate enough to find," generally at great distances. "There he is given corn bread, sweet potatoes, and ordinary pork and cabbage. In Georgia and Florida the owner of a house usually expects pay in money, while in South Carolina a mere offer of this sort would be considered an insult. The ordinary price of a dinner of this sort is 75 cents, and the price of a breakfast or a supper or tea is 50 cents."

At Tallahassee, wrote Castelnau, the tavern to which he went, while "considerably the better of the only two existing in the town, was not however in any way remarkable in regard to its luxury, for the breakfast consisted of coffee without milk, venison and corn bread, the dinner of pork, cabbage and sweet potatoes, and the supper of tea without milk and the eternal corn bread. The price of these comforts is $3.50 per day and the other expenses are all of the same character. Sometimes for a change we had boiled or roasted corn, but I admit that they added very little to my pleasure."

These prices are considerably higher than other contemporary accounts indicate.

A vivid word picture of travel accommodations, or lack of them, in 1844 was drawn by Bishop Whipple: "Jan. 27th Left St. Augustine today and after a tedious ride of four and a half hours arrived at Picolata eighteen miles from that city. We had a very quiet time, no danger being apprehended from rapid driving, & the caution appended to the head of the way bill, 'all running of horses strictly prohibited on this line,' seemed to me quite a farce. Jog, jog along more like an old scow than a northern stage coach. We were not troubled by changes of horses and drivers, by grog stations, hotels or anything of the kind and very demurely walked up to the (what shall I call it) Hotel! no! tavern! no but to the frame or skeleton of the building where weary wayfarers wait impatiently for a boat to remove them from this dreary hole."

By 1853 Charles Lanman could write that in St. Augustine "it may please future visitors to learn that the hotels and boarding houses are all under the management of southern individuals with northern principles of domestic economy. From personal experience I can speak only of one of these establishments kept by Miss Fatio, a most estimable and popular lady; and if the others are as home-like and comfortable as this, the ancient city may well be proud of her houses for the accommodation of travelers and invalids."

Nearly every town or settlement supported two or three taverns or hotels where alcoholic beverages ranging from native brews to imported rums and whiskeys were available at the bars, Dovell noted.

Practically every county was served by one or more dealers in bottled liquors.

Charles Joseph Latrobe, English author of *The Rambler in North America,* recounted his experiences of a week in Tallahassee in 1833. One night the Temperance Society held a meeting in the large parlor of Brown's Hotel, while several Negro slaves enjoyed the proceedings at the windows. "Little was accomplished," he wrote, "and after the meeting many gathered at the bar to partake of such drinks as mint julep, mint sling, bitters, hail stone, snow-storm, appletoddy punch, Tom and Jerry, or eggnog . . ."

During the years after the Civil War, the example of the widowed Margaret Fleming, at Hibernia on the St. Johns River, of opening the plantation house and adjacent cottages to Yankee guests as a means of livelihood, was common throughout the state. In Daniel Brinton's guidebook, Hibernia was described thus in 1869: "Hotel, by Mrs. Fleming, one of the best on the river, accommodates about thirty-five persons, $2.50 per day, $15 per week . . . The 'river walk' near the boarding house is a delightful promenade about three-fourths of a mile long under the spreading boughs of noble live oaks . . . Visitors can readily obtain boats, and the vicinity offers many attractive spots for short excursions, picnics, and fishing parties. Rooms should be engaged by letter."

The gifted and versatile Sidney Lanier, remembered primarily as a southern poet, was plagued during his too-short life with the necessity of making a living in some locale where his delicate health could tolerate the climate. (He died of tuberculosis in 1881 at age thirty-nine.) One financial crisis existed in January of 1875, when Lanier was offered and accepted a commission by a railway company to write a travel guide about Florida, at a salary of $125 a month, plus travel expenses for a tour of the state. That sensitive author of nature poetry felt that a guidebook would not be a very artistic contribution to the world of literature, but the pay looked good, and he agreed to research and write *Florida: Its Climate, Scenery, and History.* He subsequently spent two months of that year traveling the state to gather his facts. From Jacksonville he visited Palatka, Silver Springs, St. Augustine, Cedar Key, Key West and Tallahassee.

"A few yards from the Jacksonville railway-

In the days when river boats were a principal means of travel and communication in Florida, these were typical boat landings. Left: Grahamville landing on the Ocklawaha River, 1908. Below: Hart's Line steamer, Okeehumkee, at the Silver Springs landing, 1905.

Lower left: Typical of hotel architecture at the time, Brown House at Silver Springs in 1906 had an observation tower.

Two views of the historic Brock House at Enterprise, on Lake Monroe; above, as it appeared after Captain Jacob Brock, short of stature and heavy of beard, built in the early 1850s "a neat inn" for the entertainment of his steamboat passengers; inset, as it looked after the addition of a new wing in the 1880s. The hotel was razed in the late 1930s. The Florida United Methodist Children's Home now occupies the former hotel's riverfront site and owns some of the furnishings which were used when the Brock House was host to General U. S. Grant and other famous travelers.

Sanford House at Sanford, here shown as the New Sanford House, was built about 1880.

Looking across Silver Springs to the Silver Springs Hotel. The hotel was built in the mid-1880s and burned about ten years later.

DeBary Hall at Enterprise, built in 1871, and still standing, more than a century later.

station, across Bay Street," Lanier wrote, "the long facade of the Grand National Hotel elevates itself; wherefrom, if the traveler's *entree* be at night, he is like to hear sounds of music coming through brilliantly-lighted windows opening upon a wide balcony where many people are promenading in the pleasant evening air. Farther back in the town a few hundred yards, situated among the oaks which border an open square, is the St. James Hotel; where the chances are strong that as one peeps through the drawing-room windows on the way to one's room, one will find so many New York faces and Boston faces and Chicago faces that one does not feel so very far from home after all."

Both of these hotels were open only in the Winter.

Lanier had many good things to say about Jacksonville's accommodations for the traveler. "The St. Marks Hotel, formerly known as the Metropolitan, a quarter of a mile downtown from the depot, between Bay Street and Forsyth, blooms all the year round . . ."

These hotels were really well appointed in all particulars. The St. Marks and the St. James had been recently enlarged, the latter then being the largest hotel in the state. In addition to the hotels, pleasant accommodations could be found in some one hundred smaller public houses and private boarding homes. The Grand National and St. James charged $4 a day, the St. Marks $3; the smaller houses from $1.50 to $3 a day, and from $10 to $20 a week.

Lanier remarked on "those springy plank sidewalks which constitute a sort of strolls-made-easy over a large part of the city," and on the "splendid young oaks which border the streets, sometimes completely arching them over . . ."

Jacksonville by then had made many provisions for employing the leisure of its Winter visitors. A good circulating library was located in Astor's building, at the corner of Bay and Hogan Streets, and current publications were supplied by the Ashmead Brothers at Bay Street near Pine (Main). Visitors were welcomed also in the reading room of Ambler's Bank on Bay Street.

At a sign reading "Boats to let," on the wharf near the Grand National, sail boats could be rented at prices ranging from 75 cents an hour upward.

Several good livery stables offered first-class turnouts—saddle horses, buggies and carriages—and two shell roads afforded pleasant drives.

Visitors could spend their Winters in Jacksonville without interrupting the education of their children. Notable among the schools were the Episcopal Academy of St. Mary's Priory, and St. Joseph's (Catholic) Academy. The city also had a Conservatory of Music, recently organized, and most major churches, which were flourishing.

In Fernandina, population about 3,000, Lanier found three hotels—the Egmont, Riddell and Norwood Houses, besides a number of boarding houses. He noted also a shell road leading out of Fernandina to "its celebrated beach, where for fifteen or more miles the visitor can drive over one of the smoothest roads in the world."

Passengers from a Clyde Line St. Johns River steamer are seen walking up the company pier at Sanford toward waiting horse-drawn taxis in this photo of the pre-railroad era.

Palms and shrubs adorned the grounds of the Qui-Si-Sana Hotel at Green Cove Springs in this view, photographed about 1930.

Two keys or islands comprised the town of Cedar Key at that time, and a ferry plied between them. It had in 1875 two places of accommodation—the Gulf House and the Exchange. These hotels were described as "somewhat primitive."

On reaching what Lanier referred to as the "Tallahassee country or Piedmont Florida," the Lanier party was taken by carriage to "a genuine old-fashioned tavern" with piazzas, nooks and crannies. A "neat colored Auntie" took charge of the luggage and showed the new guests to their rooms. Lanier was charmed with the City Hotel and the hospitality there dispensed.

"The repute of these people for hospitality was a matter of national renown before the War Between the States; and even the dreadful reverses of that cataclysm appear to have spent their force in vain against this feature of Tallahassee manners . . . Genuine hospitality of this sort is indeed unconquerable. The logic of it is that if there is enough for ten, there is certainly enough for eleven; and if enough for eleven, enough for twelve; and so on *ad infinitum* . . ."

The Civil War "had completely upset the whole productive system and stunned every energy of the land; of what avail would so little be among so many? But no one has starved, and albeit the people are poor, the dwellings need paint, and ready money is slow of circulation, yet the bountiful tables looked like anything but famine; signs of energy cropped out here and there in many places." Lanier found the situation "but a reasonable one for a people who ten years earlier

The three-story Union Hotel at Green Cove Springs, pic-
red here in 1874, was favored by invalids who went there to
ake the cure" in the sulphurous waters of the spring.

A glass roof sheltered the swimming pool at Green Cove Springs, shown here about 1915.

had to begin life anew from the very bottom, with no capital."

Of the little village of Newport, located near Tallahassee, the traveler wrote: "Here, in the old days of long ago, when Apalachicola shipped its hundred thousand bales of cotton and St. Marks was a busy port, grew a thriving country trading-point; but it now contains only a few families. A hotel has recently been opened, a few feet from whose doors runs the St. Marks River, wherein there is good sport to be had with rod and gig."

Hibernia, on the St. Johns River, was found to be "a pleasant invalid resort. Mrs. Fleming's large boarding-house here usually attests its popularity by a state of repletion early in the Winter."

Farther on was Magnolia Springs, with its fine hotel, the Magnolia.

Of Green Cove Springs Lanier wrote: "The springs, with the Clarendon Hotel adjoining, are but a short distance from the river-bank. Connected with this hotel are hot and cold baths, and swimming-baths, of the spring-waters." Besides the Clarendon, the Union Hotel offered accommodations.

All of these settlements had good private boarding houses, as did most sizable communities at that time.

Seventy-five miles from Jacksonville on the St. Johns was Palatka, with a population of about 1,500. The Putnam House, St. Johns House and Palatka House were ready to welcome travelers.

Five miles above Palatka was San Mateo, a pleasant settlement. A man named Miller kept the boarding house there.

Mellonville, with two hotels, was found to be in a neighborhood beginning to exhibit much activity in settlement and improvement.

On the opposite side of Lake Monroe was Enterprise, terminus of the larger steamboat lines. The Brock House was very popular at this time, especially with sportsmen, who made it their headquarters for fishing and hunting expeditions.

Accommodations for travelers were found at the hotels of Port Orange, New Smyrna and Daytona, besides private arrangements for board which almost all settlers' families were willing to make.

Ocean travel to Florida on one of the steamers of the New York and Charleston, or the New York and Savannah line was strongly recommended by "Rambler" in his 1875 *Guide to Florida.*

These ships were in all respects the most advisable, whether for the invalid or pleasure seeker, he reported. "For those in good health, the trip is a most enjoyable one. The class of passengers availing themselves of these steamers are invariably pleasant, agreeable companions—tourists from all parts of the United States . . ."

Those traveling by steamer who did not disembark at Fernandina or Jacksonville could remain on board the *Dictator* or *City Point* and continue to Magnolia Springs, Green Cove Springs, Picolata, Tocoi or Palatka.

At Palatka, comfortable steamers were available for Enterprise, Mellonville, Sanford, or the Indian River country; or boats could be boarded for the Oklawaha River.

The steamers used on the Florida route (from Charleston *via* Savannah) were pronounced unsurpassed for speed, safety and comfort, their staterooms clean and comfortable, and their tables provided with every luxury that Charleston, Savannah and Florida markets could produce. Beef, mutton and poultry were brought from New York, while the southern coastal states furnished fish and game.

Those in poor health who did not take the ocean route to Florida from Charleston might spend "half the Winter in recovering from the fatigues of reaching the St. Johns River by land."

At Fernandina, the first landing in Florida, Rambler recommended the Riddell House and Norwood House as well-kept establishments for accommodations. Also at Fernandina, travelers could board a train for Cedar Key, where connections could be made with steamers for Havana or New Orleans. Fernandina was served by the Jacksonville, Pensacola and Mobile Railroad, which led to Quincy, Tallahassee and Live Oak, among other points.

Hotels listed in Jacksonville in 1875 by Rambler were the Grand National, the St. James, and the Metropolitan, a new hotel situated close to the landing place of the Florida steamers.

The best of the city's boarding houses were said to be Mrs. Hudnall's St. Johns House, Mrs. Buffington's, Mrs. Atkins' and Mrs. Day's.

A trip through various sections of Florida, begun in January, 1880, was the basis for a guidebook entitled *Florida for Tourists, Invalids and Settlers,* by George M. Barbour, published in 1881.

Barbour was a correspondent for the *Chicago Times* when he first visited Florida, in the party of General U. S. Grant. He moved to the state shortly thereafter and continued his explorations.

Y-shaped trusses supported the second floor veranda of the Arlington Hotel in Palatka, shown here in 1910.

Three observation towers gave a unique profile to the Putnam House at Palatka. The hostelry was mentioned by poet Sidney Lanier in 1875. Note the dangling street light above the utility pole in this turn-of-the-century photo.

Of the modern buildings at St. Augustine, Barbour found that the largest and finest were the hotels—principally the St. Augustine, fronting on the Plaza at Charlotte Street, and the Magnolia, on St. George Street near the Plaza.

Barbour told of two "very neat, well-kept" hotels at Titusville—the Lund House and the Titus House. The latter was described as a long main building with two wings forming three sides of a square, one story high. The rooms opened off the wide verandas like a row of houses in a city block. Its fare included not only seafood and game, but also "many strange and familiar fruits and vegetables, all tropical, and fresh in January."

Barbour found the Spring Garden House at Spring Garden, near DeLand, to be "quite a cozy, homelike, well-built hotel." The innkeeper was E. M. Turner of Chicago. The hotel stood in a large orange grove, surrounded by a number of pretty hotel-cottages for invalid guests. A landing pier and packing house had been built at Spring Garden Lake, two miles distant, where the St. Johns River steamers landed goods and passengers.

At Pendryville on Lake Eustis the author and his party found very pleasant accommodations at A. S. Pendry's place—the Ocklawaha Hotel.

Leesburg, then the home of about 200 people, had only fair accommodations to offer the traveler at that time. "A good Winter hotel is badly needed, and would probably be a profitable investment," Barbour observed.

Frontier conditions still prevailed farther to the west. Of his journey from Brooksville to Tampa, Barbour noted that at Fort Taylor his party reached "the humble cabin of the stage-station," where the travelers obtained lodgings which, though very rough, were acceptable after the day's ride of twenty-six miles.

On another trip, going westward across the northern part of the state, Barbour left Jacksonville by the Florida Central Railroad and changed at Live Oak to the Jacksonville, Pensacola and Mobile. From Marianna, a long ride by stagecoach brought the traveler to Pensacola *via* Vernon, Euchee Anna and Milton—"typical specimens of the better class of representative southern county-seats. A square, an old-fashioned tavern, a court-house and a few shops" described each of them. Barbour wrote eloquently of the beauties of Pensacola and "the hospitable and intelligent officers of both the garrisons."

Barbour was captivated by Tallahassee: "The 'floral city of the flowery South,' is one of the loveliest places in all America," he declared.

Its shingled exterior marked the Saratoga Hotel Palatka. On October 28, 1890, it opened for its sixth seaso with A. S. Washburne as manager.

He stayed several days in the state's capital at the "quaint, old, tavern-like City Hotel," enjoying numerous drives about the surrounding country.

Monticello, thirty-three miles east of Tallahassee, the terminus of a branch railroad about five miles long, was a flourishing town of some 2,000 inhabitants, containing two hotels, among other attractions.

Barbour described Fernandina as a popular tourist attraction, praising its three inns, the Egmont, Mansion and Riddell Houses.

Orange Park, ten miles south of Jacksonville, also had a handsome Winter hotel, which Barbour did not name, and Green Cove Springs was reported to have two large, well-furnished and finely-appointed Winter hotels.

Palatka, one of the larger cities on the St. Johns, had "numerous large stores, packing houses, warehouses, hotels, public schools and public buildings."

The Colonial Hotel at Ocala, about 1920.

Above: Ocala's Hotel Marion, about 1930.

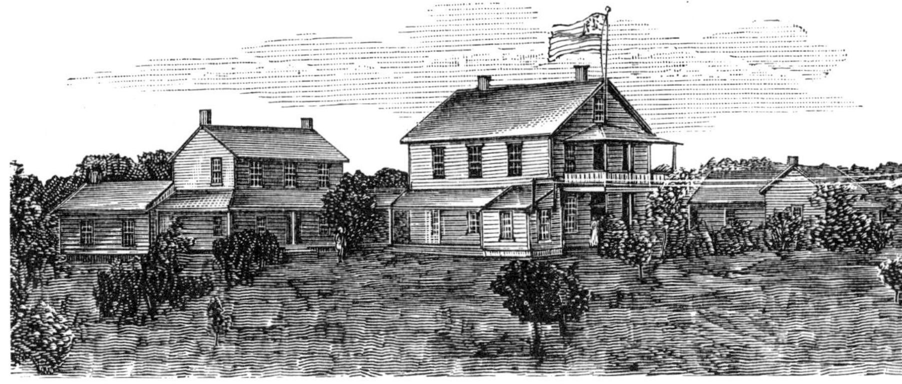

Right, top: Ocklawaha House, built by A. S. Pendry at Pendryville before 1880, provided "very pleasant accommodations," according to travel writer George M. Barbour. Second from top: The New Ocklawaha Hotel, greatly enlarged, included the original structure. Pendryville later was renamed Lake Eustis and still later, Eustis.

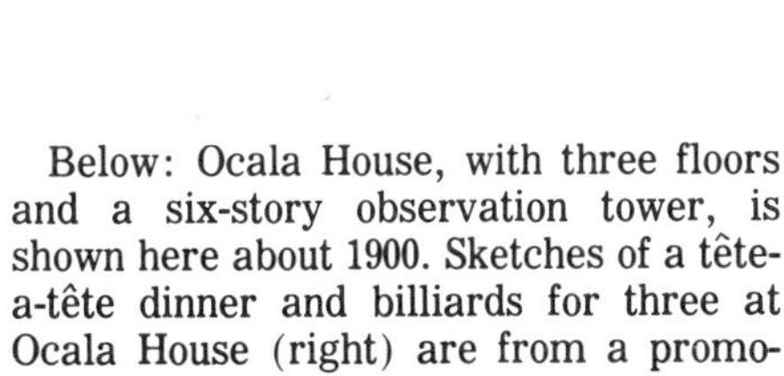

Below: Ocala House, with three floors and a six-story observation tower, is shown here about 1900. Sketches of a tête-a-tête dinner and billiards for three at Ocala House (right) are from a promotional booklet on the hotel, which was one of the Plant chain.

At Mellonville, one mile east of Sanford, were found "a pier, an old hotel, and a few dwellings." Enterprise, then the seat of Volusia County, contained a court house and county buildings, a spacious Winter hotel, three or four stores, and a large sawmill.

Long before the promoters discovered Silver Springs, Barbour called it a wonder of nature. "Boats were in readiness, and all enjoyed a row over its surface, and wondered at its marvelous clearness." From the Springs, Barbour rode westward to Ocala, six miles distant, arriving there in season to enjoy a dinner at the comfortable, old-fashioned tavern.

Barbour urged that "every visitor to Florida should make the famous excursion 'up the Ocklawaha', and no one who has once made it will be likely ever to forget a night-journey upon what has been well called 'The Mysterious River'."

In Alachua and Putnam Counties, Barbour found a "particularly attractive cluster of lakes" including Lakes George, Brooklyn, Waldo, Santa Fe, and Deep Lake. Lake Santa Fe was the largest (some 10,000 acres) and "probably the prettiest." On a bold bluff of its fertile shore the Santa Fe Hotel had recently been built, a fine, roomy structure, in the midst of a large park-like garden, with a charming lawn sloping down to the water's edge.

Barbour wrote of well-kept hotels at Lake City, described as "the most important place in this region," a prosperous and substantially built town of some 2,500 inhabitants; and at Key West, a city of 8,500 where he and his companions enjoyed "the comforts of the Russell House."

The 131-year-old Island Hotel at Cedar Key has had a varied career. It was built of tabby in 1849 as a general store for Parsons & Hale, according to Professor F. Blair Reeves of the University of Florida College of Architecture. On the second floor was a customs house; Cedar Key was then a major port. Cedar trim was added to the building later, the lumber coming from the forests which formerly grew on the island. The hotel is again open for guests in 1980, after being closed for several months prior to its purchase by a new owner.

Henry Sanford had built at his town a pier 600 feet long into the lake, large storehouses, a sawmill, machine shop, and "the elegant Sanford Hotel, standing in ample, well-kept and neatly fenced grounds, its clean, grassy surface laid out with walks and ornamented with flowers and shrubs."

Another enterprising citizen of Sanford was George H. Sawyer of Massachusetts, proprietor of the City Hotel and owner of one of the finest gardens in the state. "During the entire Winter his hotel tables are loaded with the best of squashes, cabbages, celery, cauliflower, peas, string-beans, tomatoes, potatoes, radishes, beets, etc.," wrote Barbour.

Two miles from Orlando was Interlaken, surrounded by lakes on nearly all sides, including a connected chain on which a twenty-mile boat ride could be enjoyed. "A good hotel here would be sure to attract many visitors, and there is a probability that such a one will be erected soon," he predicted.

Barbour praised Jacksonville as a "handsome and prosperous-looking city . . . covering a good deal of ground and, particularly during the Winter season, when all the hotels are thrown open to the thronging guests, presenting an animated and picturesque appearance."

Jacksonville's wide streets were "nearly all shaded by long rows of mammoth oaks, forming arcades of embowering green in Winter as well as in Summer," he wrote. "Horse-cars, connecting the railroad-depots, run along Bay Street, up Catherine to Duval Street to the St. James Hotel, down Hogan Street and back to the starting point, making a very convenient circuit . . . During the Winter season the great hotels (the St. James, the Windsor, the Carleton, the Grand National, etc.) are thronged with wealthy tourists from all parts of the world, and the place has then all the gayety and animation of a leading Summer resort at the North."

Prior to construction of the first Union Station in Jacksonville, which opened in February, 1895, each railway company had its own separate depot or loading platform. The move toward uniting them was initiated by Henry M. Flagler, who in 1893 was president of the newly-chartered Jacksonville Terminal Company. Henry B. Plant was vice-president. The handsome Tennessee marble terminal with its fourteen sandstone columns replaced the first Union Station at the same location in 1919.

Passengers rode the stage coach, bicycling was popular, and leg o' mutton sleeves were in vogue in the 1890s, according to sketches in a pamphlet advertising the Seminole Hotel at Winter Park. The hotel, shown above, was open from January to April and was managed by O. L. Frisbee. This original Seminole Hotel, another in the Plant chain, was visited by such illustrious guests as Presidents Grover Cleveland and Chester A. Arthur. It was destroyed by fire.

The New Seminole (below) was in use from 1912 to 1970. Both were on Lake Osceola, but at different locations.

Observations made on his extensive trip through Florida moved Barbour to make a prediction. Noting that most of Florida's few resort hotels were located in the northern part of the state, and that they were barely able to accommodate the increasing flood of visitors in search of health and pleasure, he wrote:

"The time is near at hand when a vast Winter 'Coney Island,' with Newport combined, must be established at some point in the southern part of the peninsula, beyond any possible danger of cold, frosts, or extreme changes; where a sea-beach drive, islands for pleasure-yachts, a race-course, polo ground, baseball park, etc., can be established." There the health seeker, the hunter, and the fisherman, the lover of strange scenes and excitement, all would be able to find their heart's desire.

His prediction came amazingly true, beginning

in less than twenty years. However, Barbour foresaw that this Shangri-La might be centered around Charlotte Harbor. Although the two men probably never met, Barbour's thought was paralleled by Colonel Isaac Trabue, a Kentuckian who came to Punta Gorda in 1883, bought acreage, took steps to have a town laid out, and prevailed on the railroad builders to extend the Florida Southern Railroad southward to Charlotte Harbor.

In that he succeeded; but by then Henry B. Plant had gained control over most of the railroads in southwest Florida, and he chose Tampa and its port, rather than Punta Gorda and its Charlotte Harbor, for his major investment.

Except for its large and luxurious Punta Gorda Hotel, which attracted sportsmen and others, Punta Gorda was left to remain a small town.

Above: One of Orlando's earliest hotels was Lake View House, built before 1879 on the south side of Central Avenue between Main and Rosalind Streets.

Charleston House (top) in Orlando, shown here in 1885, was built in 1882. In 1895 it was sawed into two parts, one half becoming part of the Tremont Hotel (left), the other half part of Duke Hall. Parts of two other buildings—the 1875 court house, built by Jacob Summerlin, and the old Methodist Church—also became part of the Tremont. Furnishings of its parlor (above) included a piano. J. W. Wilmott, an English sea captain, built the Tremont and operated it for many years. His family continued operation until 1955.

Orlando's Central House, shown here about 1890. It was located at the intersection of East Church and Court Streets. Mrs. Hollock, the manager, served "all you can eat" for 25 cents.

The Angebilt Hotel, an Orlando skyscraper which had its grand opening in 1923, is still in use.

The St. Charles Hotel, situated at the southeast corner of Orange Avenue and Washington Street in Orlando (later the site of the Bradshaw Building), was operated from 1908 to 1925 by Mrs. Charles J. Hilpert, her son Charles, and an aunt, Louise Fall. Coming from Baltimore, they bought the home and hospital property of Dr. R. L. Harris, which they converted to the St. Charles. When they sold the hotel in 1925, part of the building was razed, and part was moved and remodeled to become the Fidelity Building at 60 North Court Avenue.

Opened in 1885 by H. S. Kedney, Orlando's San Juan Hotel was rebuilt by Harry L. Beeman (son of a chewing gum king) in 1893 and extensively remodeled in 1924 and throughout the years. It was destroyed by fire in 1979. This is how it looked in the 1930s.

Twentieth Century hotels in Orlando have included the Wyoming Hotel (left), in use until the 1950s, with broad lawn and spacious, restful surroundings; the Fort Gatlin Hotel (left center), in use from 1925 to 1965, shown here in the 1940s; and the Empire Hotel (below), seen in the 1930s.

Named for an Apopka pioneer, the William Edwards Hotel at Apopka was built in 1926 by citizens of the town who formed a corporation and sold bonds to finance construction of the $180,000 hotel. A two-story brick city hall was torn down to provide a downtown site for the hostelry. The building was razed in 1963. The Apopka branch of Orlando's First Federal Savings & Loan now occupies the site. Edwards was in charge of the vast Pirie (now Errol) Estate and developed the Mount Plymouth Hotel.

The Pines boarding house, on North Orange Avenue b tween Washington and Jefferson Streets in Orlando, w. operated by Mr. and Mrs. E. B. Horner from 1913 into t 1920s.

Kissimmee hotels of the late 19th Century and early 20th Century included the Hotel Tohopekaliga with its picket fence (right); the Hotel Inn, shown immediately below in 1908; the Gray Stone Hotel (middle right), its appearance matching the name; and the prestigious Hotel Kissimmee (bottom), another of the Plant System chain.

Twin walkways led to the entrance of the Hotel Runnymede on East Tohopekaliga Lake, east of Kissimmee.

Lined up in front of the Highlands Hotel in Dundee about 1923 was a crowd potential investors, waiting to be taken to see citrus groves in the vicinity.

Under construction in 1925 was the Polk Hotel at Haines City. It has been in continuous use since completion. In recent years the name was changed to the Palm Crest Hotel.

Holly Hill Inn at Davenport is shown here in 1922. It later was used by the Holly Hill Corporation to house and entertain prospective land buyers. Now, much enlarged, it is Bishop Gray Inn, an Episcopal retirement home.

'rank Bryson, a boom-time real estate promoter, housed spects in the Groves Hotel on Ledwith Avenue at Haines y, seen here in 1925, and in several other hotels in the te. The Florida Military Institute was quartered here for a ie in the 1930s. The building has since become the Skyline 'race Apartments.

Starting life as the family home of Dr. F. W. Inman in 1887, the Florence Villa Hotel near Winter Haven had grown in the early 1900s to the size shown here. It served the public until the 1930s. The Florida Defense Force staged a farewell dance in the building on August 28, 1942, and the furnishings were sold soon afterward. When the building was torn down its last remains were sold—a million feet of lumber, 750 double windows, 900 doors.

The many-gabled Hotel Plaza in Winter Haven at the northwest corner of Central Avenue and Sixth Street Northwest, was built and originally operated by J. N. Ackley. Shown here about 1918, it was popular with tourists and Winter visitors.

Completed in 1924, the Haven Hotel (bottom left) furnished accommodations for land-seekers of the real estate boom. During the 1970s it was in use as a retirement hotel. In 1980, plans are being made by a group of business and professional men to buy the building and restore it to its former elegance.

Built in 1916 as the Eagle's Nest Hotel at Eagle Lake, this building changed hands and was renamed Coward Hotel in 1919.

Bartow's earliest hotel was the Blount House, built for a residence in 1867 by Gideon Zipprer, stepson of cattle baron Jacob Summerlin. Shown here in the 1880s, it later became the Orange Grove Hotel, and still later Tillis House.

Gracious southern hospitality was dispensed at B tow's Commercial Hotel for eighty-six years, un various names and managers. It was built in 1884, f ing the Polk County court house from the north. various times it was known as the Central Hotel . Restaurant, Buchheit House, Mabbette House, Tov House, Commercial House and finally, Commer Hotel. Meals were served family style, and for ma years it was the favorite for midday dinner among p ple who worked at the court house. Politicians . local businessmen often would take time for a rub or two of bridge in the lobby after lunch. The build was razed in 1972.

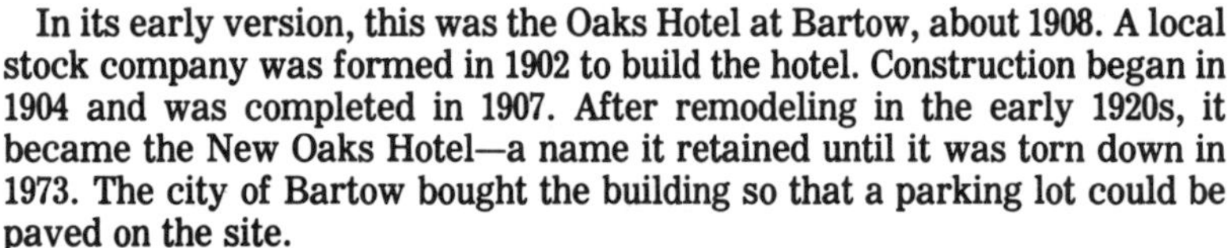

In its early version, this was the Oaks Hotel at Bartow, about 1908. A local stock company was formed in 1902 to build the hotel. Construction began in 1904 and was completed in 1907. After remodeling in the early 1920s, it became the New Oaks Hotel—a name it retained until it was torn down in 1973. The city of Bartow bought the building so that a parking lot could be paved on the site.

his was the Reif Hotel in Fort Meade, usually wn as the Reif House. It adjoined Triangle Park on south, and was popular for many years with criminating travelers. It was built in 1905 by Max Josephine Reif and had 24 rooms. The building was down in the early 1960s.

The National Hotel in Bartow was built at the corner of Oak Avenue and Pearl Street. It opened in 1887 and served the public until it was torn down in 1905.

Verandas on the first and second floors were features of the odd-shaped three-story Fort Meade Hotel. This picture was taken about 1900.

Tall pines made a picturesque setting for the Ariana Hotel at Auburndale. This hotel was being built by Contractor Paul H. Smith for a client when the land boom of the mid-1920s collapsed. Smith completed it, gave it his name, and employed a niece, Louise McLaughlin, to operate it for him for several years. Later it was sold and renamed the Ariana.

The bubble burst before this six-story hotel at Fort Meade (lower right) could be completed in the 1920s. This steel and concrete skeleton stood at the city's main intersection, Broadway and Charleston Avenue, for almost forty years. Inevitably, it was dubbed the Skeleton Hotel. It was torn down in March, 1964.

The Hotel Thelma, built in 1913 as the Kibler Hotel, was Lakeland's first modern hotel. Twin brothers A. B. and D. B. Kibler built the $125,000 structure, then sold it six years later to H. B. Carter who renamed it. It was at the northeast corner of Kentucky Avenue and Lemon Street.

Still prominent on Lakeland's M
Street is the ten-story Lakeland Ter
Hotel, built in 1924, shown here in the 1

A bird's-eye view of Lakeland, 1907-08. Massachusetts Avenue and Main Street intersect in the foreground. At left is the Tremont Hotel, built in 1886 by A. G. Munn and bought in 1888 by J. W. Emerson. In the right foreground is the Florida Hotel. Lakeland's first church building, the Presbyterian, is the steepled structure at upper right, next to the utility pole. Just to the right, with mansard roof, is Lakeland's first sanitarium, opened in 1906 by Dr. A. R. Bond.

ıkeland's massive New Florida Hotel was completed in 1926, just ɦwest of Lake Mirror. It is now the Florida Retirement Residence ɨl.

The Dixie Walesbilt Hotel in Lake Wales was another product of the boom. Civic clubs met in its dining room for a number of years. This picture was taken soon after its completion. The building still stands, its future uncertain.

The first major building in Lake Wales was the twenty-five-room ıtel Wales, built in 1911. It later became the Lake Shore Hotel, then e Plantation Inn. Famous for its fine food for many years, it was in ntinuous seasonal use until it was destroyed by fire May 24, 1979, ortly after it had closed for the Summer.

W. F. Burt's Tropical Hotel in Plant City was built about 1888, at the northwest corner of Reynolds and Palmer Streets. It became a popular dining place after Burt's daughter, Mrs. Ella Burt Strickland Crum, enlarged the building and changed the name to the Roselawn. The new Roselawn opened formally on January 2, 1908.

The elegant Chalet Suzanne, near Lake Wales, is noted for its fine cuisine, its one-of-a-kind accommodations, and its Hans Christian Andersen atmosphere. Operated by members of the Hinshaw family since its establishment in 1931, the Chalet is a perennial winner of the **Florida Trend** Golden Spoon award, and has its own private landing field. Dinner for two in 1980, including tax and tip, cost $72.

Plant City's Hotel Plant, at the northwest corner of Evers and Collins Streets, opened on November 11, 1926. Construction was financed by sale of stock to 300 local citizens. For forty years its dining room was the scene of many banquets and civic club weekly luncheons. The hotel was demolished in 1966 and a bank was erected on the site.

Mulberry's excellent Juanita Hotel originally was one wing of a department store founded in 1894 by L. N. Pipkin. This portion of the building was moved to a site east of the railroad about 1907, and named for Pipkin's eldest child. The hotel was operated for many years by Pipkin's youngest sister, Donna, and her husband, Charles Dickinson. The Tampa Electric Company office now occupies the location, 101 Second Street, Northwest.

Two of Arcadia's oldest hotels were the Arcadia House (above) built before 1901, and the DeSoto Hotel at the corner of Oak Street and DeSoto Avenue, built about 1904. The original wooden Arcadia House has been torn down, but a later brick Arcadia House Annex is still in use as a rooming house. The DeSoto was located over the DeSoto National Bank. The lobby and dining room were on the second floor and balconies faced on both streets. Private rooms were on the second and third floors. The site is now a parking lot.

7
The Gold Coast

THE FIRST PERMANENT structure in the Miami area was the Cape Florida Lighthouse, built on Key Biscayne in 1825, according to Arva Moore Parks in an article entitled "Miami in 1876," published in *Tequesta,* 1975. This project had high priority after the United States acquired Florida in 1821 because of the many shipwrecks which had occurred on the Florida reef.

By 1832 Richard Fitzpatrick of Key West had bought from the first claimants, the Egans and Lewises, about 2,560 acres on both sides of the Miami River—the choicest land in the Miami area—for $1,840. Fitzpatrick had it made into a farm, producing sugar cane, corn, pumpkins, sweet potatoes, and several kinds of tropical fruit.

The Negro slaves from South Carolina who worked the farm lived in twelve wooden houses built for the purpose. These and several other structures, all of wood, were located on the south bank of the river, while Fitzpatrick's home was on the north bank.

All of these improvements, including the lighthouse, were wiped out early in the Second Seminole War, which began in 1835. On Key Biscayne the Navy constructed Fort Bankhead, which later was taken over by the Army, moved to the mouth of the Miami River on Fitzpatrick's land, and renamed Fort Dallas.

"With Colonel William S. Harney in command, Fort Dallas became the point of embarkation for several major expeditions into the Everglades in search of the elusive Seminole," wrote Parks.

Henry Perrine, noted horticulturist, was granted a township of land in the area on which to engage in cultivating tropical fruits; but when he and his family arrived late in December, 1838, they went instead to the small island known as Indian Key, because hostile Indians were then in control of the mainland.

"The twelve-acre island was owned by the infamous Jacob Housman who in a little more than a decade had built himself a sizable empire there," wrote Parks. "Streets were laid out and at least thirty-eight structures, including the Tropical Hotel, were built on the island. It was also the temporary county seat of Dade County." By 1840, refugees from the mainland had swelled the population of Indian Key to about fifty.

The island was attacked on August 7, 1840, by more than one hundred Indians, who demolished the settlement. Among the seven persons killed was Dr. Perrine.

One of the original grantees who had not sold her property to Fitzpatrick, Mary Ann Davis of Texas, decided during this war to subdivide and offer it for sale. Colonel Harney, pleased with what he had found on Biscayne Bay, bought two lots from her for $100 in 1839.

When the war was over in 1842 and the Army left Fort Dallas, Fitzpatrick's improvements to his property had been destroyed, and he sold the land for $16,000 to William F. English, his nephew. English came, platted the "Village of Miami," advertised the settlement and began selling lots. The Dade County seat was moved to the village in 1844. In 1846 the Cape Florida Lighthouse was rebuilt.

Despite the continuing threat of Indian uprisings, more people came to the Biscayne country. George Ferguson reported that in 1850 he and his twenty-five workers had produced 300,000 pounds of coontie starch, worth $24,000, made from the roots of a palm-like native plant. This commodity, sold in Key West and elsewhere, was the only cash "crop" in those early years.

English went to California, intending to return and resume development of the village, but was accidentally shot and killed there in 1855.

Indian unrest brought the Army back to Fort Dallas that year, at the start of what would become known as the Third Seminole War. It was during this occupation, wrote Parks, that the stone buildings on the north bank, begun by William English in the 1840s, were completed by the troops. New wooden buildings also were constructed.

The first road in south Florida, connecting Fort Dallas with Fort Lauderdale, was built by Army troops in 1857. It was planned to expedite the growth of Miami, but by the time the last Seminole War was over, the Civil War was impending. The years of this conflict comprised "a period of stagnation and lost hope," noted Parks, for the few settlers who remained at Biscayne Bay were cut off by blockade from the rest of the country.

The Reconstruction year of 1866 brought to Miami a remarkable man who was to be prominent in the history of the area for the next ten years. Republican William Henry Gleason of Wisconsin and an associate, W. H. Hunt, their families, four hired men, two horses, two mules, a cow and "all kinds of other equipment" landed at Cape Florida in July of that year.

For a few months in 1868 Gleason was the state's Lieutenant Governor, from which office he was impeached for insufficient residence in the state, but not until after he had tried to wrest from Harrison Reed the office of Governor. He then returned to the Biscayne country and contented himself with dominating Dade County politics, though he encouraged continued use of the title of Lieutenant Governor, and named the mail boat *Governor Gleason* when in 1870 he moved the post office from Fort Dallas and reopened it as Biscayne, in the section that was to become Miami Shores.

But Gleason succeeded in attracting new settlers to Miami; it was his name which cropped up in the

A great deal of wall space was occupied by pictures and other decorations in the parlor of Peacock Inn at Cocoanut Grove, built by Charles and Isabella Peacock from England.

post-war guidebooks on Florida where Miami was mentioned. He was tolerated.

Daniel B. Brinton noted in his 1869 guidebook that "Lieutenant Governor Gleason resides in Miami and will entertain travelers to the extent that he can." The *Florida Gazetteer* noted that "as there is no boarding house, Messrs. Hunt and Gleason feel compelled to keep a fine hotel."

One of the more prosperous pioneers, noted Parks, was William B. Brickell from Ohio. He bought extensive property on the south side of the river and in 1870 opened a trading post, having brought with him supplies, lumber, workmen, and a tutor for the Brickell children, seven in number. With Brickell came E. T. Sturtevant, whose daughter, Julia Sturtevant Tuttle, was to write a significant chapter in Miami's history.

Among those living in the Biscayne country in 1876 were John and Ed Pent, the Frow family, Edward Barnott, Andrew Price, Charles Rhodes, John Adams, William Wagner, "Long John" Holman, William H. Benest, Andrew Bart, the Enfinger and Jenkins families, John and Mary Addison, Michael Oxer, Dan Clark, Michael Sears, Jonathan C. Lovelace, J. William Ewan, Charles and Isabella Peacock, George and Dr. Richard B. Potter, William Mettair, William J. Smith, John Harner, the Robert Rhodes family, Samuel Rhodes and his son, John Thomas "Jolly Jack" Peacock, Adam Richards, T. W. Faulkner, Charles Siebold and A. F. Quimby.

"On this tropical frontier most settlers gladly opened hearth and home to both residents and visitors," wrote Parks. "Even the Indians who came to trade were allowed to camp at Brickell's or at other pioneer dwellings, frequently sharing a meal with the family." Dinner might consist of venison steak, liver, home-cured bacon, corn bread, Johnnie cake, sweet potatoes, Indian pumpkin, coontie pudding and guava jelly.

In 1874, because of reports of privations suffered by the victims cast ashore from wrecked ships along the Atlantic coast, federal authorities built a string of five Houses of Refuge between Cape Canaveral and Cape Florida, at a cost of $2,990 each. The first of these was at Indian River, the fifth opposite the head of Biscayne Bay.

The houses were identical, thirty-five by fifteen feet in size, built of Florida pine, with roofs of cypress shingles. The ground floor consisted of a living room, dining room, bedroom and kitchen, all surrounded by a large veranda, Parks noted. The upper floor was a single dormitory for the use of stranded seafarers. The windows had no glass, but were screened and shuttered. A smaller structure nearby was a boathouse containing a twenty-two-foot surf boat and a twelve-foot skiff, with oars, masts and sails.

The middle section of Peacock Inn was built in 1882, the wings added later. In 1886, the Peacocks held a Christmas party at the Inn, inviting their hotel guests and every person who lived on Biscayne Bay. This was the first community gathering ever held in what was to become Miami, according to Arva Moore Parks in "The Forgotten Frontier—Florida Through the Lens of Ralph Middleton Munroe."

The keepers, who with their families occupied the first floor, were not expected to attempt a rescue in a storm, but to patrol the beach for survivors afterward. Also they were expected to keep enough supplies and cots to furnish food and shelter for a maximum of twenty-five people for ten days.

Gleason, whose influence waned as the Democrats regained control of Florida, had established the village of Eau Gallie in Brevard County, and promoted the construction of a two-story building there. He hoped the Legislature would use it to establish the first state agricultural college, thereby bringing the new village to life. The Democratic Legislature declined. The coquina stone building had ten rooms, a large hall, and a two-room dormitory. Gleason later opened it as the Granada Hotel and lived out his life in Brevard County, where he achieved "a type of baronial respectability," wrote Parks.

The first Winter visitors to the Biscayne country were articulate, well-educated, well-traveled folk who "exclaimed in flowery language over the colors of the bay, the sky, the colored fish, and the sea gardens," according to Helen Muir in *Miami, U. S. A.*

"They lived on boats and in tents, and finally they crowded Peacock Inn, which evolved because of their coming as the area's first hostelry, barring the Tropical Hotel back on Indian Key. This forerunner of hotel hospitality, in a region which would eventually bow to tourism as its number one industry, was built by a man named Charlie Peacock on the shores of Coconut Grove."

Charles' brother Jack had preceded him to Miami and was keeper of the House of Refuge "over in the wilds of Miami Beach," where he and his wife Martha were warm hosts to all who appeared at their door. Jack's glowing reports of tropical life prompted Charles to leave England's dampness and his meat warehouse and to set sail, with his wife and their three small sons, for Miami by way of Key West.

"It is said that his first sight of Coconut Grove in 1875 sent Charlie Peacock's stout heart to the bottom of his English boots," wrote Muir. "His wife Isabella bore up at the sight of the island-like wilderness. Perhaps she could hear prophetic voices from the future calling her the 'mother of Coconut Grove'."

The newcomers settled first at the mouth of the river, where they had for neighbors the Brickells, the Lovelace family and the "Duke of Dade" with his punctilious manners and charm, J. W. Ewan. It was seven years before they built Peacock Inn at Coconut Grove. Like other early houses, it was made of driftwood but boasted a porch, at first unscreened, and shingles of white pine from the foremast of a wrecked brig, hand made with an old-fashioned froe.

President Grover Cleveland and his bride came on the steamer Rockledge to Jupiter in 1886. The 150-foot side wheeler was built in 1859. After its boilers were condemned in the late 1880s, it served as a hotel at Jupiter until 1893. Then it was towed to Lake Worth to serve as a dormitory for Henry Flagler's carpenters; later it was bought by Captain Vail and served the same purpose in Miami; it finally became a gambling house and bordello, and in 1913 was towed out to sea and scuttled.

Five Houses of Refuge like this were built in 1874 along the east coast by the federal government to shelter shipwreck survivors. Only this one, Gilbert's Bar in Martin County, still exists.

Room and board cost $10 a week, and gourmets agreed that the food was "surpassing." Guests could rent sailboats for $2 a day.

Peacock Inn flourished from the start, and two two-story annexes soon were built. Two dressing rooms stood at water's edge, for guests who wanted to swim in the surf.

This vacation spot, wrote Muir, was in the hands of a few visitors daring enough to board the mail schooner *Flora* at Key West for a trip that might be only a day's run in a good wind, but could take a week if the wind failed.

Ralph Middleton (Commodore) Munroe, number one tourist, reactivated the dormant Coconut Grove post office name. The mail schooner began coming every week instead of twice a month, and it was no longer necessary "to sail up the bay (to Miami) on the odd chance Miss Alice Brickell would be in a mood for handing out mail," wrote Muir.

Several titled Europeans were among Peacock Inn's early visitors. Serving tea was a pleasant afternoon ritual, while dinner was ceremonious and unhurried. Isabella Peacock, later to be known as Aunt Bella, often wore a crinkling taffeta gown for dress-up occasions; the ladies dressed for dinner and took pains with their hair.

After dinner the ladies sat demurely on the porch, which they called the veranda, while the men "repaired to the rustic rockers in the small smoking room off the newly-screened dining porch, lit their pipes and Cuban cigars as a prelude to discussing the affairs of the world."

Visitors to Peacock Inn were not without medical help, as the Bay people had been in earlier days. A lady doctor named Eleanor Galt Simmons now practiced her profession by sailboat and pony.

Julia Sturtevant was married at eighteen to Frederick L. Tuttle, and they settled down in an elegant home in Cleveland, Ohio. A son and a daughter were born. Fred contracted tuberculosis, and Julia learned to manage his ironworks business when he was unable to do so. She found that she liked the business world, and was liked and admired by her male associates. "Julia could say no with a smile," noted Muir.

As early as 1873, Julia Tuttle brought her children to Miami to visit her parents, and explored the region, together with the Duke of Dade. After Tuttle's death she came south again for a Winter visit.

When Sturtevant died, Julia inherited his property. Soon she returned to the Bay and began

The Fort Pierce Hotel and Annex at Fort Pierce. The original building had broad verandas on the first and second floors, and a smaller balcony on the third. It is seen here in 1901.

Central Arms at Fort Lauderdale, advertised as a "tourist home," was the forerunner of Fort Lauderdale's glamorous hotels of a later era. Central Arms was built in 1911 in the 600 block of North Andrews Avenue. It was originally known as Progresso Inn, then Overlook Apartments, then Central Arms. Eventually it was moved to the intersection of U. S. Highway 1 and Southeast Second Street.

The Palms Hotel at West Palm Beach, shown here in a postcard view in the 1890s, was described as "a homelike hotel fronting on Lake Worth and vis-a-vis with the Royal Poinciana."

buying land on her own. In addition to knowing a deal when she saw one, the smiling Julia had fallen upon a dream, the kind that involved true vision, wrote Muir.

"Like English, when she looked at the wilderness along the mangrove-lined Miami River she saw a thriving city, and when she turned her eyes to the wild beauty of the mouth of the river where it poured into the broad, shining bay, she did not see the full-grown coconuts planted in the forties by the youthful Emanuel Acosta, a deserter from the Spanish Navy; she saw instead a hotel."

Julia, the cool businesswoman, made a point of becoming acquainted with James E. Ingraham before moving to Florida and finalizing her deal with the Biscayne Bay Company for the acreage she bought. The company was glad to unload that north bank property.

Ingraham was one of Henry Plant's lieutenants at that time, but was soon to become a key man in the Henry Flagler organization.

In the Fall of 1891 Julia, her family and belongings were floated on a barge into the bay. The party included a housekeeper named Maggie Carney and two Jersey cows. Julia moved the cows into the old Fort Dallas barracks while she and her family occupied the former officers' quarters, all located on the old Egan tract on the north bank.

From the start, her intention was to bring the railroad to the mouth of the Miami River.

She wrote to Henry Flagler, then considering the extension of his railroad southward to Palm Beach, and offered him half of her 640 acres in exchange for a railroad to Miami. His reply was non-committal. A personal visit likewise failed. Julia never gave up hope; she consulted with the Brickells, who agreed to join her in giving land to Flagler in return for the railroad.

Lake Park Hotel at West Palm Beach was on Banyan (later First) Street. The avenue once was known as Whiskey Street because of saloons in the area. In 1918 the Lake Park was owned by J. M. Pearce and managed by Frank Hirsch.

But it remained for Nature to accomplish what cupidity could not—and that by way of a disaster that none could have wished for. The Winter of 1894-95 brought killing cold to almost all of Florida—first in December, again in early February.

Groves were wiped out; many families went broke.

Flagler, his railroad's welfare tied up with the growers', moved immediately to help in such ways as distributing free seeds, crates and fertilizer, and making personal loans. He sent Ingraham out to inspect the damage.

"It was complete and Ingraham's heart sank as he made the tour," wrote Muir, "until he reached the Bay region. At Lemon City he found fruit trees untouched by the killing frost. He stopped by to see Julia Tuttle, and she was ready for him."

Restating her offer of land in return for the railroad, she handed Ingraham a small box to be taken to Flagler. Inside, on a bed of moist cotton, were fragrant orange blossoms, unharmed by frost.

Flagler acted immediately. He went south by boat and carriage, sent his compliments to Mrs. Tuttle and continued down the Bay to have lunch at Peacock Inn. He praised the food, visited the people there, and admired the royal palms at Commodore Munroe's estate, the Barnacle.

Then he had his fateful meeting with Julia Tuttle, and modern Miami was born. He agreed not only to build the railroad but also to build a hotel, clear the streets, construct a light plant and make other improvements.

He made one mistake, however, which millions would live to regret; convinced that Miami would be only a fishing village for his hotel guests, he had the surveyors lay out narrow streets, despite protests from Julia Tuttle and the Brickells.

In March, 1895, John Sewell arrived in Miami with a crew of workmen sent by Flagler to clear the streets in earnest. Sewell found accommodations at Captain Vail's Floating Hotel, just docked there.

E. E. Vail had retired as a ship's captain and built the St. Augustine Hotel in that town; the hotel had brought him a handsome income until it burned a few months earlier. He then bought the steamer *Rockledge*, one of the first steamboats on the Indian River, and made her his Floating Hotel in order to recoup his losses.

Fort Dallas had become the home of Julia Sturtevant Tuttle and her family when this picture was taken, about 1897. At center, the former officers' quarters had become the Tuttle residence. Barracks for the troops, at right, had been converted to a barn.

Built in March, 1896, by Julia Tuttle as a dormitory for workmen, this sprawling building was soon improved to become the Miami Hotel.

The second hotel to be built in the Biscayne Bay area was the Bay View Hotel at Lemon City, shown here about 1900. It was constructed by Cornelia Keys in 1892 and was moved by barge to Miami in 1899, according to Thelma Peters' "Lemon City: Pioneering on Bicayne Bay, 1850-1925."

"The men flocked to its barber shop in such droves it became necessary to make an appointment," wrote Muir. The Floating Hotel was filled within a week.

"The stake-pounding and the sawing and the sweating increased and now there were stores, Lummus', and Sewell Brothers shoe store in the rear of the Miami Hotel, and Budge's hardware store." Young Dr. James M. Jackson, son of a Bronson doctor and grove owner, was sent for to serve as house physician for the still-unbuilt hotel and to begin practice in the new town.

The railroad reached Miami on April 15, 1896. Three hundred people, gathered for the event, cheered.

The ancient hammock land along the Bay was being uprooted to make way for the Royal Palm Hotel, still in the blueprint stage while future guests chose rooms from the architect's sketches, according to Muir.

"One hundred Negro laborers, led by John Sewell, advanced into the jungle to make a smooth green lawn for the Rockefellers and the Goulds, the Vanderbilts and the Duke of Manchester. Black men marched in a V formation, black men from the Bahamas and from Georgia and Alabama, the first bunch carrying bush hooks, the next axes and the next grubbing hoes. The jungle fought back. Fumes from the poisonous manchineel tree sent men falling to their knees, heads reeling, faces swelling in the hot sun. They learned to destroy the manchineel with fire. Next the ironwood broke ax after ax until the dynamite was brought in. Then the boom-boom rang out steadily, a new accompaniment to the staccato hammering and the laughing and the bargaining."

The mosquitoes and sand flies were fierce.

At one corner of the Royal Palm site, Sewell and his workmen found a historic Tequesta Indian mound, where that long-ago tribe had buried its dead. The laborers filled six barrels with human bones, which were reburied elsewhere. They also unearthed a number of copper bowls, which were taken by the workmen as souvenirs.

Hundreds of men worked on the Royal Palm, said to be "modern colonial," wrote Muir. Thirty worked daily on the grounds alone. The dining room was to seat 500 people, and there would be another for maids and children; also a ballroom fifty feet long, a billiard room, and a swimming pool with a casino containing one hundred dressing rooms.

These casinos were standard adjuncts to the grand American plan hotels at the turn of the century. In a few instances, such as Bradley's Beach Club at Palm Beach, they were for gambling, offering roulette, chemin de fer and the like; generally, however, they were built to provide legitimate entertainment for the hotel guests, such as swimming facilities (dressing rooms for surf bathers, indoor pools), bowling, therapeutic baths, and sometimes a ballroom if there was none in the adjacent hotel. At least one, the Tampa Bay, had also a theater where live stage shows were presented.

Workmen on the Royal Palm "lived where they could," wrote Thelma Peters in an article on the hotel entitled "Pomp and Circumstance—The Royal Palm Hotel," which appeared in the April,

Workmen directed by John Sewell (in vest and shirtsleeves) broke ground for Flagler's Royal Palm Hotel on March 15, 1896. The Tequesta Indian mound in the background was leveled.

1975, issue of *Update,* the bi-monthly publication of the Historical Association of Southern Florida. The workmen's quarters might be palmetto-thatched A-frames, tents or shacks, or the dormitory-like Miami Hotel.

The women of Miami planned to celebrate Christmas, 1896, with a big community party in the casino of the Miami Hotel for the city's 155 white children of school age. This hotel was an impressive three-story structure which not only had "800 feet of broad piazza" but also was awaiting an order of carpeting for the entire building.

Early that Christmas morning, however, three blocks of the new wooden town—twenty-eight buildings—were wiped out by fire. A hose from the Miami Hotel was used to keep it from spreading further. A week later, Harry Tuttle and Tom Decker were hosts to one hundred guests who gathered at that hotel to usher in the year 1897.

The Royal Palm, completed in mid-January, measured 680 by 267 feet and had five stories, except for the rotunda, which had six, wrote Peters. "Above the rotunda was a lookout platform where every visitor of any consequence went to look at the ocean to the east and the mysterious Everglades to the west." The clapboard exterior was painted yellow with white trim, the roof red.

In addition to the main dining room and the one for guests' children and maids, the hotel had another for white hotel staff and still another for black hotel staff. Guest bedrooms numbered about 350 and another hundred took care of guests' maids and hotel staff. There were about 200 bathrooms.

An unusual feature of the hotel was a free-standing roofed veranda 578 feet long and eighteen feet wide, wrote Peters, which went around the eastern wing of the hotel connecting the north and south porticos. Situated thirty feet from the walls of the building, it served as a popular promenade where one could see and be seen. The rocking chair brigade usually congregated on the sunny south portico.

The hotel opened officially on January 16, 1897. The event was celebrated the following night when forty townspeople joined hotel guests in the spacious dining room resplendent with flowers, gleaming silver and fine linen. The gourmet dinner began with green turtle soup and ended with tutti-frutti ice cream. The assemblage moved into the rotunda after dinner and listened as the Royal Palm orchestra played such favorites of the day as "My Old Kentucky Home."

The Royal Palm Casino contained the swimming pool, which was forty by 150 feet, with water from the bay continuously flowing through it. Hotel guests paid a quarter to swim, but townspeople could swim for fifteen cents from seven to ten o'clock at night and out of season. The hotel's official photographer, J. N. Chamberlain, also had his studio in the casino.

"During its heyday the Royal Palm was host to some of the richest and most famous people in the world," wrote Peters. "The finest private steam yachts tied up at the hotel docks, and the greatest artists were brought to give concerts in the hotel ballroom. Since there was no air-conditioning and windows had to be open on warm nights, many townspeople made their first acquaintance with classical music standing among the crotons outside the windows—a custom not forbidden by the management."

At this time the Royal Palm cost $6 a day and up, the Miami $2.

For about twenty years before the land boom of the 1920s, an interesting place which received Winter guests at Coconut Grove was a rustic, exclusive group of a dozen cottages known as Camp Biscayne. Promoted by Commodore Munroe, it was the successor to Peacock Inn, according to an article by Jean C. Taylor entitled "Camp Biscayne," published in *Update* (February, 1978). In addition to the guest cottages, the camp had a central dining room and kitchen, also a library cottage and a laundry building. Numbered among its guests were several admirals and Henry R. Mallory of Mallory Steamship Lines.

Other hotels in Miami in 1904, as listed in the City Directory, were the San Carlos (G. A. Muller), Biscayne and Halcyon Hall (S. Graham), Everglades (under construction, R. S. Flanagan), Bay View (D. M. Conolly), Pioneer (E. A. Forsell), and Arcade (Mrs. Sybil Jenkins).

Also listed in 1904 were the LaBree House (Loretta LaBree), Hinson House (Jane E. Hinson), and March Villa (Mrs. W. E. March).

Peacock Inn was still active at Coconut Grove, advertised as a "rendezvous for sportsmen and yachtsmen, rather than a fashionable resort hotel." At Cutler, fifteen miles south of Miami, was Richmond Cottage, operated by Mrs. S. H. Richmond, offering fine fishing and boating.

When the railroad reached Miami, Charles H. Lum brought his wife from the home he had built for her in 1886 on the lonely peninsula that later would become Miami Beach, and they spent several weeks at the boarding house run by Mrs. Ed Chase. When the bill reached $80, Muir related, Lum asked Mrs. Chase if she would accept ten acres of Miami Beach land instead of cash.

"Land sakes," Mrs. Chase said crossly, "what in

Canoes, rowboats and sailboats were available for guests at Port Sewall's Sunrise Inn. In 1940 it offered accommodations for one hundred guests.

the world would I do with all that swamp land?"

John S. Collins had faith in that swamp land, bought 1,670 acres of it even before the trains came, and was joined by a son-in-law, Thomas J. Pancoast. They decided to build a bridge to the mainland in order to open up their real estate—almost five miles on the Atlantic and another mile along Biscayne Bay—and made a start, using about $100,000 of their own money. Then came the legendary Carl Graham Fisher, age forty, dynamic, and possessed of a solid fortune. These men, together with the Lummus brothers, J. E. and J. N., converted the mangrove swamp, "so thick a man could not get through without an ax to cut his way," as J. N. said, into some of the most valuable real estate in the world.

The Collins bridge opened on June 12, 1913. "A parade of automobiles, horse-drawn carriages, bicycles and baby carts moved over the rattling boards, many of which had not yet been nailed down," wrote Muir. "Nobody stayed at home. It was an event comparable to the puffing of the first railroad train seventeen years earlier."

Six million yards of white soil was dredged from the bottom of the bay and spread over the newly-cleared peninsula. The owners promptly planted grass and tropical shrubs—hibiscus, oleander and bougainvillea—in topsoil brought by barge from the Everglades, and in a matter of months the jungle had become a cultivated garden spot. Hardie's Casino, with its windswept ballroom, locker rooms and swim suits for rent at twenty-five cents, provided a setting for all-day family parties, when elaborate picnic luncheons were spread on the long benches overlooking the ocean.

Off to the west and south George Edgar Merrick, who came to the Biscayne country with his parents at the age of twelve, dreamed of a city of his own. Like his parents' home, which was built from native stone and had a gabled roof, it was to be known as Coral Gables. As a boy, Merrick had delivered vegetables and fruit from the Solomon Merrick grove to the back doors of the Royal Palm Hotel and Lummus grocery store.

James Deering, of International Harvester Company fame, who came to the bay country to pursue a more leisurely life, occupied his time with building the $8,000,000 Venetian *palazzo* which he called Vizcaya, two miles south of Miami.

Commodore Arthur Curtis James, of railroad fame and fortune, came south and built a hunting lodge, which he called Four-Way Lodge, farther south at Coconut Grove.

Then came World War I. At Miami Beach, Glenn Curtiss began training aviators on a strip of land near the bay—a novel notion, Miamians thought. A Naval aviation base was established at Coconut Grove, and Miami matrons outdid themselves in entertaining the servicemen who poured into the city.

A county causeway from the mainland to Miami Beach was built and opened on January 1, 1920. Carl Fisher built the Flamingo Hotel in the new beach city at a cost of $1,500,000, and engaged in flamboyant publicity stunts. He imported crack polo players and later built the King Cole Hotel to house the polo playing set.

"Miami Beach, tailored for the tourist, boasted 644 residents in 1920," wrote Muir. "That was the

The Hotel Florida at Lake Worth was built in 1913 as a fifteen-room inn. By 1924 (as seen here) it had been enlarged to include fifty rooms. Joseph H. Elliott was owner and manager.

year land began to move." By 1921, five hotels were in operation—the Wofford, Pancoast, Breakers, and Fisher's two, the Flamingo and the Lincoln.

In Miami the land boom of the 1920s began, perhaps, with the sale of the first lot in Coral Gables on November 27, 1921. The boom reached its climax in 1925, the year in which 481 hotels and apartment houses were built.

Merrick imported gondolas manned by authentic gondoliers for Coral Gables Canal and, with John McEntee Bowman, began construction of the Miami Biltmore Hotel, with its Giralda tower, at an estimated cost of $10,000,000.

The Royal Palm weathered the boom very well, its decorous opulence "providing a note of substance in a world gone mad." The Flagler trustees declined an offer of $10,000,000 for it.

Among the new hotels was the Dallas Park, built on Julia Tuttle's homesite; the historic barracks were moved to Miami's Lummus Park. Harry Tuttle built the lavish Julia Tuttle Apartment Hotel, complete with a pipe organ in the lobby, at a cost of $1,500,000.

The fires which destroyed the Breakers and Palm Beach Hotels at Palm Beach were among the

Rustic surroundings emphasized the charm of Royal Palm Lodge, built in 1915 in Royal Palm State Park near Homestead as the residence of the park naturalist, Charles A. Mosier. It was eventually destroyed by fire.

events which combined to bring about a psychological dampening of enthusiasm for Florida. However, the Roney Plaza opened with fanfare. Among other hotels completed in 1926 were the Columbus, the Everglades, and the Floridian at Miami Beach.

"The music was as loud and the fun was as fast," wrote Muir, "but when it was over and the horse-racing season ended in March, it was as though someone had turned a master switch. The town was suddenly empty."

The boom was over.

Miami's hotels and apartments provided temporary shelter for many of the 47,000 persons left homeless after the hurricane of September, 1926.

When the Orange Blossom Special reached Miami over the newly-completed tracks of the Seaboard Air Line Railway in 1927, a big celebration was held at the Pancoast. Tea dances were given at the Flamingo.

In the Spring of 1927, in a room in Key West's La Concha Hotel, a young man named Juan Terry Trippe made plans to implement a government contract to carry air mail from Key West to Cuba, and announced that he would move his infant Pan American Airways to Miami.

When the next hurricane came, on September 16, 1928, Miami suffered only lightly, being on the edge of the storm. It took 1,836 lives, mainly in the Okeechobee area.

When in June, 1930, the Royal Palm Hotel was condemned as unsound, "even the less aware of Miami's citizens recognized that an era had come to a close," wrote Muir. "Ridden with termites, the one-time symbol of hope and riches to come had outlived its usefulness and must come down. The people came and took little and big pieces of it away. Something was going from the scene and everyone sensed it."

In 1933 Henry L. Doherty, a public utilities magnate, invested heavily in Florida properties, taking over the Miami Biltmore, the Roney Plaza, and the Alba at Palm Beach, which he renamed the Palm Beach Biltmore. He hired a publicity firm and tried in various ways to "burn Miami into the public mind." Newsmen were invited "to come and bask under a palm tree with lodging and free booze" provided. Lights at the Miami Biltmore blazed in all the rooms, including the many which were not occupied. Doherty operated aero-cars between the Roney and the Biltmore to accommodate his guests, also offered helicopter rides in the afternoon and vaudeville acts with dinner. A few celebrities of the day, such as Lily Pons, Doris Duke and Rudy Vallee, were usually present "to lend authenticity to the manufactured glamor."

During the years of World War II, eighty-five per cent of the Miami Beach hotels were taken over by the Army, becoming "ready-made if somewhat glorified barracks for future officers," wrote Muir.

The simple act of shifting from tourists to soldiers saved the government the vast expense plus the delay involved in building encampments. It was one of those beautifully simple plans that worked. Owners stripped their hotels of furbelows before leasing them to the Army, but even so one officer candidate wrote home, "Dear Mom: The Army has gone very swell."

George Merrick's dream hotel in Coral Gables, the towered Miami Biltmore, became a huge veterans' hospital.

The skeleton frame of the unfinished boom-time Roosevelt Hotel was completed to become a twenty-four-hour workshop for mechanical trainees in wartime crafts. This fifteen-story Lindsey Hopkins Vocational School was a striking symbol of the change that war had made in Miami.

"The multi-million tourist industry which built the twin cities of Miami and Miami Beach may find itself in a supporting role for leading industry," wrote Muir in 1953. "Business leaders point out it was no accident that a good portion of Europe's business has been transacted in Switzerland for the same reason: hotel and entertainment facilities.

"Visualize miles of modern shining hotels, every shade and shape of hotel, block after block of colored monuments to tourism, rimming the broad Atlantic, curving as the land curves, each a contained little world designed for fancy living."

European plan hotel rates (room only) at Miami Beach in the early 1950s ranged from about $45 a day for a double ocean-front room with its own small terrace during the Winter season—January 15 to March 15—to as little as $16 a day during September and October.

The elegant Cloister Inn at Boca Raton was perhaps the *pièce de résistance* in the improbable career of Addison Mizner—a self-acknowledged genius, author of what his critics called "Bastard-Pseudo-Spanish-Mizner" architecture along the south Atlantic coast of Florida, wrote Theodore Pratt in *The Story of Boca Raton.*

In partnership with Paris Singer, one of the wealthy sons of the sewing machine king, he used his architectural skills to change Palm Beach from a hotel society to a city of "million-dollar cottages" during the early 1920s.

Addison's memory of the Spanish castles and churches he had seen and studied during his boyhood in Central America and later in Spain was prodigious. He supplemented it with a huge collection of books on the subject, and made use of this accumulated knowledge to design and build, first, the grandiose Everglades Club on Worth Avenue, which was opened in 1919, according to the Junior League book on Palm Beach.

When the Everglades Club was unveiled, Addison's future as an architect in Palm Beach was assured, and during the next six years he built hundreds of elaborate homes. His object was to make both home and furnishings look antique—to create "deteriorated magnificence."

Palm Beach loved it.

The Mizner-Singer partnership came apart about the time Addison brought to Palm Beach his younger brother, Wilson, and put him in charge of his workshop. The two brothers made a great deal of money, which they used in 1925 and 1926 to promote their dream community on the coast to the south—Boca Raton.

Addison was dubbed by his publicists as "the Aladdin of Architects" and Boca Raton was "the Golden City of the Gold Coast"—which, Pratt suggested, may have been the original application of the term, the Gold Coast, to that section of Florida. There was to be a palm-lined canal, El Camino Real, flowing between proposed Mizner-built mansions, with gondolas and gondoliers to be imported from Venice. There were to be three golf courses, a giant cathedral, and on the beach, the largest hotel ever built.

One of the full-page newspaper advertisements began, "I am the greatest resort in the world—I am Boca Raton, Florida," and ended, "My future must be glorious. I have Addison Mizner to make it so."

In twenty-four weeks after the property went on the market, $26,000,000 worth of real estate in the dream city was sold—for as much as $40,000 per lot. That is, the down payments were made on that much property.

Then the real estate boom collapsed, the Mizners and their dream resort being among the heaviest losers. A few things were accomplished: twenty-four homes were built (in the section later called Floresta) in which the Mizners had planned to house their executives; the administration building (later used to house some of the hotel staff) was constructed, and the hotel, the Cloister Inn, described by Pratt as "one of the gem buildings of the United States and perhaps the world," was completed. It reflected all of Addison's talent and $1,250,000 of Mizner money.

The great gothic dining hall with its beautiful

peaked-arch ceiling was so tall that when it was later cut in half horizontally to form two levels, each was still generously large. Space was used lavishly in the Inn's construction, and there were windows everywhere.

Red tiled roofs rambled up and down, spreading comfortably in every direction as in Old World buildings which have been added to time and again.

The Cloister Inn was completed in January, 1926, and formally opened on February 6 under Ritz-Carlton management. All that Winter it was host to many of the most famous people of that era. By the end of 1926, though, the party was over—

The magnificent Boca Raton Hotel and Club evolved from the one-hundred-room Cloister Inn, created in 1925 by Addison Mizner. Opened in January, 1926, it suffered from the collapse of the boom and was closed in 1928. Later owners expanded it enormously, while preserving the Old World atmosphere of Mizner's architecture.

Wood beams, trailing vines, an elaborate chandelier, and a circular marble table with wrought-iron legs combined to emphasize the elegance of the loggia of the Cloister Inn.

The mouth of the Miami River, as the river flows into Biscayne Bay, is seen in this turn-of-the-century photo. The Royal Palm Hotel is at left, Brickell Point at right.

for the Cloister Inn, for the dream city of Boca Raton, for most Florida boom-time promotions. The doors of the hotel were closed, and it passed into the hands of creditors. It was open sporadically until 1928.

In that year it was purchased, along with other Boca Raton properties, by Clarence H. Geist, who set out to make the Cloister Inn a part of "the most palatial private club ever known anywhere in the world," wrote Pratt. Using the Inn as a nucleus, he spent $8,000,000 making the building four times its original size, largely preserving the style of the original structure.

In 1942, the Army took over, moved the millionaires out, and used the building for two years to house Air Corps trainees.

J. Myer Schine purchased the complex from the Army in 1944 (for $3,000,000), and its period of modern elegance as a hotel began. Three years later, Pratt wrote: "If you were looking for the most prodigal public spot on the globe, there is little argument that you need go no farther than the Boca Raton."

In 1956 this plush paradise, with 1,000 acres of land surrounding it, was bought for $22,500,000—$17,500,000 more than the United States paid Spain for all of Florida in 1821—by Arthur Vining Davis, aluminum magnate. He could afford it; his fortune was then estimated at $350,000,000. Sensing that Florida was "about to boom big again," wrote Pratt, Davis spent $70,000,000 in south Florida investments within a year, including banks, cattle, an airline, and a dozen other properties.

Davis later organized the Arvida Corporation, which in 1958 acquired most of his holdings in south Florida, including the Boca Raton Hotel and Club, as the complex became known. Great enlargements and improvements have been made to the Boca, and to other Arvida properties in the city, all with sensitivity to Nature's environment, according to Henry Kinney in *Once Upon a Time.*

Thanks to Geist, Schine and Davis, Boca Raton became all that Addison Mizner dreamed it would be—and more. The tiny one-hundred-room Cloister Inn pointed the way.

This is the nucleus of the modern Driftwood Inn at Vero Beach. This charming segment was built in 1932 by Waldo Sexton from bleached driftwood and lumber from a demolished barn without architect's plans. He gave oral instructions to carpenters on the spot.

Shown about 1914 is the Over Sea Hotel at Key West, which could receive as many as one hundred visitors.

Stark whiteness of the La Concha Hotel at Key West reflects the tropical sunlight. In 1940 it offered accommodations for 127 guests. In 1980 it is vacant; it has been purchased by a hotel chain and is scheduled for restoration.

A planned agricultural development near Vero Beach, pioneered in 1912 by the Indian River Farms Company and promoted in the Midwest, brought about establishment of the Sleepy-Eye Lodge at Vero Beach, according to "Florida's Golden Sands." A demonstration farm was conducted near the town, and prospective buyers were housed in the lodge. Waldo E. Sexton, who was to build the unique Driftwood Inn at Vero Beach, began his career as a salesman for this company.

Architecture of the 1920s characterized the Hotel Del Mar, also at Vero Beach. A product of the land boom, it was razed in 1962, according to John Schumann, Jr. The site is now a landscaped parking lot.

Patio of the magnificent Breakers Hotel (present-day) at Palm Beach.

The Amphitrite, Fort Lauderdale's floating hotel from 1931 to 1942. A five-piece orchestra played for dancing at night. The Amphitrite advertised "Complete dinner from 85 cents."

One of south Florida's most luxurious 20th Century hostelries was the Hollywood Beach Hotel in Hollywood, built in 1924, seen here in the 1950s. In 1971, after a year or so of dormancy, the hotel became the home of Florida Bible College. In 1980 the building changed hands again, and is to be converted once more to a hotel-condominium, according to Reverend Graham Bell, director of admissions for Florida Bible College. The college will be relocated.

Another lavish hotel in Hollywood, the Park View, pictured in the 1920s.

Verano Hotel at West Palm Beach, "where Summer spends Winter," its promoters proclaimed. Seen here in the 1920s, hotel later became the George Washington.

Seen from Lake Worth is the Hotel Salt Air at West Palm Beach. Pictured here in 1925, it was located at the southeast corner of Datura and Narcissus Streets, later the site of a Holiday Inn.

Growth of the hotel industry in Fort Lauderdale is lustrated by these photos. Left center, Osceola Inn, 19 Upper left, Las Olas Inn, upper right, Hotel Maryla and right center, the New Tarpon Hotel, all three seen the 1920s. Lower right, Governor's Club Hotel at the c ner of Las Olas and Southeast First Avenue, 1930. Low left, Lauderdale Beach Hotel, facing the Atlantic, seen the 1950s.

Four views of the prestigious Royal Palm Hotel at Miami, at the turn of the century. This photo shows the impressive sweep of the five-story hotel, with a six-story center section.

A popular promenade. Boats arrived daily at this landing loaded with fish.

Guests take their ease or chat with acquaintances on the sunny, pillared veranda.

The hotel pool.

Soaring above its surroundings, the Miami Biltnore Hotel at Coral Gables was a landmark of oomtime opulence. Left: Tea dances were popular n 1926. Top right: the Miami Biltmore Country 'lub, an adjunct to the hotel. Its golf course is still in se. Both buildings are owned by the city of Coral 'ables, and several civic uses of them are being onsidered. Center right: the ballroom. Lower ight: This bus transported guests to the Miami 'iltmore Country Club from the Casa Loma Hotel also in Coral Gables) as a courtesy car, or (for 50 ents) a service car.

Some of Miami's early hotels: the Fort Dallas Hotel at Avenue C and 13th Street (upper left); the Hotel Biscayne (upper right); the San Carlos Hotel and Annex (center); the turreted Halcyon Hall, designed by Stanford White (lower left); the Hotel Vereen at 313-315 North Miami Avenue (lower right).

Eight skyscraper Miami hotels, pictured in the 1920s and 1930s. Clockwise from top left: Henrietta Towers, divided by air shafts into four structures; the Cortez Hotel, with ornate window treatment on the top floor; the Ponce de Leon Hotel, hooded with awnings; the Everglades Hotel on Biscayne Boulevard, surmounted by an exotic tower; the Robert Clay Hotel; the Venetian Hotel, overlooking Biscayne Bay; the Hotel Patricia, and the McAllister.

Some Miami hotels of the 1940-50 era: looking up Collins Avenue, the Sans Souci, 3101 Collins; the Saxony, 3201, and the Versailles, 3425.

Another Biscayne Hotel, of much later vintage than the shown on page 170.

"Where the river meets the bay" was the advertisi slogan of the Granada Hotel.

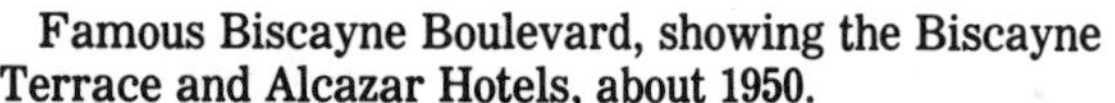

Famous Biscayne Boulevard, showing the Biscayne Terrace and Alcazar Hotels, about 1950.

The 1920s catapulted Miami Beach into becoming one of the world's great playgrounds, and the area's hotel industry mushroomed. Top left, the Mare Grande Hotel; top right, the Floridian, on the Bayfront; middle left, the Lincoln Plaza; middle right, the elegant reception room of the Nautilus Hotel; lower left, the Belvedere; lower right, the Ambassador.

More Miami Beach hotels of the 1920s and 1930s. Top ro
Hotel Monterey (left) and Biscayne Plaza. Second row: t
Miami Beach Hotel, with distinctive striped awnings, and t
Hotel Rex. Third row: the Biscayne-Collins Hotel, and t
beachside Strath-Haven. Bottom: Essex House, gracefu
rounding the corner of Tenth Street and Collins. Several
these hotels typify the much-ornamented architectural st
of the 1920s, designated as Art Deco. The Essex illustrat
the streamlined style of the 1930s.

The stately Roney Plaza Hotel, the Grand Dame of Miami Beach in the late 1920s and 1930s. Newton B. T. Roney personally greeted many of his guests. For years, Walter Winchell was prince regent at the Roney. It was one of the first—in the 1950s—to offer television in every room. The hotel was razed about 1970, and the site is now occupied by Roney Plaza Apartments and other structures.

Palm trees and striped umbrellas partly shaded the many who attended a tea dance in the Oriental Tea Garden of the Flamingo Hotel at Miami Beach on March 17, 1923.

Hotels on Miami Beach, 1954. The view is north from just above the Roney Plaza. On the ocean side, just above the center of this picture, is the towered Pancoast Hotel with grounds in front—once called the most exclusive hotel in America, according to Dr. Thelma Peters of Coral Gables. The Fontainebleau is not in this picture—it was built later that year in the patch of trees between the beach and Indian Creek at the top of the picture.

Appendix

These promotional statements of general information about hotels along the route of the Florida East Coast Railway appeared in a booklet on that subject published by the FEC in 1901.

The latest and most popular of out-door sport to find a home at the Florida East Coast resorts was the ancient and royal game of Golf. As to this exhilarating and health-giving recreation the wishes of tourists were anticipated, for in 1897 links were laid out at St. Augustine, Palm Beach and Ormond. One year later, links were added to the attractions of Miami and Nassau. Thousands of dollars were spent in making this system of links the best in the South, and the venture has proved a tremendous success.

The tournaments held last Winter were well attended, and at some of the events there were as many as eighty entries for the preliminary rounds. In the annual games that followed on the northern links in the Spring the advantage of the Winter's play proved wonderfully effective.

Should a visitor wish to remain but one day at the resort at which links have been established, he can obtain a membership card for that day. Should he hold a card for a longer period, the card obtained at one place is good for membership on each and all of the links under control of the Florida East Coast Hotel Company. A lover of golf can land at the station with his clubs and start play half an hour afterward if he chooses.

St. Augustine

Hotel Ponce de Leon: Open during January, February, March and April. Robert Murray, manager.

Hotel Alcazar: Open November to May. Joseph P. Greaves, manager. Connected by indoor passage with the new Hydro-Therapeutic Baths.

Hotel Cordova: Open November to May. Suites, three to ten rooms each, furnished or unfurnished, for housekeeping or not, as desired.

The Hydro-Therapeutic Baths: Open December to April, inclusive. The finest baths in the world. The only baths in the United States whose patients can have all Winter, from December to May, every day, out-door air and sunshine, and enjoy with their families the life of a great Winter resort. Treatment under the supervision of a skilled medical attendant.

Hot and cold Saline and Hydro-Electrical Baths for rheumatism, gout, and all nervous diseases. Complete Electrical Baths, Static, Sensorial, Galvano-Faradic currents with Hydro-Electrical Douche. Massage in all its branches by graduates.

The Schott system for heart disease.

The Nauheim Baths.

The famous Hydroiodided Mineral Water from Clarendon Springs, Vermont, will be the drinking water furnished the patrons of the Baths. After a long series of experimental tests, this water, which is scientifically bottled at the spring, so that its gases and other evaporating but efficacious properties are retained, is selected, as it produces throughout the digestive tract, and in anemia, kidney and liver disorders, obesity and cutaneous affections, the most advantageous effects.

The Casino: Open November to May. Entertainments, dancing, theatricals, concerts, cake walks, semi-saline swimming pool, bowling, billiards, tennis, bicycles, and bicycle riding academy.

Furnished Cottages: Delightfully located and of different sizes, for rent for the Winter season, October or later to May or June.

Fresh Milk: A dairy of registered Jerseys is owned and controlled by the Florida East Coast Hotel Company so that guests and children in the St. Augustine hotels and cottages may be supplied with milk equal to the best obtainable at the North.

Golf: Links open December to May 1. While northern links are snowbound, frozen or muddy, the links of the Florida East Coast Golf Club are in prime condition.

New Club House.

Links on which were held the Winter championships of 1898, 1899, 1900. Elegant condition from constant work throughout the Summer.

Drives and Bicycle Paths: Many miles have been added to those on the peninsula, on the mainland and on Anastasia Island.

Launches and Sailboats: St. Augustine still holds its own as the ideal spot for sailing parties.

Schools: Accommodations for children, with competent instructors in kindergarten as well as higher branches.

Miami

Hotel Royal Palm: Open during January, February, March and April. H. W. Merrill, manager. Tropical gardens enlarged and improved. Special bachelor accommodations with shower baths, etc., added.

Swimming Pool: Salt-water, open-air swimming pool, and hot and cold salt-water tub baths.

House Boats and Fishing: Specially located for bone and tarpon fishing. Fitted for fish dinners and luncheon parties.

Golf: Finest links in the South, covering seventy acres of tropical prairie. Club house; lockers; professional instructor.

Ormond

Hotel Ormond: Open during January, February, March and April. Anderson & Price, Managers. Enlarged, remodeled, rearranged; 130 new bath room suites; new dining room and kitchen; electric lights throughout; electric elevators.

Beach Pavilion: Midwinter ocean bathing; dressing rooms for bathers.

The Tomoka River: New 12-knot Daimler Launch, capacity for 150 passengers, making round trip daily between 3 and 10 o'clock p. m. Wonderful day and night scenery without having to be out all night. The Oklawaha of the east coast.

Golf: Links will be in elegant condition from continuous work throughout the Summer.

Bicycle Paths: New paths laid out, old paths extended and repaired. Lockers arranged in beach pavilion for beach bicyclists.

Drives: Livery enlarged and improved. Number of drives increased. The most beautiful and typical Florida drives in the South, through the palms and palmettos, moss and dense foliage.

Launches, Canoes and Sailboats: The Halifax River is an ideal spot for all these excursions, and boats of all kinds are moored in front of the hotel.

Palace electric launches, fitted with searchlight for night trips and fishing, made by the Electric Boat Company, New York.

Palm Beach

Hotel Royal Poinciana: Open during January, February, March and April. Fred Sterry, manager. Enlarged and rearranged. Now the largest hotel in the world.

Golf, Gun Club and other Sports. Links will be even better than last year.

Salt-Water Swimming Pool: And midwinter ocean bathing in the surf. Hot and cold salt-water baths.

House Boats and Fishing: For fishing parties, and fish dinner or luncheon parties.

Bicycle Paths and Walks: New trails. Old ones cut and widened. Cycle chair livery very much enlarged and improved.

Alligator Farm: Very interesting feature at end of cycle chair ride through the jungle trail.

To the Sportsman

Hunting all along the East Coast is good. Quail, pigeon, snipe and small game are abundant near the railway; but larger game is more shy and must be hunted in localities less thickly settled. Snipe are more plentiful south of New Smyrna, particularly near Titusville, on what is known as the Indian River prairie. Water and shore birds, such as ducks, plover and the crane species, are found everywhere. Deer and wild turkeys are numerous a short distance from the towns and settlements.

Florida is one of the most celebrated states in the Union for fishing as well as hunting, and no part of the state can equal the east coast, particularly the lower section. Tarpon feed as far north as New Smyrna, but are only taken in large numbers from the St. Lucie River, near Fort Pierce, Palm Beach, Lake Worth Inlet and the inlet to Biscayne Bay. These waters are warm and tarpon and other large fish come inside to feed. Kingfish and jewfish, often weighing 200 to 300 pounds, and other large varieties are abundant about Jupiter Light and southward, through the Florida Keys.

The fish of commerce are the mullet, mackerel, cavalia and a few other varieties. Nothing is more interesting to a tourist than a day's outing with a crew of professional fishermen.

Directories

Three directories of Florida hotels are offered on the following pages. A few known errors have been corrected, and probably there are others. However, the lists represent the best information available. In 1882 the newly-invented typewriter was still a novelty, and records were kept in longhand.

The first list was published in the 1883-84 edition of the **Florida State Gazetteer and Business Directory,** compiled and published by Monroe D. Cushing and T. J. Appleyard, Jacksonville, Florida, in 1882. The 1912 list came from **A Guide to Florida,** by Harrison Rhodes and Mary Wolfe Dumont, published by Dodd, Meade and Company, 1912.

Both of these purport to be all-inclusive. The third list, from **Cue's Guide to What to See and Do in Florida** by George W. Seaton, published in New York by Prentice-Hall in 1940, is only a selected list of hotels either known to the author personally or recommended from various sources. The omission of any hotel from this list is "in no sense to be considered derogatory," he asserted.

Note in the 1882 list, the now-obsolete use of abbreviated names, such as Geo. for George, Jno. for John, and Thos. for Thomas, for example.

FLORIDA HOTELS, 1882

Altoona—Altoona House, J. P. Miller; Jackson House, J. H. Jackson

..**Anclote**—DeLong House, W. N. Conoley; Mark's House, Gulf Coast Reserve Co.

Anthony Place—W. S. Hemingway

Apopka City—Morgan House, Mrs. P. Morgan.

Argyle—Mrs. A. McDonald

Astabula—Mrs. Ann Snyder

Baldwin—Mrs. E. Coy

Bartow—Mrs. G. E. Mann; W. T. Carpenter

Bay Port—Mrs. L. M. Garrison; J. W. Whisenant

Branford—Branford House, Coffee & Branard

Callahan—Booth & Booth; John O'Donald

Campbelltown—I. W. Calloway

Carrabelle—Hall & Kelley

Cedar Keys—O. Bettelini; Gulf House, Capt. Parker; Magnolia House, T. L. Carter; Prevatte House, J. A. Erickson; Suwannee Hotel, Dr. McIlwaine

Chipley—D. J. Williams.

Citra—Citra House, Mrs. Park

City Point—Mrs. W. H. Sharp

Clear Water Harbor—Orange Bluff Hotel, M. C. Dwight

Cove Bend—J. M. Baker

Crescent City—Lakeside House, ——— Harlow; Putnam House, M. M. Potter

Darbyville—McClenny & Co.

DeLand—DeLand Grove House, J. Minot; Seaman House, A. Seaman

Dunedin—J. H. Gunn

Enterprise—Brantley House, A. Harold; Brock House

Eustis—Henderson House, H. W. Wood; Lake Eustis House, A. D. Key; Ocklawaha House, Edw. C. Gable

Fernandina—Egmont Hotel, G. W. Kettelle; Florida House, Mrs. A. Laddy; Mansion House, F. C. Shurer; Strathmore, W. H. Clay; Tourist's Hotel, W. H. Clay

Fort George—G. W. Gilbert

Fort Mason—Lake View Hotel, ——— Erman

Fort Meade—C. B. Lightsey

Fruitland—Fruitland House, J. A. Austin

Gainesville—Arlington House, J. B. Wistar

Glen St. Mary—Miss T. M. Tilton

Green Cove Springs—Clarendon Hotel, Harris & Applegate; Orange Cottage, Mrs. Walls; Riverview Hotel, Lucius Muchoberaz; St. Clair Hotel, Gluck & Rogers; Riverside Hotel, A. G. Morgan; The Pines, Bemis & Brazier

Gulf Hammock—Mrs. C. B. Wingate

Hawthorne—Tennessee House, W. S. Moore

Jacksonville—Fred. Bettelini; Carleton House, Stimpson & Devnell; Elmwood Hotel, Geo. A. Hoover; Grand View Hotel, G. W. Smith; Mattair House, Mrs. M. A. Mattair; Sledge House, Mrs. C. A. Sledge; St. Clair House, Mrs. P. Pratt; St. Marks Hotel, Fred. E. Foster; St. James Hotel, J. R. Campbell; St. Johns House, Mrs. E. Hudnall; Sunnyside Hotel, S. M. Hall & Co.; The Duval, McIver & Baker; The Everett, J. M. Lee; Tremont House, Mrs. A. R. Sweetser; Windsor Hotel, F. H. Orvis

John's Pass—Chas. Archer

Key West—Ranal & Zunsten; W. A. Russell

Kissimmee—Lake House, W. A. Patrick; Okeechobee House, J. B. Goff; Tropical Hotel, J. M. Mabbette; Tahopkabaga Hotel, Robert Bass

Lake City—J. F. Appell; Thrasher House, M. P. Thrasher

Lake de Funiak—John C. Garrett; A. P. Jones; Mrs. J. T. Waldo

Lake Jessup—Mrs. A. E. Howell

Lake Maitland—Bigelow Hotel; Park Hotel

Leesburg—Kentucky House, Mrs. Watts & Lanier; Leesburg Hotel, Jos. Miller; Milan House, J. B. Milan

Live Oak—Ethel House, John Fraser; Railroad House, Reuben Jones; Suwannee House, W. H. Slate

Lloyds—Mrs. L. W. Whitfield

Longwood—E. W. Hanck

Madison—Florida House, Mrs. S. M. Hankins; Froleigh House, Mrs. M. A. Froleigh

Magnolia—Magnolia Hotel, O. D. Seavey

Manatee—Gates House, Mrs. M. M. Gates

Mannville—R. J. Spence

Marianna—Marianna Hotel, T. E. Hearn; National Hotel, Mrs. Charlotte Pittman; Richardson House, Mrs. M. A. Richardson

Mayport—L. S. Burrows

Melrose—M. L. Lambkin

Micanopy—Knox House, Mrs. S. E. Knox; Jacob Winecoff

Milton—Santa Rosa Hotel, Jos. Ames; Eagle Hotel, E. H. Dixon

Molino—J. B. Vaughn

Monticello—Madden House, Mrs. Skipper

Mount Dora—B. M. Bruce; Madam Guller; Hotel Co.

New Smyrna—Ocean House, Frank W. Sams

Norwalk—Gove House, H. S. Gove

Orange City—Deyarman House, H. H. Deyarman

Orange Lake—Lake View House, W. P. Carr

Orange Park—Park View Hotel

Orlando—Central House, B. H. Derby; Luckey House, S. A. Luckey; Magnolia House, T. W. Shine; Palmetto House, C. & I. A. Claflin; Summerlin House, J. W. Loring

Palatka—Carleton House, Andrew Shelly; Graham's Hotel, S. Graham; Florida House, A. P. Carnova; Larkin House, Larkin & Allen; Putnam House, F. H. Orvis; St. Johns House, P. & H. Peterman; Westmoreland, Mrs. L. T. Wiley

Palma Sola—L. Y. Jenness

Pensacola—City Hotel, Edward Sexauer; Lindsay House, Mrs. Lindsay; Merchants Hotel, M. Kryger; St. Johns Hotel, Mrs. C. Pfefferle

Pinecastle—W. H. Macy

Port Orange—E. A. McDaniel

Quincy—Mrs. M. S. Zeigler

Rosewood—S. C. Corson

St. Augustine—Benedict House, Mrs. Hamilton; Florida House, G. L. Atkins; Edwards House, Mrs. John T. Edwards; Magnolia House, W. W. Palmer; Sunnyside Hotel, Mrs. Thos. F. House; St. Augustine Hotel, E. E. Vail

St. Lucie—Mrs. M. S. Jones

Sanford—Nolan House; Sirrine Hotel, Wm. Sirrine; Sanford House

Sanitaria—R. Fuller

San Mateo—Idlewild Hotel, A. Barrelle; Kirkland House, Jno. L. Le Salley

Snowville—Altamount Hotel Co.

South Lake Weir—O. H. Paddock

Spring Garden Center—Turner House, E. M. Turner

Starke—Kentucky House, J. R. Martin; Railroad House, J. Kleinschmidt

Sumterville—Hamilton House, J. R. G. Hamilton; Hamilton Hotel, Mrs. M. E. J. Hamilton

Tallahassee—City Hotel, W. P. Slusser; Leon Hotel, W. H. Howerton; St. James Hotel, G. A. Lamb

Tampa—Collins Hotel, Phil. H. Collins; Orange Grove Hotel, H. L. Crane; Isaac D. Craft

Tangerine—W. F. Redding

Titusville—Mrs. M. E. Titus

Volusia—Volusia Hotel, T. S. Pillsbury

Waldo—Sunnyside Hotel, Jennie Richards; Waldo House, Mrs. A. Lagara

White Springs—T. F. Wesson

Winter Park—A. E. Rogero

Yalaha—Eubanks House, Mrs. Eubanks

FLORIDA HOTELS, 1912
(With number of rooms or capacity, if listed)

Alachua—Sheffield Hotel, Mrs. J. Powell, 12; Transient House, J. M. Powell, not listed; Transient House, A. R. Griffin, 4.

Apalachicola—Franklin Hotel, C. H. Montgomery, 100; Fuller Hotel, S. Jenkins, 60.

Altamonte Springs—The Altamonte, F. M. Scheibley, 100.

Apopka—Apopka House, Mrs. W. K. Williford, 15.

Arcadia—Arcadia House, Mrs. A. Roe, 35; Southern Hotel, Mrs. S. J. Faulks, 20; Florida House, Mrs. S. Stewart, 20; Cottage Hotel, S. N. Harward, 20; DeSoto Hotel, M. S. Woodson, 50.

Archer—Magnolia House, S. Frie, 30.

Atlantic Beach—The Continental, H. E. Bemis, 250.

Avon Park—Hotel Verona, Dr. J. H. McCartney, 100.

Bartow—Hotel Oaks, H. M. Wear, 50; Wright House, J. C. Wright, 20; Bartow House, Mrs. J. H. Gardner, 25; Glen Oak, Mrs. I. L. McRory, 50; Orange Hotel, Mrs. N. Tillis, 50; Commercial Hotel, Mrs. Z. Towles, 25.

Bayard—Wings, Mrs. Wing, not listed.

Belleaire—Belleview, W. J. Fleming, 450.

Belleview—Boarding House, O. M. Gale, 12; Boarding House, R. C. Ridge, 10.

Boca Grande—Hotel Boca Grande, C. B. McCall, 25.

Bowling Green—Bowling Green Hotel, Mrs. D. Vestal, 30.

Boynton—Boynton Hotel, Boynton Hotel Co., 100; The Vera, Mrs. W. H. Funck, 15.

Bradentown—Wyman House, A. F. Wyman, 25; Manavista Hotel, Marven & Pearsons, 200; Le Chalet, John Holder, 25; The Oaks, Mrs. Morris, 15; Garr House, V. A. Garr, 30.

Buena Vista—Courley House, Mrs. Ida Courley, 25.

Captiva—Captiva House, C. Eyber & Son, 25.

Cedar Keys—Schlemer House, A. Schlemer, 20; White House, S. T. White, not listed.

Citra—Boarding House, W. A. Redditt, 6.

Clearwater—Verona Inn, Mrs. C. W. Joseph, 75; Sea View, T. Kamansky, 40; Sea Ora, Lewis Fitzgerald, 25; Phoenix, Misses Scranton, 50; Amspaugh Cottage, J. L. Amspaugh, 15; Clearwater Inn, Thos. Gladding, 50.

Clermont—Clermont Inn, Wm. Kern, 30.

Cocoa—Cocoa House, E. E. Grimes, 110; Cranbrook Cottage, Jane M. Smith, 20; Home Cottage, not listed, 15; Singleton Cottage, Mrs. G. S. Singleton, 10; Thomas Cottage, Mrs. M. A. Thomas, 20.

Cocoanut Grove—Camp Biscayne, R. M. Munroe, not listed.

Coleman—Coleman House, Mrs. R. L. Gowdy, 25.

Coronado Beach—Atlantic Hotel, T. B. Demaree, 75.

Crescent City—Grove Hall, W. C. Norton, 75; Sprague House, E. B. Coutant, 25; Turner House, Miss M. M. Turner, 30; The Southfield, S. A. Kinard, 35.

Cutler—Richmond Cottage, Mrs. S. H. Richmond, not listed.

Dade City—Woods' Tavern, I. A. Woods, 25; Embry House, W. E. Embry, 25; Osceola, Mrs. M. D. Cochran, 20.

Dania—Webb Hotel, F. W. Palmer, 20.

Daytona—The Austin, H. H. Manwiller, 100; Bennett House, A. H. & E. Lane, 85; Brown Cottages, J. G. Brown, not listed; City Hotel, J. C. D. Dohn, 20; The Cedars, Mrs. Wm. Jackson, 30; The Cleveland, Mrs. Sarah Austin, 20; Despland, L. M. Waite, 200; Fairview, Miss N. L. Lynch, 25; The Gables, S. H. Moseley, 30; The Glenn, Mrs. Glenn, 30; The Hamilton, J. M. Mabbette, 20; The Howard, J. C. Howard, 50; The Islington, Mrs. J. B. Parkinson, 50; Ivy Lane Inn, W. W. Foltz, not listed; Lyndhurst, R. W. & J. H. Ball, 40; Magnolia, Mrs. Celeste Hinks, 40; Myrtle, Chas. Kost, 35; Oaks, E. M. Sammis, 80; Orange Villa, Mrs. Clara Cass, not listed; Osborne House, Amelia Osborne, 20; Palmetto, C. O. Chamberlain, 100; Parkinson, Mrs. Montana S. Ludlow, 45; Pines, Mrs. J. B. Hinsky, 60; Prince George, Hilyard & Holroyd, 125; Prospect, P. J. Doyle, not listed; Ridgewood, E. D. Langworthy, 150; Rosedale, E. M. Brown, not listed; Saratoga Inn, John J. Maguire, 20; Schmidt's Villa, Henry Schmidt, 100; Stanley House, S. H. Moseley, not listed; Troy House, Mrs. Mary Troy, 50; Wayside Inn, W. W. Abercrombie, not listed; Western, J. S. Rainsford, not listed; Willmer, W. C. Branch, 30.

Daytona Beach—Daytona Beach Hotel, Thos. H. Keating, 60; Glenwood, E. F. Britton, 35; Lone Bay Inn, Mrs. Ichabod Dougherty, not listed; New Seaside Inn, H. F. Stewart, 125; Pinehurst, W. H. Freeman, 25; Van Valzah, J. A. Van Valzah, 60; White House, E. L. Howard, not listed.

DeLand—Boarding House, Mrs. Dunbar and Miss Dunn, 30; Carrollton Hotel, G. A. Dreka, 100; College Arms, I. T. Whitcomb, 125; Douglas House, Mrs. A. J. Sembler, 30; Hutchinson Hall, George Hutchinson, 25; LaVilla, Mrs. W. J. Austin, 25; McLeod's, Mrs. E. B. Smythe, 40; Melrose, Mrs. W. W. Alcott, 50; The Oaks, S. P. Hays, 50; Putnam Inn, B. E. Brown, 125; Sembler Cottage, Mrs. A. J. Sembler, not listed; The Sutherland, M. J. Bennett, 40; The Waverly, Mrs. Drake, 35; Winter Home, J. E. Cone, 25.

DeLeon Springs—DeSoto, F. O. Rudd, 50.

Delray—Ocean View, M. Bennett, 15; Sterling House, H. J. Sterling, 15.

Dunedin—Club House, M. N. Thomson, 100; Jordan Hotel, J. D. Jordan, 25.

Dunnellon—Dunnellon Hotel, Mrs. Jennie Smith, 35; Marion Hotel, Mrs. L. Buse, 35; Willacoochee Hotel, H. W. Stalker, 25.

Enterprise—Epworth Inn, Florida Christian Assembly Association, 100.

Eau Gallie—Indian River Inn, J. R. Mathers, 20; Private Home, J. C. Boyer, 10; Private Home, W. H. Gleason, 10; Private Home, J. W. Rosetter, 10; Private Home, C. L. Taylor, 10.

Eustis—Ocklawaha House, J. S. Lane, 50; St. George Cottage, Mrs. Staton, 30; Wyman House, A. A. Wyman, 25; Eustis House, H. W. Bishop, 40; Grand View, M. T. Baulet, 40.

Federal Point—Groveland House, F. F. Tenney, 20.

Florence Villa—Florence Villa, H. Guy Nickerson, 300.

Fort Pierce—Atlantic, Faber Bros., 25; Carlton, Mrs. L. L. Carlton, 15; Chester House, Mrs. Harbin, not listed; Ft. Pierce Hotel, Mrs. F. M. Tyler, 75; Riverview Hotel, Mrs. S. W. Jennings, 35; Spring Cottage, F. C. Adams, not listed; Stetson Hotel, Lucian Baker, 25.

Fort Lauderdale—New River Hotel, P. N. Bryan, 60.

Fort Meade—Reif House, Mr. and Mrs. J. C. Reif, 24; Lightsey House, Mrs. J. C. Reif, 10; Southern Hotel, M. H. Wilson, 35.

Fort Myers—Royal Palm, F. H. Abbott, 200; Hotel Bradford, E. F. Wyatt, 85; Hill House, Mrs. M. F. Hill, 50; Thorp House, Mrs. L. G. Thorp, 30; Florida House, W. A. Nelson, 30; Cottage Home, Mrs. S. W. Sanchez, 20; River View, Mrs. A. M. Brandon, 40; Sellers House, J. I. Sellers, 20; The Everglades, Mrs. K. B. King, 150.

Gainesville—Brown House, J. A. Ettel, 75; Magnolia Hotel, J. S. Goode, 40; White House, W. R. Thomas, 60; Commercial, W. R. Richardson, 25.

Grant—Jorgensen House, L. Jorgensen, 30.

Green Cove Springs—Hotel Quisisana, not listed, 200; Tyler House, Mrs. J. W. Lucas, 30; Mohawk, Mrs. C. W. Tyler, 30; Riverside Hotel, Mrs. M. Hancock, not listed.

Hastings—Hastings Hotel, J. W. Sealy, 60; Homes' Place, A. M. Homes, 10; The Fox House, B. F. Fox, 10.

Hawks Park—Bay View House, M. R. Mendell, not listed.

Hobe Sound—The Wigwams, J. H. Grant, not listed.

Homosassa—Rendezvous, T. D. Briggs, 100; Crescent Lodge, E. B. Richardson, 20; Carpenter Hotel, I. C. E. Carpenter, 18; Palmetto Inn, R. O. Stephens, 12; Crescent Lodge, S. R. Udell, 15; Whitehall, J. J. Williams, 15.

Indianola—Hotel Indianola, Ballard and Maxfield, 60.

Island Grove—Carlton House, Mrs. Carlton, not listed.

Jacksonville—Seminole, Wm. H. Marshall, 250; Windsor, C. H. Montgomery, 400; Aragon, J. A. Newcomb, 250; Duval, W. M. Floor, 250; Everett, George Mason, 225; Albert, W. A. Guill & Co., 200; Park, W. H. Lowry, 100; St. Albans, K. H. Conroy, 50; The Royal Palms, Mrs. M. J. Morgan, not listed; Grand View, D. E. Cooper, 60; Waverly, Mrs. L. Wilson, 150; New St. James, W. E. Alexander, 125; Atlantic, George Morford, 175; Windle, W. W. Smith, 100; Victoria, M. Ingalls, 75; Travelers, Mrs. H. W. Hancock, 100; Riverview, T. Griffith, 60; Westmoreland, John F. May, 75; Lenox, W. M. Teahan, 65.

Jupiter—Carlin House, M. M. Carlin, 20.

Key West—Cripe and Annexes, not listed, 60; Edgar House, not listed, 20; Island City Hotel, not listed, 50; The Jefferson, J. P. Vining, 80; The Victoria, Alvarez & Co., 20.

Kissimmee—Park House, A. Rose, 50; The Inn, H. W. Thurman, 60; Greystone, H. W. Thurman, 60; Lake House, J. Hyde, 50; Groves House, R. Groves, 20.

LaBelle—Ft. Thompson Park Hotel, E. E. Goodno, 50; Hotel Everett, E. E. Goodno, 25.

Lake City—Blanche Hotel, J. W. Ettell, 75; Central Hotel, J. T. Briere, 50.

Lake Helen—Harlan Hotel, P. E. Stone, 10; Hotel Webster, J. A. and M. I. Jeferys, 200.

Lakeland—Tremont, John S. Bowen, 75; Glenada, U. Blount, 35; Sidney, J. E. Lee, 35; Arlington, Mrs. M. E. Rice, 30; Matanzas, Mrs. McIntosh, 20.

Lantana—Lantana House, M. B. Lyman, 10.

Lawtey—Redding House, Mrs. Redding, 12.

Largo—Hotel Largo, F. M. Campbell, 30.

Leesburg—Lakeview Hotel, E. C. Worrell, 125; Magnolia, J. A. McCormack, 12; Hotel Heights, L. E. Dozier, 50; Commercial Hotel, W. & M. C. Folson, 15.

Little River—Douthett House, Miss Douthett, 15.

Live Oak—Suwannee, Pearson & Letcher, 100; Ethel Hotel, J. R. McDonald, 40.

Long Key—Long Key Fishing Camp, L. P. Schutt, 100.

Lloyd—Whitfield House, Mrs. I. H. Dennis, 10.

Loughman—Wray Camps, neither listed.

Madison—Merchants Hotel, Mrs. J. P. McCall, 60.

Magnolia Springs—Magnolia Springs, O. D. Seavey, 300; Magnolia Inn, O. D. Seavey, 30.

Maitland—Maitland Inn, D. T. Judd, 50; The Oaks, M. E. Simmons, 10; Moreman House, Mrs. L. A. Moreman, 25.

Manatee—The Central Hotel, H. L. Ringo, 200.

Marco—Hotel Marco, W. D. Collier, 50.

Melbourne—Brown House, Mrs. George M. Brown, 40; Carleton, John M. Ferguson, 85; Myrtle Cottage, G. G. Cummings, 20; Sunny Rest, Mrs. M. A. Brown, 20.

Merritt—River View, neither listed; The Pines, Mrs. Gertrude T. Duff, not listed.

Miami—Arcade, Mrs. J. E. Ogle, not listed; Bay View, Mrs. E. C. Miller, 30; Biscayne Hotel, H. G. Keith, 150; Boyd Cottage, Mrs. J. W. Boyd, 30; Commercial, Conrad Schmid, 20; Ft. Dallas Hotel, Mrs. Lillie L. Flanagan, not listed; Gralynn House, S. Graham, 40; Green Tree Inn, M. H. March, 50; The Gautier, Mrs. T. N. Gautier, 10; Hinson House, Mrs. J. E. Hinson, 12; Hotel Iroquois, R. T. Daniels, 150; Minneapolis, J. P. Sawtelle, 40; New Everglades, Mrs. I. M. Wells, not listed; The Rocklyn, P. C. Hainlin, 20; Royal Palm, J. P. Greaves, 400; The Rutherford, Mrs. V. A. Rutherford, 15; San Carlos, Gus A. Muller, 60; White Palace, C. D. Smith, 300.

Montbrook—Davis House, Mrs. J. R. Davis, 50; Piney Woods Inn, Mrs. J. S. Sistrunk, 20.

Monticello—St. Elmo, H. W. McRory, 100; Scott House, Mrs. R. Scott, 15.

Morriston—Cox House, J. P. Cox, 50.

Mount Dora—Lakeside Inn, Geo. D. Thayer, 75; Bruce House, B. M. Bruce, 40.

Naples-on-the-Gulf—Hotel burned.

New Smyrna—Alba Court, C. W. & J. F. Pennell, 45; Byrd House, J. W. Byrd, 22; Fox House, Dr. B. F. Fox, 15; Magnolia, Mrs. G. A. Demmick, 25; Ocean House, Sams & Sams, 100; Palmetto, Mrs. J. W. Ashton, 15; Paul Cottage, Mrs. Paul, 20.

Oak Hill—Barker House, H. S. Barker, 20.

Ocala—Montezuma, J. A. Dewey, 170; Ocala House, E. L. Maloney, 200; Hotel Metropole, Mrs. C. A. Liddon, 20.

Orange City—Orange City Hotel, R. L. Fenn, 50; The Trues, J. L. True, 2.

Orange Park—Cottage Inn, Mrs. A. L. Evans, 20; Twin Cottage, Miss VanEmburg, 25.

Orlando—San Juan, H. L. Beeman, 150; Tremont Hotel, Capt. J. W. Wilmott, 120; The Pines, J. T. Horner, 25; New Lucerne, Mrs. R. S. Rowland, 75; The Windermere, Mrs. Bryant, 25; Duke Hall, Mrs. J. K. Duke, 30; Eola Cottage, Miss H. T. Paul, 20; The Summerlin, Mrs. C. V. Caldwell, 25; The Windsor, Mrs. J. Q. Myers, 25; The Wyoming, A. T. Miller, 75; The Childs Cottage, Mrs. J. P. McBride, 15; The Keystone, Mrs. H. B. Myers, 15; The St. Charles, Hilpert & Faul, 60.

Ormond—Granada, F. R. Moore, 30; Mildred Villa, A. M. Watson, 20; Ormond, J. D. Price, 600; Rose Villa, Mrs. Frank Mason, 20; The Inn, Anderson & Price Co., 75.

Oviedo—Argo House, Mrs. J. Argo, 25; Cushing House, T. L. Cushing, 30.

Palatka—Arlington, E. L. Wilbur, 75; Devereux Home, Mrs. Devereux, 10; The Howell, R. C. Howell, 100; Kimball House, Mrs. J. A. Granger, 20; Metcalf House, Mrs. Willie Metcalf, not listed; Saratoga, M. B. Jacobson, 75.

Palm Beach—The Breakers, Leland Sterry, 600; Hibiscus, not listed, 125; Palm Beach Hotel, Sidney Maddock, 300; Royal Poinciana, H. E. Bemis, 2,000.

Palmetto—Oaks Hotel, J. N. Green, 50.

Pass-a-Grille—The La Plaza, Mrs. A. C. Hartley, 75; The Bonhomie, Geo. H. Lizotte, 60; Mason Hotel, J. A. Mason, 25; Page's Hotel, C. C. Page, 25.

Pensacola—Escambia, G. W. Sims, not listed; Manhattan, A. Goldbach, not listed; San Carlos, G. H. Hervey, 175; Southern, K. I. Bowen, not listed.

Plant City—City Hotel, Mrs. W. A. McQuaig, 25; Palmetto Hotel (being rebuilt); Roselawn, Mrs. E. B. Crum, 100.

Ponce Park—Pacetti House, G. A. Pacetti, not listed; Park Hotel, J. R. Ellison, not listed; Pacetti's, B. J. Pacetti, 15.

Port Orange—Port Orange House, S. Fred Cummings, 45; The Illinois, D. W. Winn, 18.

Punta Gorda—Dade House, S. I. Huffman, 40; Travelers Hotel, Mrs. J. C. Johns, 40.

Punta Rassa—Shultz Hotel, Geo. R. Shultz, 60.

Quincy—Lorrance Hotel, J. W. Baschal, 20; The Quincy, W. M. Mabson, 100.

River Junction—Shepard House, W. L. Shepard, 50.

Rockledge—Indian River, Hotel Indian River Co., Inc., 300; New Rockledge and Cottages, D. L. & W. H. Wood, 200; Oak Cottage, F. D. Baldwin, 50; Plaza Hotel, not listed, 200; Singleton Cottage, Mrs. George L. Singleton, 20; White's Cottages, J. J. White, 30.

St. Augustine—Alcazar, W. McAuliffe, 400; Arlington, Mrs. Emma McL. McKeen, 60; Barcelona, Miss A. N. Blair, 70; Bay State Cottage, W. P. Oliver, 15; Bennett House, S. F. Bennett, 60; Buckingham, Wachenhousen & Maust, 75; Campbell House, Jno. T. Campbell, 30; Central Hotel, C. W. Johnson, 50; Craddock House, Mrs. E. West, 40; Dunham House, Mrs. D. L. Dunham, 25; Florida, O'Connor & Mahon, 250; Granada, S. Thomas Penna, 150; Hotel Clairmont, Mrs. A. Boutelle, 75; Keystone, L. J. Boyes, 60; La Borde, Mrs. E. Cowan, 40; La Posada, Mrs. John Center, 50; Lyon Building, O. B. Smith, 150; Magnolia, Palmer & MacDowell, 300; The Marion, H. Muller, 100; Monson House, A. V. Monson, 75; Neligan, Mrs. H. Neligan, 20; Ocean View, H. E. Hernandez, 75; Palmetto, not listed, 50; Ponce de Leon, Robert Murray, 500; San Marco, not listed, 100; Spear Mansion, Mrs. A. R. Spencer, 50; St. George, M. B. Montgomery, 200; Valencia, Miss E. Frazier, 75; Villa Flora, Mrs. Alanson Wood, not listed.

St Cloud—New modern hotel will be opened and operated during season 1911-12.

St. Lucie—Killcaire, Benj. Sooy, not listed.

St. Petersburg—The Detroit, C. N. Crawford, 225; The Hollenbeck, S. D. Hollenbeck, 225; The Huntington, C. S. Hunt, 225; The Manhattan, Staples & Lyman, 200; The Central, J. C. Thorn, 200; The Ansonia, F. E. Cole, 150; The Belmont, Mrs. C. B. Tippetts, 125; The Livingstone, Mrs. L. F. Livingstone, 100; The Chautauqua, F. H. Wilcox, 100; The Allen House, Mrs. M. R. Allen, 75; Dusenberry Villa, Mrs. W. P. Dusenberry, 75; The Paxton House, Mrs. W. W. Coleman, 75; The Panama, G. M. White, 75; Planters Hotel, A. J. Knight, 75; The Bon Air, W. W. Birchfield, 50; Overman House, W. J. Overman, 50; The Olud House, Mrs. C. Wilson, 50; The Albion, Mrs. L. H. Strum, 50; Pinellas Hotel, Mrs. F. Field, 50; Whitfield House, C. Whitfield, 50; Sarven House, H. Sarven, 50; Norton Flats, neither listed; Tonnelier Flats, neither listed; Chapman House, M. W. D. Chapman, 50; Davis House, Mrs. C. M. Davis, 50; The Bell House, Mrs. R. P. Bell, 30; Almon House, Mrs. M. L. Stroger, 25; Bramlitt House, Mrs. M. Bramlitt, 25; Bon Air House, Mrs. C. S. Pepper, 25; Majestic House, W. H. Jett, 25; The Palms, Mrs. W. L. Straub, 25; The Jenkins House, Mrs. A. D. Jenkins, 20; The Ark, Mrs. F. Graham, 20; The Dow House, Mrs. A. Dow, 20; Roberts House, Mrs. W. A. Roberts, 20; The Henry House, Mrs. W. C. Henry, 20; The Bay Shore House, Miss L. Mangold, 20.

Sanford—New Sanford House, Harry P. Driver, 100; Bye Lo Hotel, W. L. Fielding, 50; Gate City House, J. D. Parker, 20; Pico Hotel, Mrs. Tackach, not listed; Comfort Cottage, Mrs. M. Martin, 50; Chandler House, Mrs. Chandler, 10; Robins Nest, E. Robins, 25.

Sanibel Island—Casa Ybel, Duncan & Barnes, 60; The Matthews, Mrs. M. J. Matthews, 50; The Gables, The Misses Nutt, 10; Sanibel House, Mrs. J. B. Daniels, 25; Woodring House, Mrs. A. E. Woodring, 10.

San Mateo—Byrlyn Place, J. A. Crosby, 10; Idlewild, Dr. J. E. Cochrane, 10; The Palms, Mrs. F. A. Bailey, 10.

Sarasota—Belle Haven Inn, Dr. John Halton, 200; Halton Hotel, Dr. John Halton, 100; The Sarasota, H. S. Smith, 25.

Seabreeze—The Clarendon, E. L. Potter, Propr., W. F. Kenney, Mgr., 300; The Glenwood, E. F. Britton, 40; Cherokee Cottage, H. L. Kochersperger, 100; The Nautilus, E. D. Langworthy, 225.

Sebastian—Braddock House, G. A. Braddock, 20; Private Board, W. F. Baughman, not listed.

Silver Springs—Brown House, Mrs. M. F. Brown, not listed.

Stuart—Danforths, Mrs. C. Stephenson, 25; Stuart House, Wm. M. Erhart, not listed; Private Home, Broster Ketching, 30; Private Home, Mrs. U. S. Robinson, 10; Private Home, G. W. Thomas, 10.

Suwannee—Suwannee Springs Hotel, not listed, 75.

Tampa—Tampa Bay Hotel, David Lauber, 500; DeSoto Hotel, W. L. Parker, 200; Almeria Hotel, C. H. Hawes, 60; Hotel Hillsboro, J. L. Tallevast, 100; St. Charles, C. Mexis, 75; Hotel Palmetto, A. Paleveda, 75; Hotel Commercial, Mike Makres, 50; Marlboro, E. G. Smith, 50.

Tarpon Springs—The Ferns Hotel, C. H. Lee, 25; Homeworth Inn, Theo. J. Petzold, 15.

Tavares—Fitch Hotel, Mrs. E. J. Fitch, 20; Osceola Hotel, B. F. McCormick, 50.

Thonotosassa—Grand View, D. E. Hazen, 30.

Titusville—Hotel Dixie, W. F. Green, 150; Deisner's Boarding House, Mrs. E. J. Renaker, 40; Myers' Cottage, Mrs. W. H. Myers, 30; Palm-Hurst, A. F. Falck, 25; The Sterling, P. G. Walton, 25.

Useppa Island—Useppa Inn, F. Lyon Roach, 70.

Walton—The Walton Inn, F. G. McMullen, not listed.

Wauchula—Peace River Hotel, A. C. McCall, 200; Wauchula House, J. L. Bush, 30; DeSoto, G. Tompkins, 40.

Weirsdale—Lake Side Hotel, L. T. Clawson, 60; Pleasant Hill House, Mrs. E. S. Upham, 20.

West Palm Beach—Briggs Cottage, Mrs. H. E. Briggs, 20; Earman House, Mrs. S. E. Earman, not listed; Gables, W. M. & N. B. McGriff, not listed; Holland, J. D. Lockwood, 75; Hotel Jefferson, neither listed; Ivy Cottage, Mrs. T. D. Brown, not listed; Keystone Cottage, Mrs. Benj. Cook, 30; Minaret Cottage, Mrs. Frank Darling, not listed; Palms, J. C. Stowers, 125; Sans Souci, A. R. McKelvey, 20; Seagle House, F. V. Seagle, 40; Seminole Hotel, not listed, 100; The Tiffany, Mrs. C. Tiffany, not listed; The Virginia, Mrs. A. L. Haugh, 20.

Winter Garden—Orange Hotel, W. R. Dixon, 28; Bell House, W. S. Bell, 10.

Winter Park—Seminole Inn, R. P. Foley, 60; Batchelor Cottage, D. N. Batchelor, 15; Ingram Cottage, Mrs. Ingram, 10; The Chautauqua, B. S. Trude, 10.

Winter Haven—Lake View, J. N. Ackley, 75; Waulola Hotel, W. W. Mann, 25.

A SELECTED LIST OF FLORIDA HOTELS, 1940
(With number of rooms, if listed)

Altamonte Springs—Altamonte Hotel, 100

Apalachicola—Gibson, 50

Apopka—Palms, 40

Arcadia—Arcadia House, 60; Plaza, 97

Atlantic Beach—Atlantic Beach, 60

Avon Park—Highland Lakes, 117; Jacaranda, 120; Pine Crest Lakes Club, 58

Babson Park—Hillcrest Lodge, 30

Bartow—New Oaks, 75; Stewart Hotel, 35

Belleaire—Belleview Biltmore, 415

Boca Grande—Boca Grande, 200; Gasparilla Inn, 116

Bonita Springs—Bonita Springs, 36

Bradenton—Dixie Grande, 175; Keswick Arcade, 63; Manatee River, 200; Manavista, 87; Robert Whitney, 90

Captiva—Captiva Lodge, 40

Cedar Key—Cedar Key (not listed)

Clearwater—Borden, 27; Clearwater Beach, 100; Fort Harrison, 253; Gray Moss Inn, 100; Osceola Inn, 25; West Coast Hotel, 45

Cocoa—Brevard, 55; Cocoa House, 50; Knox, 49

Cocoa Beach—Ocean Lodge (not listed)

Coral Gables—Antilla Hotel, 65; Casa Loma, 80; Miami Biltmore, 400

Crystal River—Crystal River Inn, 25

Daytona Beach—Barbe, 30; Breakers, 50; Clarendon, 160; Daytona Terrace, 150; Geneva, 75; Gilbert, 80; Osceola, 150; Prince George, 70; Princess Issena, 200; Seaside Inn, 70; Seville, 40

DeLand—College Arms, 150; Putnam, 125; Stetson Lodge, 35

DeLeon Springs—DeSoto House, 40; Ponce de Leon Springs, 27

Delray Beach—Bon Air, 69; Colony, 150; Sandoway East, 25; Seacrest, 60

Dunedin—Dunedin, 30; Fenway, 116; Yacht Club Inn, 38

Dunnellon—Rainbow Springs Lodge (not listed)

Eau Gallie—Oleanders, 62

Eustis—Grand View, 59

Everglades—Everglades Inn, 50; Rod and Gun Club, 40

Fort Lauderdale—Broward, 100; Champ Carr, 125; Garden Court, 35; Gilbert-Maryland, 50; Governor's Club Hotel, 125; Lauderdale Beach Hotel, 150

Fort Myers—Franklin Arms, 102; Morgan, 62; Royal Palm, 150

Fort Myers Beach—Fort Myers Beach, 29

Fort Pierce—New Fort Pierce, 125

Gainesville—Gilbert, 40; Thomas, 100; White House, 70

Green Cove Springs—Qui-si-Sana, 50

Haines City—Polk Hotel, 70

Hobe Sound—Jupiter Island Club, 62

Hollywood—Casa Blanca, 40; Hollywood Beach, 540; Park View, 100; Surf Hotel, 50; Villa Hermosa, 48

Jacksonville—Andrew Jackson, 100; Aragon, 125; Burbridge, 150; Flagler, 125; George Washington, 300; Gilbert, 78; Mayflower, 300; Roosevelt, 300; Seminole, 250; Windsor, 220

Jasper—Hewitt (not listed)

Key West—Casa Marina, 200; La Concha, 127; Overseas, 100

Kissimmee—Gilbert Arcade, 40

Lakeland—Gilbert-Washburn, 44; Lakeland Terrace, 150; New Florida, 175

Lake Wales—Chalet Suzanne, 25; Lake Shore Hotel, 50; Seminole Inn, 36; Walesbilt, 96

Live Oak—Suwannee Hotel, 66

Melbourne—Indialantic, 50; Melbourne, 74.

Miami—Alcazar, 250; Alhambra, 85; Columbus, 300; Dallas Park, 300; Dolphin, 125; El Comodoro, 250; Everglades, 600; McAllister, 550; Miami Colonial, 200; Miramar, 100; Roberts, 150; Villa d'Este, 90

Miami Beach—Anglers, 50; Atlantis, 150; Barclay-Plaza, 100; Breakers, 38; Embassy, 100; Flamingo, 239; LeRoy, 100; Pancoast, 137; Roney Plaza, 300; Surfside, 125; Whitman, 150; Wofford, 150

Mount Dora—Lakeside Inn, 125

New Smyrna—Alba Court Inn, 50; New Smyrna Hotel, 75

Ocala—Harrington Hall, 74; Highlands, 35; Marion, 100

Orlando—Angebilt, 250; Avalon, 60; Jefferson Court, 135; Orange Court, 279; San Juan, 250; Wyoming, 125

Ormond Beach—Coquina, 121; Ormond, 300

Palatka—Gilbert, 36; James, 50

Palm Beach—Brazilian Court, 180; Breakers, 500; Everglades, 60; Mayflower, 250; Palm Beach Biltmore, 550; Villa Atlantique, 60; Whitehall Hotel, 300

Pass-a-Grille Beach—Don Ce-Sar, 327; Pass-a-Grille Beach, 50
Florida's Fabled Inns

Pensacola—Gilbert, 40; San Carlos, 500

Pirates Cove—Pirates Cove Fishing Camp, 40

Pompano—Hillsboro Club, 75

Ponte Vedra Beach—The Inn, 80

Port Sewall—Sunrise Inn, 100

Punta Gorda—Charlotte Harbor, 200

St. Augustine—Gilbert-Plaza, 40; Monson, 100; Ponce de Leon, 250

St. Petersburg—Alexander, 75; Allison, 126; Gilbert, 65; Huntington, 125; Jungle, 100; Poinsettia, 100; Princess Martha, 250; Vinoy Park, 375

Sanford—Gilbert, 50; Mayfair 75

Sarasota—Bay Island, 40; Gulf View Inn, 52; John Ringling, 150; Orange Blossom, 125; Sarasota Terrace, 125

Sebring—Harder Hall, 150; Sebring, 100

Silver Springs—Silver Springs Court, 39

Tallahassee—Cherokee, 100; Floridan, 150

Tampa—Bay View, 150; Floridan, 400; Gilbert, 40; Hillsboro, 326; Mirasol, 146; Tampa Terrace, 225

Tarpon Springs—Stratford, 40; Villa Plumosa (not listed)

Useppa Island—Useppa Inn, 140

Vero Beach—Royal Park Inn, 50

Wakulla Springs—Wakulla Springs Lodge, 25

West Palm Beach—Alhambra, 100; Dixie Court, 132; George Washington, 200; Royal Worth, 260

Winter Haven—Florence Villa, 125; Haven, 136

Winter Park—Alabama, 80; Hamilton, 40; Seminole, 82; Virginia Inn, 80

Bibliography

Abbott, Karl P., **Open for the Season,** Garden City, N. Y.: The Country Life Press, 1950.

Amory, Cleveland, **The Last Resorts,** New York: Harper & Brothers, 1948.

Barbour, George M., **Florida for Tourists, Invalids, and Settlers,** New York: D. Appleton and Co., 1882.

Bartram, William, **Travels of William Bartram,** 1791, edited by Mark Van Doren, New York: Dover Publications, Inc., 1955, Dover edition, republication of the work published by Macy-Masius in 1928.

The Florida Bicentennial Trail: A Heritage Revisited, Bicentennial Commission of Florida, 1976.

Bickel, Karl A., **The Mangrove Coast—The Story of the West Coast of Florida,** New York: Coward-McCann, Inc., 1942.

Bill, Ledyard, **A Winter in Florida,** New York: Wood and Holbrick, 1869.

Bothwell, Dick, **Sunrise 200—A Lively Look at St. Petersburg's Past,** illustrated by Jack Barrett.

Bryant, William Cullen, **Letters of a Traveller,** New York: G. P. Putnam's Sons, 1850.

Cabell, Branch, and A. J. Hanna, **The St. Johns, A Parade of Diversities,** New York: J. J. Little and Ives Co., 1943.

Carrère & Hastings, **Florida, The American Riviera — St. Augustine, The Winter Newport,** New York: Gilliss Brothers & Turnure, The Art Age Press, 1898.

Cash, W. T. and Dorothy Dodd, **Florida Becomes a State,** Tallahassee: Florida Centennial Commission, 1945.

Chipley, W. D., compiler, **Pensacola (the Naples of America) and Its Surroundings,** Louisville: Courier-Journal Press, c. 1877.

Cox, Merlin G., and J. E. Dovell, **Florida From Secession to Space Age,** St. Petersburg, Fla.: Great Outdoors Publishing Co., 1974.

Davis, T. Frederick, **History of Jacksonville, Florida, and Vicinity, 1513 to 1924,** published by the Florida Historical Society, St. Augustine, Fla.: The Record Company, 1925.

Douglas, Marjory Stoneman, **Florida: The Long Frontier,** New York: Harper & Row, 1967.

Dovell, J. E., **Florida: Historic—Dramatic—Contemporary,** Volume II, New York: Lewis Historical Publishing Co., Inc., 1952.

Dunn, Hampton, **Yesterday's St. Petersburg,** Miami, Fla.: E. A. Seemann Publishing, Inc., 1973.

Dunn, Hampton, **Yesterday's Tallahassee,** Miami, Fla.: E. A. Seemann Publishing, Inc., 1974.

Edwards, Virginia, **Stories of Old St. Augustine,** St. Augustine, Fla.: C. F. Hamblen, Inc. Printed by Paramount Press, Jacksonville, Fla., 1973.

Estey, Winifred W., **Tangerine Memoirs,** The Tangerine Improvement Society, 1957.

Forbes, James Grant, **Sketches of the Floridas,** Quadricentennial Edition of the Floridiana Facsimile & Reprint Series, Gainesville, Fla.: University of Florida Press, 1964.

Fritz, Florence, **Unknown Florida,** Miami: Center Printing Co., 1963.

Gilkes, Lillian, **Cora Crane—A Biography of Mrs. Stephen Crane,** Bloomington, Ind.: Indiana University Press, 1960.

Gill, Joan E., and Beth R. Read, editors, **Born of the Sun,** the Official Florida Bicentennial Commemorative Book, 1975.

Gold, Pleasant Daniel, **History of Duval County, Florida,** St. Augustine: The Record Co., 1928.

Grismer, Karl H., **Tampa—A History of the City of Tampa and the Tampa Bay Region of Florida,** ed. by D. B. McKay, St. Petersburg: St. Petersburg Printing Co., Inc., 1950.

Groene, Bertram H., **Ante-Bellum Tallahassee,** Tallahassee: Florida Heritage Foundation, 1971.

Hanna, A. J., **A Prince in Their Midst,** Norman, Oklahoma: University of Oklahoma Press, 1946.

Hanna, Alfred Jackson and Kathryn Abbey Hanna, **Florida's Golden Sands,** The Bobbs-Merrill Co., 1950.

Harner, Charles E., **Florida's Promoters—The Men Who Made It Big,** Tampa: Trend House, 1973.

Hurley, Frank T., Jr., **Surf, Sand, & Post Card Sunsets,** St. Petersburg, Fla.: Great Outdoors Publishing Co., 1977.

Hurley, June, **The Don Ce-Sar Story,** ed. by Ken Hurley, St. Petersburg, Fla.: Partnership Press, 1974, second printing, 1975.

An Invalid (anonymous), **A Winter in the West Indies and Florida,** New York: Wiley and Putnam, 1839.

Kinney, Henry, **Once Upon a Time—The Legend of the Boca Raton Hotel and Club,** Arvida Corporation, 1974.

Kjerulff, Georgianna Greene, **Tales of Old Brevard,** Kellersberger Fund, South Brevard Historical Society, 1972.

Lanier, Sidney, **Florida: Its Scenery, Climate, and History,** 1875, facsimile reproduction, Gainesville, Fla.: University of Florida Press, 1973.

Leonard, Irving A., **The Florida Adventures of Kirk Munroe,** Chuluota, Fla.: The Mickler House, Publishers, 1975.

Long, Ellen Call, **Florida Breezes or Florida, New and Old,** Floridiana Facsimile & Reprint Series, Gainesville, Fla.: University of Florida Press, 1962.

Longstreet, R. J., **The Story of Mount Dora, Florida,** Mount Dora Historical Society, 1960.

Maitland Historical Society, **Maitland Milestones,** 1976

Martin, Sidney Walter, **Florida's Flagler,** Athens, Ga.: University of Georgia Press, 1949.

Martin, Sidney Walter, **Florida During the Territorial Days,** second edition, Philadelphia, Pa.: Porcupine Press, 1974, first edition, Athens, Ga.: The University of Georgia Press, 1944.

Mathews, Mrs. George G., Chairman, The Junior League of the Palm Beaches, Inc., **Palm Beach Entertains, Then and Now,** New York: Coward, McCann & Geohegan, Inc., 1975.

McGovern, James R., **The Emergence of a City in the Modern South: Pensacola 1900-1945,** DeLeon Springs, Fla.: E. O. Painter Printing Co., 1976.

Official Directory of the City of Miami, 1904, Reprint and Facsimile Series, Historical Association of Southern Florida, 1974.

Morris, Allen, compiler, **The Florida Handbook, 1971-1972,** Tallahassee, Fla.: Peninsular Publishing Company, 1971.

Morris, Allen, **Florida Place Names,** Coral Gables, Fla.: University of Miami Press, 1974.

Motte, Jacob Rhett, **Journey Into Wilderness—An Army Surgeon's Account of Life in Camp and Field During the Creek and Seminole Wars, 1836-1838,** edited by James F. Sunderman, Gainesville, Fla.: University of Florida Press, 1963.

Mowat, Charles Loch, **East Florida as a British Province, 1763-1784,** Floridiana Facsimile & Reprint Series, Gainesville, Fla.: University of Florida Press, 1964.

Muir, Helen, **Miami, U. S. A.,** Coconut Grove, Fla.: Hurricane House Publishers, Inc., 1953.

Mullen, Harris, H., **A History of the Tampa Bay Hotel,** University of Tampa Foundation, 1966.

Mullen, Harris H., **Florida Close-Up,** Tampa, Fla.: Trend Publications, Inc., 1972.

Parks, Arva Moore, **The Forgotten Frontier—Florida Through the Lens of Ralph Middleton Munroe,** Miami: Banyan Books, Inc., 1977.

Patrick, Rembert W., **Florida Under Five Flags,** Gainesville, Fla.: University of Florida Press, 1945.

Webb's Pensacola City Directory, 1885-86.
Pensacola City Directory, 1893-94.
Maloney's Pensacola City Directory, 1898, Vol. 1.
Peters, Thelma, **Lemon City: Pioneering on Biscayne Bay, 1850-1925,** Miami: Banyan Books, 1976.
Pettengill, George W., Jr., **The Story of the Florida Railroads, 1834-1903,** Bulletin No. 86, The Railway and Locomotive Historical Society, Boston, Mass.: Baker Library, Harvard Business School, 1952.
Phillips, Morris, editor of the Home Journal, **Abroad and at Home, Practical Hints for Tourists,** New York: Brentano's, c. 1892.
Parks Arva Moore, **The Forgotten Frontier—Florida Through the Lens of Ralph Middleton Munroe,** Miami: Banyan Books, Inc., 1977.
The Plant System, **Florida Resorts,** Buffalo, N. Y.: The Matthews-Northrup Co., c. 1899.
Pratt, Theodore, **The Story of Boca Raton,** St. Petersburg, Fla.: Great Outdoors Publishing Company, 1963.
Pratt, Theodore, **That Was Palm Beach,** St. Petersburg, Fla.: Great Outdoors Publishing Company, 1968.
"Rambler," **Guide to Florida, 1875,** Floridiana Facsimile & Reprint Series, Gainesville, Fla.: University of Florida Press, 1964.
Rerick, Rowland H., **Memoirs of Florida,** Vol. 2, edited by Francis P. Fleming, Atlanta: Southern Historical Association, 1902.
Rhodes, Harrison, and Mary Wolfe Dumont, **A Guide to Florida for Tourists, Sportsmen and Settlers,** New York: Dodd, Mead and Company, 1912.
Romans, Bernard, **A Concise Natural History of East and West Florida, 1775,** reprint, New Orleans, La.: Pelican Publishing Co., Ltd., 1961.
Seaton, George W., **Cue's Guide to What to See and Do in Florida,** New York: Prentiss-Hall, 1940.
Sewall, R. K., **Sketches of St. Augustine,** Bicentennial Floridiana Facsimile Series, Gainesville, Fla.: The University Presses of Florida, 1976, a reprint of the 1848 edition published by Putnam, New York.
Simmons, William Hayne, **Notices of East Florida,** 1822, Bicentennial Floridiana Facsimile Series, 1973.
Simons, Norman and James R. McGovern, **Pensacola in Pictures and Prints,** Volume IV, the Pensacola Series Commemorating the American Revolution Bicentennial, Pensacola: Mayer Printing Co., 1974.
Smiley, Nixon, **Yesterday's Florida,** Miami, Fla.: E. A. Seemann Publishing, Inc., 1974.
Smiley, Nixon, **Yesterday's Miami,** Miami, Fla.: E. A. Seemann Publishing, Inc., 1973.
Smith, Earl L., **Yankee Genius—A Biography of Roger W. Babson,** New York: Harper & Brothers, 1954.
Tebeau, Charlton W., **Florida's Last Frontier—The History of Collier County,** Miami: University of Miami Press, 1957.
Tebeau, Charlton W., **A History of Florida,** Coral Gables, Fla.: University of Florida Press, 1971.
Thrift, Charles T., Jr., **The Trail of the Florida Circuit Rider,** Lakeland, Fla.: Florida Southern College Press, 1944.
Webb's Historical, Industrial and Biographical Florida, Wanton S. Webb, editor and compiler, New York: W. S. Webb & Co., Publishers, 1885.
White, Louise, **Key West—A Guide to an Enchanting City,** St. Petersburg, Fla.: Great Outdoors Publishing Company, 1965.
Williams, John Lee, **A View of West Florida, 1827,** facsimile reproduction, Gainesville, Fla.: University Presses of Florida, 1976.
Wilson, James Grant and John Fiske, editors, **Appleton's Cyclopedia of American Biography,** New York: Appleton, 1888.

Index